# BABES IN THE WOODS
## With a Little Child to Guide Them

William L. Roth, Jr.

Foreword by Timothy Parsons-Heather

The Morning Star of Our Lord, Inc. is a nonprofit, tax-exempt, 501(c)(3), religious and charitable organization which is incorporated under the Laws of the State of Illinois. It has been established for the dissemination of various apologetic works in defense of the Truth of the Holy Gospel of Christianity. It is the intrinsic role of this Corporation to provide pastoral consolation to those lacking in faith, the infirm, homebound, incarcerated, deprived, dejected, and those who are otherwise suffering humanity for the sake of the Glory of the Kingdom of Jesus Christ. All proceeds from this book are being donated to other charitable causes to help feed, clothe, and house the poor, and for the reproduction of this spiritual manuscript for distribution on every continent of the world. If anyone would like to contribute to this worthy cause, you may do so through the following postal and website addresses.

The Morning Star of Our Lord, Inc.
Post Office Box 8854
Springfield, Illinois 62791-8854
www.ImmaculateMary.org


Published by The Morning Star of Our Lord, Incorporated
Used with permission.

Publish date:          February 22, 2003

Cover photograph:      Curtis Roth Cave
                       Adam Dean Cave

ISBN: 0-9671587-4-5

Printed in the United States of America

*Dedicated to the Memory of...*

Harry Dean Cave

September 21, 1958 - November 10, 1958

A Pentecost Child
For 50 days, the Earth was Blessed
Saint Harry, Pray for Us!

Introit
## *Holy Thursday*

*Is this a holy thing to see,*
*In a rich and fruitful land—*
*Babes reduced to misery,*
*Fed with cold and usurious hands?*          4

*Is that trembling cry a song?*
*Can it be a song of joy?*
*And, so many children poor?*
*It is a land of poverty!*          8

*And, their sun does never shine,*
*And, their fields are bleak and bare,*
*And, their ways are filled with thorns;*
*It is eternal winter there.*          12

*For, wherever the sun does shine,*
*And, wherever the rain does fall,*
*Babe can never hunger there,*
*Nor poverty the mind appall.*16

William Blake   (1757-1827)
English poet, engraver, and painter
From *Songs of Experience*
1794

# Babes in the Woods
*With a Little Child to Guide Them*

## Table of Contents

### Section I
### *All Creatures Great and Small*

### Section II
### *Return the Age of Innocence*

### Section III
### *The Rite of Passage*

## Section IV
### *With a Little Child to Guide Them*

## Section V
### *The Mother and Child Reunion*

## Memorial Citations

## The Morning Star of Our Lord, Incorporated
## Other Titles Available

*In Our Darkest Hour*
*Morning Star Over America*

*At the Water's Edge*
*Essays in Faith and Morals*

*When Legends Rise Again*
*The Convergence of Capitalism and Christianity*

*White Collar Witch Hunt*
*The Catholic Priesthood Under Siege*

See address on Copyright Page
for ordering information.

*At that time, Jesus said to God in reply, "I give praise to you, Father, Lord of Heaven and Earth; for although you have hidden these things from the wise and the learned, you have revealed them to the little ones."*

Saint Matthew 11:25

# Foreword
## *A Cause for Contemplation*

---

Thirty years ago this Fall, in September 1972, I drove my little Ford Falcon automobile to Jacksonville, Illinois into a parking lot behind the Blackstock House dormitory at MacMurray College to move into my room and begin my undergraduate studies. I was commenced from high school along with just-over two dozen other students in the Village of Ashland that previous May; and I had no idea what God, the Earth, society, and all the Hosts of Paradise had planned for me from that moment beyond. There is no reason to conceal the fact that I really did not want to be there in the first place; but my parents had wished so dearly that I might earn a college degree and succeed in life in ways that time, fashion, circumstances, and opportunity never allowed them to enjoy. I was their seventh of seven sons, and the only one to apply for admission to a formal college at the age of eighteen years. I was always somewhat of a homebody at the time, and very stubborn about demanding my own space in which to engage the physical universe on my definitive terms—not so much that it was always that way back home with all my brothers and sisters; but I knew that my folksy desire for living was about to be infringed upon by an institutional setting in which I would be anonymous amidst a group of total strangers. This filled me with a certain sense of anxiety and trepidation because, after just having been one of the mature seniors of my little prep-school, I knew there were many powers and forces with which I would thereafter have to grapple to regain control of my immediate world. However, it seemed a lot better than traipsing-off to the Viet Nam war, groveling in a minimum-wage job at the downtown grocery store everyday, or getting myself filthy working at my father's autobody repair shop. So, there I was; glaring around at the Georgian brick buildings which housed the various fields of study that my little midwestern college had to offer. I knew I had to come to learn more about myself, to discover the systems of ethics and academics in the land of the free and the home of the brave, and to somehow decipher what it was that I wanted to achieve as a young male of the early 1970s in terms of finding gainful employment and making my mark on Creation as a uniquely conceived individual of God. Millions of people before us have stated that if we were ever so advanced that humankind might be capable of foretelling and predicting the future, do we reckon we might attempt to change our present courses of action and our ways of thinking so as to avoid repeating the same tragic mistakes of the past, or perhaps amend our unmitigated error and make-up for lost time in securing that elusive inner-peace and long-sought good will among the foreign nations of the Earth? I knew that I would never succeed in learning what I was supposed to know by staying there on campus, so I moved back home with my parents and commuted the 20 miles to class for the next four years; and my childhood desire for my own self-autonomy was not completely lost to me.

When William L. Roth, Jr. approached me and said that he had written a manuscript that he wanted to publish about little children, he also said, *Tim, I think I have composed a piece of work about the youth in all of us that everyone can read without having to look-up too many words in the dictionary.* He was referring to many of his previous books that were written and directed toward American intellectuals, theologians, politicians, philanthropists, scientists, and philosophers in which he had to employ the use of their own vernacular to bring them to a closer understanding of the simplicities of human love. Indeed, this has been the focus of his writing and the purpose of his life for over a decade, now. He has addressed the ecclesiastical phonetics of Scriptural Truth, the origin of the meditations of our hearts, the ideals of a legitimized democracy, and the reason why we should not be too quick to judge others, lest our Divine Lord holds us to the same critical fashions once we see His Glorious Face. It is true beyond all telling that we still hunger for that same innocence which has seemingly become only a shadow and a distant memory for us now—the instances in life when we looked as children into the world with great wonder, curiosity, and a stifling awe. We seemed not to be so stringent back then because we knew very little about the distinctions of human existence with which we would be forced to compete and overcome. Is this not, in itself, the essence of the fears I felt when I arrived on that college campus 30 years ago? All of God's children are called to somehow return to this unassuming nature of raw anticipation as we ponder the Second Coming of Jesus Christ. We are expected to assume an attitude as His disciples so as to be marked by the receptivity and trustful dependence that is so characteristic of little children. William told me that he wanted the subtitle for his manuscript to be, *With a Little Child to Guide Them.* If we look into the Book of Isaiah 11:6-9, we discover the passages where God has prescribed our interior consciousness as needing to be not unlike His own Son's from His Birth in Bethlehem, all the way through the kind congeniality that He took to His Death on the Cross on Good Friday. He speaks about the traditional names of the gifts of the living presence of the Holy Spirit in Jesus Christ in Chapter 11 of Isaiah, referring quite overtly and explicitly to the Rule of Immanuel,...*The Spirit of the Lord shall rest upon Him: a Spirit of Wisdom and of understanding, a Spirit of counsel and strength, a Spirit of knowledge and of fear of the Lord.* And, with all this power, the Christ-Child who would be born as the King of all Creation is described as being so valorous that He would cast-out the ruthless with a subtle word, slaying the wicked with His holy breath. And, then, to address the great commission wherein God would provide that perfect innocence of He who was so Crucified for our Salvation,....*Justice shall be the band around His waist, and faithfulness a belt upon His hips. Then, the wolf shall be a guest of the lamb, and the leopard shall lie down with the kid; the calf and the young lion shall browse together, with a little child to guide them.* (ff) *The baby shall play by the cobra's den, and the child lay his hand on the adder's lair.* Is our world anywhere near approaching such humble solemnity that these things might come-to-pass in our age? These passages from Isaiah are prophetic of the idyllic harmony that Heaven brings to us through the Resurrection of Jesus Christ, overwhelmingly drawing us closer to the universal peace and justice of the Messianic times.

    It was only upon reading the entirety of *Babes in the Woods* that I was finally able to understand what God was saying in the Book of Isaiah about the Rule of Immanuel. Growing-up in America today, or anywhere else in the world for that matter, little children must not be made to feel as though their souls are being scoured with hydrochloric acid and steel wool. They should never be forced to fear their parents because they might be physically or emotionally punished by them, but because we as their mothers and fathers have made the definition of *love* so distinct and clear to them that they willingly obey our instructions with reverence, instead. It always seems like our understanding of Divine Truth must be the product of untold human suffering before we ever come to realize what it means to extract ourselves from situations where mortal sin may engulf us again. However, if we live in accordance with the Holy Gospel, this need not be true at all; for I am convinced that peace in every form, full reconciliation, justice, prudence, humility, and holiness are willed into existence by the invincible nature of God through His Eternal desire to exercise His dominion over us. His is a wholesome manifest of endearing guidance; but humankind is much too arrogant to believe that we will ever need to be led into the unknown future by anything or anyone—be it God, mortal, beast, or brawn—whom we cannot yet see with our physical eyes. But, if we become the little children whom Jesus wants us to be, we will rise as the stewards of every phase of Creation, in service for Him under the Cross and before the Throne of our Triune God. Therein rests the peaceful accord of all humanity; reclaimed in our own day as time immemorial continues to expire. Who can say that the next baby we might see on a sonogram screen being nourished in its mother's womb, or one sitting in a high chair at the local Pizza Hut, or another being pulled by the hand down the sidewalk as fast as his little feet can carry him by a harried babysitter might not become a future Roman Catholic pontiff, another Mother

Teresa, the likeness of President Lincoln, or a great healer of an ailing sector of quarantined lepers?

It is for these critical reasons that we must be vigilant against any malevolent forces which may try to hinder the health, safety, and spiritual well-being of our little children.  There is an entire bevy of wanton evil swirling about the world, trying to convince us that none of this is true.  Satan and his scoundrels would have us believe that our children are not really a gift from God, but rather a blight and burden upon our upward mobility and social relationships, inhibiting our status before other men and the accumulation of material wealth.  This is the type of selfish posturing which has led to the horrific scourge of abortion, which William addresses in this book with great explication in Chapter XIII.  He makes it quite clear that we must understand that any species of life which refuses to nurture and protect its young is destined for extinction; and we civilized human beings are certainly no exception.  By all means, we are further culpable to God in the role of protecting our innocents because we have been afforded the grace of great intellectual brilliance that always accompanies rational judgement.  It is toward this provocative sense that William L. Roth speaks in *Babes in the Woods*, as his message of love inspires the revealing aspects of the human heart and the tenderly charitable attributes of our little ones, i.e., knowing how they are reluctant to indict or prejudge their peers, almost always open to constructive new ideas, willing to learn about the facets of nature and the Sacred Mysteries of God; and they are, above all things, very good listeners when they really choose to be.  In the Chapters you are about to read, William takes us on a vast journey inside the juvenile psyche and through the cataclysmic endeavors of their puberty and adolescence.  He surveys the cultural divides between our stoic elderly retirees, the millions of Baby Boomers, and our ofttimes outlandish Generation X.  The venues he employs to extract humor from under some of the most extraordinary conditions is a work of art for every 21st century reader.  His contention that a certain artifact is a more valuable stroke of genius according to how labor-intensive it is harks back to the age of our grandfathers; who themselves were never too much given to creative originality.  But, they were certainly aware that a poor rapport and public humiliation never discriminate in favor of those whom our enemies might choose to deride.  William's writing pulls us together within our social commonness, revealing that he is deeply troubled by our many misguided youth—those who are tortured by drugs, licentiousness, and alcohol abuse; the thousands more who are abandoned by their parents every year, and just as many who are left alone to fend for themselves on the not-so-friendly streets of crime and poverty.  Indeed, it is the human heart that brought him to pen *Babes in the Woods;*

researching all the avenues down which our broken children travel for attention, relief, entertainment, mischief, their search for new identity, and comradery with their friends. He calculates the reasons why so many of them take their own lives and resort to violence as a means of excommunicating the ghosts that haunt them from within. And, he arrives at the proper conclusion: that the cause of error in our children's existence has been, and remains to be, that these youngsters do not feel loved in the way that we are commanded to embrace them according to our Christian faith.

Our nation's progeny see their country as being much too absorbed by politics and division, and not engulfed by friendship and compassion. There is no doubt that each and every one of them has confronted the same reticence that I felt when my foot first hit the ground as I stepped out of my Ford Falcon in September 1972. We must begin to understand that they are the proverbial seedlings of our American future, the hope for our renewed democracy, and the obvious sign that our Almighty Father in Paradise has proclaimed that human life must go on. William promised that he would place my *Foreword* into his book with no editorial amendments of his own. Therefore, I feel comfortable knowing that I can add herein the text of a brief essay that he penned while in the Second Grade with a fair amount of prompting from his father and elementary teacher, way back in 1969. Let us recall that such little people are only about seven or eight years old; but the following paragraph is what he humbly wrote regarding, *What Should I Do To Be A Good American Citizen?*

*Being a good American citizen starts in the home, by teaching your children to become responsible, respect other people's properties, and teaching them Christian morals and values. They should be responsible in getting chores and other duties done, and must obey authorities in schools, churches, homes, and many other places.    When you get old enough, become involved in community organazations* (sic) *in order to help on projects that will improve your city or town. Some of these organazations* (sic) *are the Lions Club, Jr. and Sr. Women's Clubs. If the town authorities are doing something you don't think is right, first, find out what the position of the town is.    Then, if necessary, work to correct these unjust situations.    Be objective first, listen to all sides of the story.    Then, see if it would help the town, then last of all, object if you don't think it's right.    Whenever there is an election, go and vote, not just for a Democrat or a Republican, vote for the person you think is best qualified for the job.    You should keep up with and be informed of government matters and current issues.    These thoughts add up to basically one thing, truly loving your fellow man.*

No other conclusion can be drawn than to realize that William L. Roth, Jr. learned at an early age that civility, peace, and social justice are vested in the power of the individual person to force a change in making this a better world; and that is why he has written so many books about spiritual power, moral character, personal integrity, public service, and Christian religiosity. Indeed, his own father, the elder William Roth, son of (the late) John J. Roth (1896-1977) and Eula Monica Reiser Roth (1902-1964) was elected mayor of the Village of Ashland, Illinois just twelve years after teaching his own son to embrace God's Divine Wisdom when dealing with the responsibilities we all bear as American citizens; having served from 1981-1985 after a long tenure on the Board of Trustees. Our greatest leaders knew this, too—our poets, playwrights, presidents, physicians, and millions of ordinary citizens who have made the best of their practical dreams to churn our nation and the entire globe into the sweetened vessel of Christian affection which will, in due time, overcome all and everything that stands in the way of our final reconciliation. There are many stepping stones along that pathway; and *Babes in the Woods* is one upon which we can pause to see the best of what our little children must become.

Timothy Parsons-Heather
BS, MPA, PHM
Spring 2003

# Section I
## *All Creatures Great and Small*

---

# Chapter I
## *Dawn Breaks Past the Reckoning*
## *Will the Future Uphold Our Helplessness?*

There must be dozens of analogies that have been drawn by modern romantics in an effort to describe the art of communicating our expressions of the heart; from an author sitting in front of a page with pen-in-hand like Pablo Picasso with a palette, or an opera house composer with blank lines on the treble staffs atop his piano, and even an eloquent speaker refining his thoughts prior to delivering an extemporaneous speech to a hall filled with ears. No one will ever be able to affectionately accuse me of being a great anthologist, a practitioner of music in the lineage of Mozart or the likes of Mendelssohn, and not even close to being an orator fashioned after the numerous Winston Churchills of the world. My purpose has always been more simple than that; wishing only to express the rudimentary purposes of our infant Christian faith; hoping against hope that at least someone, somewhere, might garner a momentary understanding about what it means to bow in deference to Jesus Christ, the Son of God, the healer of our age. If ever there was a time for the resonance of an octave of spiritual docility to descend upon the Earth, surely we must be living it in our parenthetical passage of history while the 21st century is only now beginning to crack ajar like a chicklet emerging from an egg. There are too many injustices and brash emotions bringing us to tears these days; the awkward young who are too undeveloped to compete with their affluent friends and peers, or ostentatious veterans of social etiquette trying to put their names in lights on the bright marquee of Carnegie Hall, and witty profiteers who look like hamsters running on wheels in an effort to make another buck; all ignoring with equal apathy the elderly and infirm who lay in their own excrement because few among us ever choose to remember them inside the secluded quarters of their musty nursing homes. I sometimes wonder why we cannot see our way clear to reverberating the call of righteousness that springs from the Divine Love that Our Lord gave us the very moment He was born. It seems to have been properly absorbed and reflected by our ancestors and predecessors, exalted and regenerated by them, and thereafter passed-along to us for the glory of God. It is a ringing of this spiritual Truth that is sorely lacking in us now; the mutual intonations of goodness, charity, forgiveness, and peace. There should be no broken links in the bonds of such virtues from whence God first dispatched His only begotten Son from the Womb of Mary into our exiled world below Him; but we are doing our worst to try to breach it anyway. Whether we like it or not, we are not quite omnipotent creators of our own accord because we are still sinners in the flesh, walking blindly and haphazardly askew through a valley of dark shadows to the certainty of our deaths without a proper sense of the purpose of charismatic hope. We own no kingdom with which to castigate the perils of the world unless we moor our final legacies to our Messianic Savior and accept the transforming Light still emanating from His Cross.

Without giving every facet of our mortal constitution to the Son of the Blessed Virgin Mary, there is nothing inherent in us that will ever yield the admiration of the Angels or the accolades of the Saints. We are born to our parents as orphans from our Almighty Father until the moment we are baptized by Holy Water in His Trinity of Names, willfully predisposed to His Crucifixion on Good Friday and His Rising from the dead; commended with such exemplary piousness through the advocacy of His Mother, Our Immaculate Virgin Queen and Patroness of the reconciliation between the Heavens and the Earth. It is toward this sacred purpose that I have written *Babes in the Woods*, knowing in Truth that we are meant to become like little children to regain the innocence we have lost, to discern in invariable terms what Christian simplicity should really mean; and to make the case, at least for now, that we are failing by woeful quanta to protect our innocent progeny from the scandals of the world. How many reasons do we require to justify the engagement of this discussion to prove our outright errancy? There is a cardinal number represented in the U.S. and France that is called an *octillion*, which is a *one* followed by an unbelievable 27 zeros, and in Great Britain and Germany by 48 zeros. Even if we ever exhausted such an audacious number of excuses why we should never engage a cause of action to ameliorate the lives of our little ones, the King of Creation would have us understand that not a solitary one would justify our reluctance to proceed. Our children are weeping pitifully while crouching on their knees before a humankind that mysteriously despises them from the moment they are conceived, especially in America. We can see and hear them crying into the eardrums of their impassive elders who yield to them but a haughty facade of insolence, while briny tears roll down their cheeks as they beg only to be fed their share of irreproachable human love. They persistently scratch upon our doorways like pets left out in the rain, scrawl the messages of their suffering in blood onto our city sidewalks, and protest with rocks thrown through our windows that they find in the ditches where they hover together for the night. When they become old enough to speak clearly for themselves, the calling of their voices is ignored by housewives who often abandon the challenges of motherhood in favor of getting rich and by stuffy businessmen whose corporate covetousness takes them to the airways for weeks and sometimes months at a time, instead of to the campuses of their offsprings' middle schools. Then, while they sit inside their tinted-windowed limousines waiting for a passing train, they see for themselves the exasperation of their younger sect; broadly, beautifully, and defiantly displayed in aerosol graffiti on the sides of the railcars in rainbow-colored paint. Ironically, the cast-iron links of these powerful locomotives have become our children's copy books, their empty music staffs, and their bullhorns to the world. There is a destined finality of Eternal Judgement and proportionate Wrath in the arsenals of God that He will unleash upon His enemies for having led His children astray. He has never been too much interested in how we value our friendships when we get to our workplaces for the day, whether we ultimately keep pace with the lifestyles of the upper-elite, that we set-aside forest reserves for our hunters to seek their kill, or if we travel at the speed of sound to contract a capital debt. Indeed, His focus is more concentric as to whether our faith in Him is ever deployed, how we comply with His Beatitudes from the Sermon on the Mount, whether we have caused anyone to take shelter in abject poverty beneath the trestles of those same passing freight trains in the starkness of the night, and how many lonely children fall asleep in the corners of their orphanages with no one there to comfort them, or give them a bedtime kiss, or somehow offer them hope by telling them that, tomorrow, everything will be alright.

Christians and Gentiles, alike, keep repeating the same mantra everyday that all-in-all will be justified and fully revealed once the Son of Man returns by breaking past the horizon of our lost hopes and dreams; but far too many of us decline to look any further than our upstairs bedrooms to search for the remainder of His little ones whom we are also supposed to embrace. I believe that if we wait for the arrival of such a day, it may be too late for many of them to be consoled by then; or nourished, uplifted, and guided; and that God will judge us *in advance* for forsaking His weakest ones as though our duty to tend to them is somehow none of our concern. Are we not setting our own Eternity afire before He has a chance to destroy it with the power of His Love on behalf of those whom we are allowing to starve and shiver in the cold? Oh!—how He wishes that the world were already blazing in such flames! Are we who live lavishly in America today so confident that we have earned His Divine Mercy rather than stirred His raw contempt that we are willing to draw upon His kindness with such bold pride and vanity in our hearts? Is not His vat of forbearance drawn nearly to the dregs; and are we not hoping to be able to sneak through the cracks beneath the backdoor of Heaven someday like thieves crawling on their bellies under the cover of the dark, rather than marching arm-in-arm with stately brightness alongside those whom He has vested with the dignity of its Hosts?  Let us not be deluded about this anymore—He knows exactly who we are, what we are doing, and the wanton malfeasance of our plans!  Let us never be too quick to patronize an absolution we have never really earned; for He may choose to etch the epitaphs announcing our final condemnation into marble slabs and headstones before we've ever died!  This does not imply that our faith will let us down or that Christ will not wash clean the most wretched from the crevices in our midst by the power of His Blood.  Beneath it all, we are the military-industrial complex who has placed our patriotic flagstaffs above His Holy Sacrifice; exchanging trillions of dollars in municipal bonds between the nations of the world, but simultaneously forcing 60 million of our own sick and dying citizens to lay flat on their backs without sufficient medical care and in agony in their homes; many of them little children who are suffering malnutrition because our corporate ethicists have placed their hopes on constructing new skyscrapers to block our view of Paradise, commissioning statues to commemorate the wealth they inherited from their dead, and procuring new fleets of private jets so they can spend the winter months tanning on the beaches of the Bermudas instead of landing like resurrected saints in C-5 cargo planes with fuselages packed to the bulkheads with food upon the shores of Bangladesh.  Indeed, ours is the country that struts about the outer-spacial void in billion-dollar shuttles and dispatches distant satellites to see whether life exists on other cosmic worlds.  Oh!  There is going to be a reckoning, alright!—just in time to see the error of our ways flash before our eyes when Jesus Christ reveals where, when, and in whom His Flesh and Spirit resided in those forgotten little children we have left dying on the streets!

We boast quite prolifically about having a firm grip on the future in America these days, and how self-sufficient and independent we have become from the other continents of the globe; fully autonomous from their particular kinds of domestic plight, rampant social unrest, and untold civil wars.  Many Christians are fearing the very same concerns about which I have written in this book; that the entrance into Paradise for some who live around us is going to bear the likeness of a Belmont Stakes photo-finish.  Jesus Christ knows exactly who they are; for He has already snapped the photograph, but has yet to develop the film in the realm of the spiritual unseen to reveal it to the world.  If there is predestination in anything for sure, we can stand in confidence that anyone who suffers harm upon His little innocents that does not repent and seek His final pardon will never allow *themselves*, by the self-adjudication of their very own souls, to see any farther inside the New Jerusalem than the glistening diamonds on the outer Gates of Paradise on their way toward the pit of lasting grief and strife in a fiery perdition called Hell. Everything in the creative genius of the human intellect should tell us that the strong should protect the weak, the wise are called to enlighten the ignorant, the fit to carry the frail, and the enriched to lift-up the indigent from under their dinner tables and give them an equal share of the bounty of the Earth that our Divine Lord has proffered to us all. It is possible for the world's entire population of starving little children to be rescued from their awful fate of nibbling bread-crumbs off their brothers' earthen floor into carving veal cutlets in stately dining rooms beside every prince and princess who was ever so fortunate to draw the breath of life. Ours is the task of discovering where our poor youth are huddled together in masses and by the dozens in single-family huts, having no running water with which to take a bath or to even quench their thirst. We must begin a concerted effort to liberate the millions of children around the world who are being sold as prostitutes, or held captive as slaves in sweat-shops for wealthy capitalists, and incarcerated in cages like wild animals to keep them from escaping into freedom and their search for dignity. Anything less than restoring their pristine innocence in return for God's blessings upon us will not suffice for *Thy Kingdom Come, Thy Will Be Done*; and God Almighty shall have the final say when His Truth is ultimately sifted from beneath the ruins of our scornful indignance on the last day of the world.

In the final analysis, whatever time we invest, no matter how many resources are expended or miles traveled, hours spent, schedules revised, and priorities rearranged, our children are worth every last pitch of effort that their parents or guardians might be required to share in order to sculpt their lives around the needs of their little ones who are so dependent upon them. America does not necessarily deserve a reprimand from people like me to realize that we are almost failing in the pursuit of identifying with the needs of our younger generation; and we discover this every time another one of them surrenders to temptation and sin. When a teenager is caught with crack cocaine lodged in the toe of his shoe, or gets a grisly-looking body piercing, or is found to be in possession of any kind of contraband, the rest of us are probably just as responsible for not addressing the conditions that led them into such delinquent conduct in the first place. We recognize their lack of peaceful guidance in the sounds of their head-banging music from their car stereo speakers next to us at the intersection of State Street and Broadway, by their purple hair sticking-out like a sore thumb a row or two ahead of us in the movie theatre, and by the horrendous columns of failing grades that appear on their report cards at the conclusion of another academic term. The truth is, our children need us long after the moment they are old enough to know they are alive. They discover that freedom means that they own the right to deign a fate for themselves—either good or bad; and they will be faced with the consequences of their actions if they do not learn in advance which avenues to shun and avoid. Our youth are often confused by our seeming lack of concern in directing them toward the proper courses of conduct because they are apprehensive about our ulterior motivations. In other words, they can read between the lines that we are trying to control them. We have a great deal more to do to convince our offspring that they are not just another deduction from our annual income taxes and that we believe them to be capable of learning right from wrong in the virtues of spiritual Truth as we force them into a pair of slacks and a necktie and send them off to listen to the preacher on Sunday morning. However, we discover in the long-run that teaching our children to be holy is just as important as whether we, ourselves, ever succeed in the labor force so we can purchase a retirement home when we grow older or are able to save an adequate nest-egg so we can travel to the Florida Keys in the wintertime. There is no doubt that millions of American parents are more worried about the balance of their 401(k) accounts right now than whether their children gain a closer relationship with God. Consequently, when we are called out of bed at the stroke of midnight to bail one of our wayward sons out of jail for getting into a ruckus after having worked the late-shift at the nearby Burger King, we look upon them with outright disdain and wonder why they never do anything to make themselves more productive for once in their lives. All of this occurs while we remain silent about the counter-cultural fad shops in many neighborhood precincts where they sell the latest in tobacco paraphernalia, bongs and one-hitters; pewter craftware depicting skulls, crossbones, and screaming eagles; posters of the most popular punk-rockers on stage these days sporting nose rings and spiked hair, erotic and pornographic movies, risque lingerie, incense burners, off-colored birthday, wedding, and anniversary cards; and the hottest Heavy Metal music CDs with a written warning against their graphic lyrics in bold stickers on the front of their labels.

All of this is to the detriment of the stability of our nation's spiritual health. Should we not, instead, be instilling into our children's psyches the pious images of Christian baptismal fonts, statues of the Saints, mosaics of the Stations of the Cross, murals of the lives of Jesus, Mary, and Joseph; and the stately platforms which contain the Holy Oils that are blessed by our Roman Catholic Bishops every Spring during their solemn Chrism Masses? Sadly, our children's search for Truth is already dead beneath the water or is slowly foundering; and it is their adult counterparts who are ultimately to blame for allowing it to die. Can we force our Christian values upon them against their will? Probably not. But, we can surely show them the fruits of our own piousness and bring them to pine for the inner-peace we enjoy by setting before them the best example of holy love that they will ever see in their natural span of life. We can be kind to them, and address and admonish them without robbing them of their dignity. We can teach them that hatred, indiscretion, violence, and lust are unnegotiably wrong; and that their identification with immoral infatuation is by no means a source of true freedom. Our American spiritual leaders and teachers of Christianity must explain to them in absolute terms that homosexuality, lesbianism, premarital sex, contraception, abortion, and suicide are mortal sins that are hanging like albatrosses around their necks; trying to take their souls into the fiery pit of eternal condemnation. Thereafter, if they howl in protest against our orthodoxy, should we not place the manifestation of supernatural miracles before them as evidence of God's Grace, such as the extraordinary apparitions of the Blessed Virgin Mary in places like Fatima, Lourdes, and Guadalupe to prove to them that Jesus Christ really does exist, and that He sees them as being worthy to be blessed by the extension of His Love into our present day and time? Indeed, if the scripted message hidden in their scrawling gang symbols is ever etched into the facade of the downtown Municipal Building to express their indignation against our indifference, should we not erect a Messianic Cross in front of it that is so mammoth in size that no one would ever be able to decipher their coded hieroglyphics? We should anticipate and preempt their assaults against the decency and dignity of humankind by ensuring that they also become the epitome of Christian piety for themselves. The taste of our civil liberties will not take a bitter turn if we teach them that it is not a violation of the First Amendment to hold their tongues about the things they do not like or refrain from throwing a tantrum every time we ask one of them to carry-out the trash. The advancement of Creation will not take a giant leap backward if we require them to politely and respectfully address their elderly neighbors as "Mr. and Mrs. Smith," rather than "Yo! Dudes!"

We are not according our sons and daughters one whit of good by laughing in the face of their tawdriness, upholding their socially malignant rituals, sustaining their objections to Divine Truth, or turning our backs on their intentional discourtesy just because we want to be regarded as their personal friends. It may not be true that our children learn their distasteful habits from what we might say and do, but they can certainly be led astray by their imitation of our imprudence and omissions. So, what does this implicate for their future? The answer depends upon whether we ultimately recognize that nothing in the world can supplant the guidance, leadership, and exemplary love that our younger generation must somehow glean from us. We seem to be getting nowhere fast in making a measurable difference toward achieving this goal. We rise every morning to the news that another group of children has taken-up cigarette smoking, binge-drinking alcoholic beverages, chasing the record for eating the most cheeseburgers in a day, and being the first to drop from a certain height while wearing a measured bungee-cord around their waist. One of these days, our whole misalignment of priorities is suddenly going to snap—literally and figuratively; and our entire society will land flat on its head in corruptive oblivion without a scintilla of spiritual decency for our grandchildren to inherit; or anything else implied, spoken, or written that would prove to our posthumous critics that we were anything other than morally bankrupt. A great portion of the reason behind our lack of focus on the intrinsic value of the human person is the existing lack of equality between our families, societies, and nations of the world. I have placed a list of the top dozen capitalist billionaires from *Forbes Magazine* on the sixth page of Chapter V in this book to address the issues of our great cultural inequity, but such a phenomenon as the disproportionate distribution of material wealth is not the only cause of the degradation of the nobility of our children. Not too many statistics are as obvious in divulging to our children that things are not always as they seem as the prospect of who is confiscating our money. While it is never a toss-up as to whether a 4-year-old child would rather munch on a Snickers candy bar than be forced to choke-down a helping of Brussels sprouts, most of their choices in life are not as simple to decide. The physical environment, our social classes, certain scandalous people, and our immediate senses often skew their vision of reality; and this is why *we must be there* to lead them toward the righteous paths. Many insecure parents go to great lengths, too, to overprotect their children; like reminding them to never brush their teeth when they have the hiccoughs for fear of choking on the toothpaste. Our concerns for such microcosms sometimes make our vision so narrow in scope that we fail to remember the millions of others around the globe who have never known the meaning of oral hygiene, flossing, or gargling with Listerine; let alone ever having been told what a professional dentist does. Are we so lacking in dimensions of Love that we cannot tend to the personal needs of our offspring and the paupers of our neighboring countries, too? While we are deciding whether to use goose-down feathers in our pillows or some type of synthetic foam, hundreds-of-thousands of little children in far-off lands fall asleep every night with their heads resting on anthills and their feet tucked beneath fallen tree branches. Are we such crass isolationists that we are closing our eyes to their needs by reason of the proverbial sarcasm,...*better to end the suffering before us than to address any agony we know not of?* Unfortunately, such a plea of ignorance of the law is not going to do much to exonerate our souls once we hear the piercing voice of the Son of God in the Halls of Justice someday.

I attended a Roman Catholic prayer service on December 11, 1999 where the sponsors dispensed a small pamphlet that had a very hopeful supplication for little children on one of its pages. The author was listed as being unknown, but he or she must surely be very blessed. I have recorded it with the same awkwardness and broken sentences in which it appeared in the booklet. The text reads, *We pray for children who sneak Popsicles before supper. Who erase holes in math workbooks. Who can never find their shoes. And, we pray for those who stare at photographers from behind barbed wire. Who can't bound down the street in a new pair of sneakers. Who never "counted potatoes," who are born in places we wouldn't be caught dead in. Who never saw a circus. Who live in an X-rated world. We pray for children who bring us sticky kisses and fistfuls of dandelions. Who hug us in a hurry and forget their lunch money. And, we pray for those who never get dessert. Who have no security blanket to drag behind them. Who watch their parents watch them die. Who cannot find any bread to steal. Who don't have any rooms to clean. Whose pictures aren't on anybody's dresser. Whose monsters are real. We pray for children who spend all their allowance before Tuesday. Who throw tantrums in the grocery store and pick at their food. Who like ghost stories. Who shove their dirty clothes under the bed, and never rinse-out the tub. Who get visits from the tooth fairy. Who don't like to be kissed in front of the car pool. Who squirm in church and scream into the telephone. Whose tears we sometimes laugh at, and whose smiles can make us cry. And, we pray for those whose nightmares come in the daytime. Who will eat anything. Who have never seen a dentist. Who aren't spoiled by anybody. Who go to bed hungry and cry themselves to sleep. Who live and move, but have no being. We pray for children who want to be carried, and for those who must be. For those we never give-up on, and for those who never get a second chance. For those we smother with affection, and for those who will grab the hand of anyone who is kind enough to offer it.*

It must be a source of both solace and consternation to think that the conduct of our little children can be such a strange contradiction for us who are their caretakers. They can make us laugh and cry in the brief span of only five minutes; and our anger toward them can be eradicated with their simple, "I promise I will never do it again." I sometimes wonder whether their fear of punishment is as great a factor in their thoughts and actions as what they think we would do if they suddenly surprised us by conforming to our wishes upon our first command. It may not always be easy to determine the workings of the mind of a child, but we can always anticipate the tenderness of their impressionable hearts. It seems as though we are constantly having to forgive them for something; which should never be a great strain upon us once we realize that their behavior is rarely the product of any serious premeditation. Wasn't it the great English poet Alexander Pope (1688-1744) who wrote the famous maxim,...*to err is human, to forgive is Divine*? Perhaps he was referring to the Biblical passage from the Holy Gospel according to Saint Matthew where Jesus responds to a question that is put before Him by one of the Apostles, *...Then Peter came up and asked Him, "Lord, when my brother wrongs me, how often must I forgive him? Seven times?" "No," Jesus replied, "not seven times; I say, seventy times seven times."* (Mat. 18:21-22). Our Lord's admonishment here directly precedes the parable about the merciless official who was forgiven his debts by the king, then went to seize and throttle one of his own debtors. When his master found it out, he handed the man over to the torturers until he repaid the entire account. Jesus concludes His parable by saying, *...My Heavenly Father will treat you in exactly the same way unless each of you forgives his brother from his heart.* Now we are discovering the reason why Jesus asks us to become like little children before we are allowed entrance into the Kingdom of Paradise. Do we not find them spatting upon one another on the playground at midday and playing checkers on the back porch by night? Do not our little ones say things that pierce their friends' feelings to the core; but such offenses are forgotten upon the occasion of our taking them each and every one to the malt shop for a treat? If we ponder the text of the petition that I discovered inside the pamphlet at that Catholic prayer cenacle, would we not be remiss if we refused to expunge the record of our children's errors within moments after they occur? Would we not hold their little hearts closer to our breasts if we did not bear a grudge against them for the mistakes we see them make? It is quite obvious that Our Divine Lord requires us to forgive anyone who trespasses against us, as is witnessed by Peter in the Holy Gospel of Saint Matthew. But, such pardoning should not be restricted to certain adults from whom we might have something to gain. Our children need a definitive reassurance that we harbor no ill-feelings against them; and this is how they grow to be the likeness of Christ in their older years.

It oftentimes seems like we do not realize the commonness of our exile from Heaven as one unified species of man. We are the perpetrators and victims of a catastrophic proceeding called human existence—which is a miraculous and mystifying gift that only God, Himself, can ultimately explain and refine. Our life on the Earth is somewhat synonymous with a nocturnal convulsion from which we will all awaken someday and see how He has developed and shaped unseen Creation while we were asleep. Our childhood flashbacks and spontaneous brainstorms are an inherent part of the climax of this sublime crucible. It is true that we are helpless, and that anything we might do in order to excavate a more productive purpose from under the burdens of our transgressions is only an exercise in futility if we decline to engage the Holy Spirit of God to help us. The future will uphold our actions and responses if we refer our plight to our higher guardians, regardless of our age; because they who are the Hosts of Paradise in the realm of the Firmament who seem to be so elusive sometimes will actually intercede for us.  If our pondering is fashioned upon the predicate that the Dawn of the Son of Man will follow the reckoning which He has already laid-out for us, is it not true that we have already been judged outside the element of time?  Is our present age simply a moment in a series of many others during which we are maintaining our allegiance to His Sacred Heart of Love, or proving once and for all that we shall never be true to our oath in following Him?  Of all the facts, figures, premises, and opinions that *Babes in the Woods* will produce, the most significant premonition is that we are given both supernatural power and indomitable strength through our obedience to Jesus Christ for amending the way we live, comforting those who are afflicted, especially our little children; inhaling a fresh breath of Christian reverence wherever we can, and telling the enemies of the Holy Cross that they are dead-wrong about their presumption that humankind is failing or can never be elevated in our relationship to God and the physical universe.  All we need to do is look around.  There are signs and indicators of the Sacred Plan of our final repatriation into the Mansions of Paradise everywhere.  But, we must clarify our vision through the power of the human heart; for from such is where we see the metamorphosis of the best of all possible worlds.  We are obviously the keepers of our precious little people; and they are the naive innocents who live in our midst with the invincible Love of Jesus Christ seeded deeply within their souls.  A humble recording artist by the name of Tom T. Hall penned a song in the early 1970s entitled, *Old Dogs, and Children, and Watermelon Wine* in which he asks God to bless all little children who are still too young to hate.  I did not really know what he meant until I grew older and discovered that despising our fellow man is not a congenital defect of our newborn babies.  We actually *learn* to hate our brothers by what we see them do, how they speak in our midst, by the prejudices we inherit from those around whom we are reared, and an atmosphere in America today which is wholly lacking in the fruits of the very Christianity that most of us claim to avow.  Indeed, our hatred is a sad by-product of our disingenuous habit of saying that we are Christians, but behaving in quite the opposite terms.  The most dire consequences occur when our children see this happening and perceive us as being character role-models with whom they should identify, and respect, and emulate.  Perhaps we would be better followers of Christ if we heeded both the letter and the Spirit of His New Covenant Gospel.  Then, America's youth will not be so confused anymore; they might see the entire globe with inclusive hearts instead of an arrogant western hemisphere that believes we must be pacified by patrons from far-distant shores.  If we claim to be Christians in the likeness of the Apostles, we have yet to prove it to the rest of the world. Let us instill this into the consciences of our children, evoke it from the atheists whose souls are already dead, and take Our Divine Lord's Creation back again with a righteousness that is so holy and profound that Saint Peter, himself, will crawl from beneath his towering Basilica in Rome with a bottle of champagne in his hands.

# Chapter II
## *Bassinets, Bathtubs, and Baseballs*
## *The Comedic Life of Infancy*

I suppose one of the things that makes our little children so memorable is that they own a penchant to be extremely humorous without really trying; and this is the innocence that seems to pass so swiftly during the progression of their formative years. We do not help much when we tease them all the time or use their clumsiness as the butt of our jokes. If ever there was an image of how we do this, it would surely be the scene of the father and his four-year-old son sitting in two front row seats at a baseball game, somewhere along the third-base line. Oh yes, we have all seen it happen. A batter fouls a pitch into the stands near them, the man catches it for a brief moment, after which he bobbles it and accidently lets it tumble back down the retaining-wall onto the field and roll around. So, what does he do before it has a chance to get completely away? He grabs his son by the ankles, lowers him over the wall above the foul territory and tells him to outstretch his arms and pick-up the baseball with his fingers. And, as soon as the little boy has hold of it, his father reels him back into the stands with the souvenir baseball in tow so they both will have a remnant of their day at the park. They sit back down with their catch in their laps, laughing at the top of their lungs, along with the 38,000 other baseball fans in the grandstand, and millions of television viewers who just witnessed the entire event. Going from the sublime to the ridiculous, we then hear a witty commentator on the sidelines remarking about the spontaneous act and posing the question of what might have happened if the little boy's tennis shoes would have slipped off. We also get a big charge out of watching the syndicated TV program *Kids Say the Darndest Things* that was made popular by the great interviewer Art Linkletter from the 1950s through the 1980s, and continued into the 1990s and beyond by the hilarious entertainer, Bill Cosby. Why are such exchanges between these children and their host so comical? Because, when questioned, little people will nearly always reveal the truth about their home lives, their parents, their school mates, and their personal habits and preferences. It is a fact that nothing is as funny as such unique details when they are presented by the speech of an unassuming innocent child. I sometimes think that the word "impish" was created especially to describe both the looks on their faces and their cackling demeanor when I see them in such extemporaneous settings. There is a lesser-known humorist who hails from my hometown of Ashland, Illinois by the name of Reverend Alf Anderson, a Protestant minister and jeweler by trade, whose life and wit have generated various short stories and puns about the unintentional comedy that our little children often extol. Mr. Anderson was a feature reporter for the *Ashland Sentinel* newspaper, which is a small and almost irrelevant weekly edition that has been a part of the Ashland iconography for over a hundred years. It was printed by the William Bast family for generations, and has since changed hands and is now produced by another local owner. Anyway, the following two stories appeared in the *Sentinel* in January 2002.

*For his part in a Sunday School program, a four-year-old was to say the line, "I am the Light of the world." Because he had difficulty remembering his line, his mother sat in the front row. When his turn came and his face was a blank, his mother mouthed the words. Suddenly, his face lit-up, and with a loud confidence in his voice, he exclaimed, "My mother is the Light of the world!"*

And, another...

*There were five kindergarten boys with a part in a school program where each boy was to receive a large letter written on a placard and hold it up while standing in line to spell the word, "hello." The boy holding the letter "o" became confused and stood at the wrong end of the line. Proudly holding-up his big letter, the word did not spell "hello," but something else quite different altogether. The audience response was a mixture of muffled guffaws and various expressions of dismay. Not a soul in the room really knew what to do with this one.*

I also received an electronic mailing about the same time that Mr. Anderson's funnies appeared in the local newspaper from someone named Janet Cook that had some additional comical stories in it that I think ought to be shared with the rest of the world.

*After the Christening of his baby brother in Church, a little boy sobbed all the way home in the back seat of the car. His father asked him three times what was wrong. Finally, the boy replied, "That priest said he wanted us to be brought-up in a good Christian home, but I would rather stay with you guys."*

This little fellow had no idea that he was inadvertently insulting his unsuspecting parents by accidentally suggesting that they were not really Christian—notwithstanding the fact that he had yet to learn the meaning of the term. His sudden shedding of tears was based upon the truth as he knew it to be, as skewed as it may have been. But, his purpose was to tell his mother and father that he loved them and never wanted to live with anyone else. Such loyalty is what makes our little children so affectionate, honest, devoted, dependent, and innocent. Inside their hearts lives the essence of humankind at our highest clarity before the Eternal Throne of God. When we lay a baby on its back in a wooden crib beneath a dangling carousel of various-shaped objects that are suspended by a string, we can see how mesmerized he is by their curious movements as he reaches to haphazardly tap them with the tips of his fingers. Is this not how Jesus was also capable of shaping, bending, altering, and redirecting the disposition and composition of the entire solar system that He saw at His Birth as being no larger than a carousel of objects from His lowly manger in Bethlehem? The world watched as Our Divine Lord developed and grew from an infant child into the vast maturity of Love and Truth that over 75 billion people who have lived and died throughout history have ultimately come to know. Is God telling us that our best emulation of His Divine Love is to be like His Child-Jesus in our acceptance of His Kingdom, and by growing our dependence upon His Immaculate Mother to make Creation aright? And, too, has He warned us by virtue of His piety within the parameters of His sinless Flesh that the world will reject us, too? It so often seems as though children have a wholesale amount of more courage than we do because they are brave enough to dream their own miracles into being, to reach-out into the wilderness of the world without fearing that it will harm them, and to evoke from those around them the desire to be as trusting, unassuming, receptive, and benign. They seem to own an incorrupt perception of the Truth as it is spoken outright by God because their hearts have not yet been hardened by the seemingly inevitable offenses of other men. We can learn how to be like Jesus from His littlest ones because they have not chosen to defy Him in defense of their own personal defections. To be clear, they are entirely open to accept what human life has to offer through the blessings of God from the interior of their souls. Aside from all the comedy, we are the inheritors of a generation of newborn people who can flatten mountain ranges with their tears, convert multitudes of the spiritually blind with the innocence in their eyes, restore the happiness of entire continents of despondent mourners with the genuineness of their laughter, dispatch battalions of Angels to the suffering and forsaken, and console the destitute-of-heart with their prefigured kindness. Rarely have we ever approached a child sitting in a highchair eating a cookie who did not ask us to take a bite, as nibbled and soggy as it might have been. However, even herein, scores of their elders continue to cast them aside as being no more than underdeveloped creatures whose fate is but a matter for future conjecture, or giddy little nuisances with nothing tangible to offer such a mature lot of materialized men as we have become today. We adults place more honor in our autonomy to breach the rules that God has laid before us than we do in upholding the sustainable perfection He has placed inside the hearts of our own little children.

There is a Divine nature to the comedy of our infant children that no motion picture screenplay writer or producer can ever replicate because we somehow lose our honesty trying to make the finished product a precise reflection of their attributes as we *wish* them to be. We are reminded of the little boy who was watching his father, a pastor, handwriting a sermon onto a piece of paper. "How do you know what to say?" he asked. "Why, God tells me," his father replies. So the boy continues, "...then why do you keep crossing things out?" We have been told that facts are very stubborn things, and this is the dilemma that the pastor faced in the wake of such an obvious question. He could have gone into detail about how the Holy Spirit shapes our thoughts and writes our entreating recitations by virtue of the solemnity of our prayers and our openness in understanding the Wisdom of the Sacred Scriptures. But, that would only have led to additional queries from the boy that his father did not really have time to answer. Indeed, what does this say about the many theological manuscripts of such legends as SS. Thomas Aquinas, Augustine, John Baptiste-Vianney, Bonaventure, and Ignatius? How does the premise that they were all children of God in the likeness of Baby Jesus play alongside the fact that they were capable of writing so evocatively about the Cardinal Virtues and the Fruits of Divine Love? The answer is quite simple: they wiped the slate of the secular world completely away from their senses; they forced themselves to forego the materialism that has plundered the lives of so many decent men; they wept openly to better understand the guidance from an Almighty Father whom they could not yet see from within the blindness of their mortal years; and they reached upwardly with their hearts and hands to take hold of a Creator whose intentions for their lives had not altogether been revealed. In essence, they had the courage it takes to surrender to the power of Jesus Christ to heal humanity through other broken hearts, to alter the face of the globe with the hands of the descendants of the very people who first corrupted it, and to enlighten an entire world of darkness by the glow of holiness which has sprung-forth like wildflowers from under the boot-heels of a quite haughty army of sinners. These Saints were despised by those who placed no trust in the omnipotence of God to suspend the laws of nature with the blink of His eyes, to set entire races of oppressed people free as briskly as a passing summer breeze, and to annihilate the obstinance of His detractors through the Love of an Immaculate Child whom the faithful around Him deemed fit to crown as their incarnate *Emmanuel*. This is the intersection of our kaleidoscope childhood and the stationed genius of Heaven above—to be able to cast-out our worries in the same way that an anonymous child might take a hapless swipe at a carousel from the sanctuary of his crib. There is no greater evidence of the domination of our Proverbial God to instruct His people in charity, goodness, piety, self-denial, sacrifice, and service than for Him to have given His great Saints the grace to underscore the invincibility of His renewed Creation through their own personal suffering and to commission them as valorous conquerors in order to defeat every last parcel of atheistic intellectualism they encountered with their childlike faithfulness to the Eternal Wisdom of His Messianic Son.

The new identity we have gained in the empowered providence of Our Lord's well-intentioned purposes comes to us only after we relinquish our prejudices against the Sacred Mysteries of the Salvation of our souls in the Bloodshed of Jesus on the Holy Cross. The predestined awareness that we have garnered in Him transcends our material scrutinies, overwhelms the capacity of our courses of thought, brings closure to our corporal lust, dissolves the networking of capitalist profiteers, and tips the playing-field of spiritual warfare in favor of the Christian elect so we can always be victorious over the enemies of Godly Love who often retreat in cowardly agnosticism behind their ivy-covered walls. So, let there be no mistake about it: to remain simple in our allegiance to the Son of God never implies that we must be naive about the deceptive ways of the world. We know who our adversaries have become because they are the beastly bullies on the playground that refuse to lend an ear to the deafening reveille of Christ's horn of plenty, who would rather take a beating than say *I love you* to their worst enemies, and who believe that brutal force is always more powerful than interpersonal reconciliation. Little do most of them know that the next newborn baby in the OB room at the hospital downtown can wield more power to amend the Earth and reshape Creation than they will ever have if they should live ten-thousand more years. Why? Because our children's innocence mirrors the same Godliness and spiritual fortitude that has already uprooted the repugnance of our sinful underworld to reveal the glowing apple-blossoms of Our Lord's gleaming eyes. It would take more words than we could possibly imagine to describe how Jesus wishes this to be true—just look at the two innocent little children whose angelic faces appear on the cover of this book. They are my nephews whom God has chosen to be the offspring-sons of my younger sister Lisa and her husband, Larry Cave. Jesus is asking us to believe that Saints Peter and John would have posed for such a similar photograph if they would have had the means and opportunity back when they lived; and we know the legacy of their Christianity as they faithfully imparted it across their exile in His behalf for the conversion of humankind and the ushering of the Kingdom of God into the physical world. All the Apostles were once little children in the likeness of Curtis and Adam Cave; and so are the rest of us who look at their picture now and wonder how anyone so diminutive could ever have a meaningful effect on the stature of this earthly life and the miraculous Dominion of the next. They grow-up too quickly to suit us sometimes; and it costs a small fortune to feed and clothe them, to keep them in social competition with their peers, to provide them dependable transportation, and to send them to school. But, in the depths of all this, they never lose their desire as little children to be loved and comforted by us. They retain their affection for the souls who first begot them, who nurtured and cared for them in their infancy, and for the academic institutions that gave them their start toward surviving on their own. Are they as innocently witty after they have grown? Perhaps more of the latter applies, sometimes. Another one of Janet Cook's stories interjected here might be rather apropos.

*We are told about the college drama group that presented a staged morality play in which one of the characters would stand on a trapdoor and announce, "I descend into Hell!" A stagehand below him would then pull a rope, the trapdoor would open, and the character would plunge through. The play was very well received. When the actor playing the part became ill, however, another one who was rather overweight had to take his place. When the new actor announced, "I descend into Hell!" the stagehand pulled the rope, the boy began his plunge, but he became helplessly stuck in the opening. No amount of tugging on the rope could make him descend. All of a sudden, another student in the overhead balcony jumped to his feet and yelled, "Hallelujah! Hell is full!"*

There have been innumerable early-childhood psychoanalysts, psychiatrists, sociologists, and educators who have studied and written about the inner-workings of the mind of a child. What is it, they ask, that each of them has in common? What forces direct their motivations, shape their erratic behavior, and provide unforeseen details about how a certain youngster will develop and evolve? Are these counselors and doctors not really making an attempt to discover the impact of a world of contradictions upon the untouched divinity of the infant psyche? Is the way that the world affects our children less important than it is that we should learn from their mistakes? We keep focusing upon some type of internal "jet stream" that may have a discernable influence on the atmosphere of their well-being in later life. Such cause-effect reasoning is the very thing that is making our diagnosis of them so difficult to conclude. Unfortunately for those whose profession is to decide how to mold and shape the conduct of our children, our little ones do not harbor a vast conspiracy or clandestine agenda like most clinical psychologists choose to believe. They do not awaken in the morning and lay-out certain plans toward the continuation of a fashioned mission that may take weeks or months to accomplish. They live from one moment to the next, and from one social encounter to another. The entire expanse of their internal purposes can usually be contracted into the period of daybreak until dusk on any given day. And, this is exactly what makes them seem so peculiar to us. Parents are concerned about what projects are required to be finished by next week, when the utility bills come due, what kind of automobile to buy, and what nursing home they will have to put Grandma in before too long. Their younger counterparts, on the other hand, are fully absorbed in choosing the starting pitcher for this afternoon's softball game, what kind of fruit topping to put on their ice-cream sundaes, whether or not to wear socks inside their tennis shoes, and how to avoid getting into any serious relationships with the neighborhood boy or girl who lives next-door. Do we envy them for never having to wonder who is going to pay for their supper tonight or wash the pillow-cases where they will lay their heads, and not having to face the realities of salaries, taxes, and the rumors of war all the time? There are probably very few of us who would not wish to return to the simplicity of our childhood, whether or not we received an occasional spanking or two, so as to reverse these inexorable forces of adapting to human life in a materially-oriented world which is filled to the brim with the memories of so many sorrowful losses. No one can grow into adulthood and be unfazed by these things because the tender heart which is given to us at our birth struggles like a madman drowning in a waterfall to survive. Our innocence ends only after we surrender to the callousness of infighting to be the best in a competitive whirlpool of social stratospheres, imperialist stock brokers peddling their wares, and narrow-minded financiers coveting our goods. Just once, I wish a corporate board chairman would open a meeting of investors with the famous story about his little grand-daughter sitting on his lap while he reads her a bedtime story. From time to time, she would take her eyes off the book and reach-up to touch his wrinkled cheek. She would alternately stroke her own cheek, then his again. Finally, she speaks up, "Grandpa, did God make you?" "Yes, sweetheart," he answers, "God made me a long time ago." "Oh," and she pauses, "Grandpa, did God make me too?" "Yes, indeed, honey," he says, "God made you just a little while ago." Feeling their respective faces again, she observes, "God is getting better at it, isn't He?" Suddenly, it would seem that the purview of his corporate chair would not be as important to her grandfather anymore. Whose mind would not come to parade-rest upon hearing such a comment and wonder what had taken them so far from the simplistic vision of that little child?

I once wrote an *Essay* in one of my earlier books about Christianity, *At the Water's Edge: Essays in Faith and Morals,* in which I subtly rebuked the United States for straying such a great distance from the unintentional holiness which is an intrinsic part of the psychology of our little children. I described how they ride around the supermarket in our grocery carts like miniature grand marshals in the parade of daily life. I touched upon the fact that they care little about the role of our police and fire departments, or what a man in a pleated robe does when he takes a seat behind the bench in a federal courtroom. Thinking back upon it now, I still maintain that they can look at a four-star general in full uniform and not be as moved as they might be by seeing someone dressed as Santa Claus in the foyer of the local JC Penney store. But, can we not sense with greater enlightenment how even the littlest among us are brought to understand the reasons why adults wear silver badges and big black rubber boots to work everyday? Has our world of mutual hatred which brought America to suffer the horrible civilian atrocities that we endured on September 11, 2001 forced this issue upon our children as they were made to watch the Port Authority and New York City policemen and firemen from dozens of units in Lower Manhattan serve, suffer, and die; and their fire trucks and other equipment being smashed, burned, and buried beneath the smouldering rubble of two Twin Towers tumbling to the ground like a pair of dinosaurs without any bones? Indeed, did they not see airplane pilots wearing uniforms with gold epaulettes on their shoulders trying to describe what the moment must have been like for their executed colleagues to have their respective jetliners commandeered by a gang of terrorist thugs and forced to fly headlong into these same two skyscrapers, the rings of the U.S. Pentagon, and onto an isolated field in rural Pennsylvania? So, we sit our children down at the dinner table or in front of the fireplace and tell them that our admired men and women who they never knew before, those who were wearing those decorated uniforms, were suddenly summoned by our adversaries to sacrifice their lives, their loved ones, and the utter dignity of their families in order to protect the very country in which all of our little children are being raised. Tragically, their innocent hearts are too early taught the grief of death long before they ever conquer life; and they encounter the loneliness of being separated from our newest martyrs prior to knowing why they were ever so stately clad in the selfless vestments of true American heroism. They do not comprehend the meaning of hatred; they have not grasped the purpose of political unrest; the religious conflicts around the globe seem absolutely surreal to them; and the world continues-on without their input until we believe they are old enough to join in the battles against our common enemies whom *we* have already chosen for them. Why can we not become more like them? Why are we not as tolerant and lacking in social vindictiveness as a kindergarten class or a room filled with giggling preschoolers? For them, the comedy of human errors continues every day; and we must rediscover the gene inside their little hearts that causes them to be influenced by it, the one that we have somehow allowed to die in our process of growing-up.

The most endearing aspects of our personal nobility should teach us that the "childlike" nature that Jesus Christ is summoning from us is not a gullible deference to the influences that are vile enough to take advantage of our Christian innocence. Moreover, it is not necessary that we break the laws of Divinity in order to completely understand them. By all means, the more we talk about evil works, the less time we have for evangelizing the virtues of peace, reconciliation, and spiritual Love. Being a child of God is always about *new beginnings*, so that we never lose hope that the very next tomorrow might bring the culmination of all our dreams and aspirations. No matter how much time passes-away, the mission of our transition from this life into the next can never be muted or destroyed—whatever conflicts we may have to enter and conclude, notwithstanding how many divisions of Christ's enemies we are eventually forced to conquer, and regardless of the numerous undercurrents of daily life we must ford or swim against to streamline the wakes for goodness and Light. We see our little children kneel like angels around a Christmas nativity scene as they play with their toy cars under the shade trees in the back yard. And, the Bible tells us that they sit like olive plants around our dinner tables. We must never, *ever* bring harm to them or make them feel as though they have no purpose in our present-day world. They should always be consulted as being special participants in the vastness of our human experience, never remanded to the margins where we cast so many inanimate things, and brought close to our breasts in affection and respect. Whatever negativity we might feel toward our children, we should always remember how Jesus loves them. The forethought of our actions should be to include them in our decisions about where we live, what Church we choose to attend, where they will be sent to get a formal education, and how we will provide for their personal development with an emphasis upon remembering the experiences of our own. Under no circumstances should we ever allow our children to believe that their presence is irrelevant in the unfolding of the history of the world. God has given them to us as a gift of Holy Love, whether we believe it or not; and His is the choice to make us their stewards and guardians. He places His Holy Spirit inside them because, as the great lyricists Randall Thompson once wrote; we are all required to give them *The Best of Rooms* alongside Him in our devotions and to be their protectors, to openly display that they are worthy of our respect, and to prove it outright by elevating them to the highest pinnacle inside our solemn heart-of-hearts. It is true that our children are their most impressionable and vulnerable while they live beneath the umbrella of our loving trust. Sustaining them as they grow means a great deal more than just feeding them a couple of times a day, changing their diapers, or putting a pacifier in their mouths when they are crying too loud. Responsible parenting means valuing the power of filial affection over assertive physical discipline, offering them redirection by positive encouragement despite their mistakes, declining to resort to corporal punishment, commending them when they have complied with the most modest of our expectations, and literally placing our arms around them to tell them with the compassion of God in our souls that we Love them beyond all description. Any mother or father who refuses to physically hug their children to express their thankfulness that they have been born are cold and cowardly enemies of the very God who brought their precious little progeny into being. They will laugh and play with us when they are not otherwise distracted by our refusal to shield them from the cruel hatred of the lost. Parents and guardians are required to Love all little children, no matter their origin, race, color, or creed; for our hearts are the fertile soil in which Jesus Christ has sown them as seedlings to bloom into future saints while the mortal Earth becomes increasingly more holy and beautiful by the hour.

There have been many artists, manuscript writers, TV producers, cartoonists, and actors who have attempted to portray the way reality ought to be by invoking the innocuous behavior of little children to make their position more clear. We have been both entertained and instructed by their renditions because, deep inside, we still wish we could live in the make-believe world of our childhood for the rest of our days. The actor Jay North played "Dennis the Menace" in the late 1950s TV series that allowed us to see just how vexing youngsters can be for those around them. And, even as his elderly neighbor, Mr. Wilson, placed his palm on his forehead when he would see Dennis coming and say, "Oh, good grief," we still knew that he bore no grudge against him simply because he was being a tenacious little boy. Additionally, of course, we saw a young Jerry Mathers play the role of "The Beave" on "Leave it to Beaver" during that same time period, and all the Brady Bunch kids whom we watched struggle through their adolescent years in the mid-1970s. The common thread in each of these characters was their brash unpredictability, impishness, and ultimately the harmless humor that most of them, even as little pranksters, focused toward their parents for the entertainment of their audience. During none of these episodes did we ever witness their elders resort to physical aggression as a means of teaching the differences between right and wrong. Even when their intellectual reasoning and social sanctions failed in helping them to understand, we were always left with the impression that human Love was the catalyst in changing them for the better. Furthermore, do we remember the late 20th century cartoonist, Bill Watterson, whose comic-strip characters *Calvin and Hobbes* appeared in over 2,400 newspapers across

America from 1986 until December 1995? His work entertained millions of people by exploring the antics of an imposing 6-year-old boy with an overactive imagination — believing that his stuffed tiger was able to speak and move, that he could be in contact with space aliens anytime he needed a quick distraction, and who futilely tried to convince his parents that he was the most maligned and underrated child-genius on the block. Although Bill Watterson has been rather reticent about being interviewed by anyone to discuss his comic strip, no one has any doubt that he holds a firm grasp on the facts about the insightful motivations of our children.

One of my favorites was published on February 8, 1993 in which little Calvin appears to be standing waist-deep in a snowbank holding a fresh ball of ice between his mittens. The first three panels show him striking various poses and reciting, *Oh, lovely snowball packed with care, smack a head that's unaware. Then, with freezing ice to spare, melt and soak through underwear. Fly straight and true; hit hard and square! This, oh snowball, is my prayer.* He immediately turns thereafter as if to be looking at us, the reader, and says, *I only throw consecrated snowballs!* Do we suppose that because of his shallow attempt at piety, we might grant him forbearance in advance should he carry-out the mission he has planned? Of course, he always liked to use the powers of authority to his own advantage, too. A comic from December 2, 1994 has him speaking on the telephone in the first three panels, although we do not yet know to whom; and he is saying, *Look out the window! It's snowing! There must be almost half an inch! By morning, I'll bet there's tons of snow! Do you think the schools will close?* Then, whomever he is speaking to on the other end of the line must say something he does not like, so Calvin screams into the receiver, *What? Oh, yeah? Well, same to you!!* The final frame shows him climbing back into bed with his stuffed tiger and saying, *I wonder how a crabby guy like him got to be superintendent?* A similar comic published on March 11, 1995 shows him talking on the telephone again, saying, *Hello? Yes. I'd like to speak with the Chief of Police.* Apparently, the officer gets on the line, and Calvin continues, *Hello, Chief? Is it a law that your socks have to match anything else you're wearing?* The party on the other end is either quite irritated by the call or is saying exactly what little Calvin wants to hear because the last panel shows him holding the telephone away from his ear while he turns his face in another direction, cups his hand around his mouth to serve as a makeshift megaphone, and yells at the top of his lungs, *Hey Mom, listen to this!* Lastly, I was quite amused by Watterson's July 22, 1995 publication that shows Calvin walking past his father who is sitting in a livingroom lounge chair, saying on his way by, *Oh, just so you know, I am the downhill tumble and roll champ, king of the toad finders, captain of the high altitude tree branch vista club, second place finisher in the 'round the yard backward dash, premier burper: state division, sodbuster and worm scout first order, and generalissimo of the mud and mayhem society!* We then see his father place a book he has been reading onto his lap, rest his chin on his palm with his elbow on the arm of the chair, and say to his little boy with great tolerance in his voice, *Busy day?* And, Calvin says, *About usual. Want to hear what Hobbes is?* We are led to assume that his father has opened a pandora's box by inviting his son to continue his senseless exhortations about his stuffed tiger, whom he believes with all his heart to be a breathing and moving striped feline.

It often seems like there is an invisible tug-of-war going on between Heaven above us and the Earth here below. Everything that is immortally Divine is part of the treasure trove of God's blessings we see everyday, and Jesus Christ is doing everything in His power to coax us into reaching into the depths of our souls and launching the very purpose of human life into the Firmament beyond the stars. What the Scriptures appear to be telling us is that we are not forced to wait until the end of time to retrieve our portion of the perpetual Glory that ultimately belongs to us. Jesus has already been Crucified, descended among the dead, and was Resurrected by His Father on the Third Day. It is through the miracle of our faith that we realize that we are heirs of His immortality, and that He has bequeathed to humankind the riches of His Kingdom in Paradise in advance. We own the additional benefit of knowing that we will see the Light of His Glorious Face someday soon, as well. When we take our rightful place among the Angels and Saints, the Almighty Father will ratify everything we have ever done for our children, the entire world of nations, and His Kingdom in an overwhelming display of Grace. He is quite obviously communicating the message to us right now that our conduct, temperament, and demeanor are supposed to reflect that of His little ones; and at the same time and in the precise way we are supposed to be teaching them to be humble and holy, so does He likewise instruct us. We must keep our sense of humor through the perils of life while we concurrently adhere to His strict admonishments to rid the world of all sin and suffering. Our faith must be not unlike that of our believing little children—come what may—as we approach and receive the Holy Sacraments of the Church and, ultimately, the purifying Sacrifice of His Life on the Cross. If we allow Him to cleanse our souls like infants splashing our palms against the surface of the water in a claw-foot bathtub, He will know that we are not afraid to have our mortal lives laid bare before Him with great faith and trust in the Sacred Mysteries of His Holy Crucifixion. Once we have been fully clad in the armaments of His Love by which our imminent perpetuity is sustained, we will know with pristine clarity what He has been saying all along through the wailing voices of our little children, to *Feed My Lambs,* and *Tend My Sheep.*

# Pastoral

*When I was younger,*
*it was plain to me,*
*I must make something of myself.*
*Older now,*
*I walk back streets,*
*admiring the houses*
*of the very poor:*                                         7
*roof out of line with sides,*
*the yards cluttered*
*with old chicken wire, ashes,*
*furniture gone wrong;*
*the fences and outhouses*
*built of barrel-staves*
*and parts of boxes, all.*                                  14
*If I am fortunate,*
*smeared a bluish green*
*that properly weathered*
*pleases me best*
*of all colors.*
                    *No one*
          *will believe this*                              21
          *of vast import*
          *to the nation.*

William Carlos Williams  (1883-1963)
U.S. poet and pediatrician, excerpted from
*Al Que Quiere*  1917

# Chapter III
## *Either In or Out!*
## *Could You Repeat That, Please?*

There is a great deal of truth in the prospect that children who do not seem to be much in tune with reality will often seek to create a pretense of their own in which to live. Such is the basis for an inordinately active imagination, believing in illusions of greater grandeur, hallucinating about a perfect world that will probably never exist in their time, and crawling into the backwoods of their daydreams to escape the perilous facts. There is no general consensus about how to reach beyond the confusion they face in their adolescent years with any hope for success; but there is nothing to be lost in setting-out to try. We have seen both the tragedy and humor that engulfs their lives sometimes, but we have also done precious little about prescribing solutions that will take them to seeing the world more clearly, challenging the errors in their midst, and conquering the ghosts that seem to keep their desires for constructive change at bay. Their meandering thoughts and senseless "psychobabble" might often seem to be their way of talking just to be heard, but deep inside them rests a greater need to be touched to the core of their hearts. Some younger people enlist their talents in works of art and literature; others in music, academia, and athleticism. But, far too many resort to the misguidance that is the product of personal rejection, sensationalism, sexual eroticism, and outright evil influence. The fact is, they revolve in and out of a mindset of awkward indiscretion and, thereafter, retreat into mysterious behaviors of darkness and delusion. And, in this, we must know that there is no cause for levity or reason for looking away with the assumption that they are just being temporarily immature. Whether we wish to accept it or not, every single action that is taken by our children is based upon their reaction to us, their dependence upon the values of accidental judgement, and their struggle for the meaning of moral right and wrong. They learn to be wise and strong by watching their elders overcome their own fears; not with some strange unbridled brashness, but with reason and a carefully constructed process of rational thinking. If our little ones become too afraid of the world as a whole, it is perhaps because we have not taught them enough about spiritual courage. This is not to say that we should not remind them of the malevolent forces of the universe, but how to respond when they see them first-hand. I have been a long-time subscriber to our local newspaper in Springfield, Illinois; and I am never unfazed by some of the ironic articles I read in it sometimes. A story that appeared in November 1994 reminds me of the good intentions that we often have in teaching our children how to keep themselves safe against the harmful elements of the everyday world. However, this particular article shows, perhaps, the paranoiac side of "stable" adults as we try to gain leverage against the dangers to our children. A minister in Enfield, New Hampshire who started buying guns because he feared that the Brady Law would infringe upon his right to bear arms accidently shot and killed himself while demonstrating firearm safety to his family, according to the Associated Press. The AP reported that the pastor died at his kitchen table in front of his wife, daughter, and their son-in-law. According to another daughter, her father did not know that the gun was loaded. Police reported that the family had recently purchased as many as four other registered hand-guns during the prior month of October 1994.

This speaks directly to the point that the protection of our family should be as prayerful as it is practical. We prompt our children when it is appropriate to sit, kneel, or stand; but we somehow cannot get the message across that we need not fear our fellow humanity to the point that we wrap lethal weapons around our waists to ultimately survive. Even as I write this particular chapter in this book, the Eastern seaboard of the United States has been terrorized by the sniper killings of nearly a dozen innocent people who were only carrying-out the ordinary motions of their lives. What are we supposed to do? Was that preacher who accidently suffered a self-inflicted fatal gunshot wound telling us something about prevailing against the evils inherent to a democratic nation of mentally deranged shooters and flying lead? Where is the National Rifle Association when we ask them whether they will ever step-forward to pay the salaries and overtime expenses of our law enforcement agencies who are required to investigate such matters as criminals who abuse their privilege to buy and bear arms? Can we not see the overt contradiction in this that keeps hitting our children in the face when they see or hear the news on TV or over the radio at the end of the day? We tell them not to be afraid, and then remind them that it would be prudent to own a firearm, just in case they may need to shoot anyone who might seem overly suspicious to them. And, although it is legal for the general population to purchase guns, most states pass laws making it illegal for people to ever carry them for their own protection for fear that they, themselves, might potentially turn into thugs. Does this not seem eerily reminiscent of what we screamed at our youngsters in their toddler years when they would slam the back screen door too many times in rapid succession, ...*either in or out*!? What facts are they supposed to glean from us when we remind them that we live in the safest nation on Earth, but are forced to explain to our littlest ones why a certain president has been assassinated, what happened to Pope John Paul II on May 13, 1981, and why their uncle had to be called to the courthouse for jury duty when the next-door neighbor suddenly turned-up missing for a week, and was then found stuffed lifeless into the trunk of his own car with a bullet wound in his left temple?

Such contradiction and hypocrisy are the worst enemies of our struggle to teach our children right from wrong. If we decline to persist in the principles of Christian Truth, they will have no foundation upon which to walk in complying with their adulthood responsibilities. America espouses the nobility of sovereign peace and justice, but we send army tanks and smart bombs across the borders of foreign nations in an effort to conquer their resistance to our domestic Constitution. Again, what message does this send to our impressionable youth about how to speak softly and sustain the dignity of all human life? Dozens of our States and Commonwealths utilize capital punishment as a means of deterring violent crime. However, what do we tell our eight-year-old son who asks what the purpose of the lethal injection was in Texas late yesterday? "Well," we say, "the man was found guilty of killing somebody; and that is against the law. So, they decided to kill him, too." And, about that time, our son looks at us with a twisted expression of disbelief on his face, saying, *Could you repeat that, please?* Thereafter, we are placed in the awkward position of trying to explain to him that the government has the right to execute condemned prisoners because they believe that it somehow decreases the chance that somebody else will take an innocent life; even though there are no valid statistics to prove that this has ever been true. What we cannot really tell the curious boy is that state-sponsored execution is all about vengeance and our mutual reluctance to feed somebody for the rest of their natural life whom our judicial system has arbitrarily deemed unfit to live. I there any doubt that most of us who have reached adulthood are forced to spend our time covering-up for the lies that we have manifested about the reality of the world, albeit many of them unintentional; or about how we are all supposed to be Christians at heart, but invest so much of our time wiling-away the hours plotting our course for securing more riches and exacting retribution against people we hate that we have never even met? It would be an Herculean task to gain our children's trust again if we ever allowed them to see the true patterns of our motivations that elicit the responses we often command from those who work under our employ or who are otherwise subordinate to us on the rungs of the social ladder. Our children's apprehension about our intentions eases just a little every time they see us keeping our word, be it something of slight importance or of grave concern. This, therefore, is the foundation in which their trust in Christianity must be garnered from us. It is imperative that we stop giving our offspring those proverbial cerebral knee-jerk answers to their various questions that they have heard so many times before. Is it any wonder that they seem so indifferent toward the things we expect from them nowadays? They do not always understand the musings of middle-aged men because we baffle them by the mixed signals that we, ourselves, embrace as being the proper way to conduct our affairs. They often see us sitting craftily on the cutting edge of higher reasoning, making inroads in technology and human development, at the same time our interpersonal outrage makes us no greater peacemakers than our teenagers on a playground. We give them orders and expect both their compliance and accolades while we provide them only the bare necessities to survive under our roofs; and this strange and evocative process is what we have limited ourselves to become as their "parents and guardians." We once staged sit-ins and walk-outs to protest established institutions that seemed so elitist and corrupt when we were in high school and college, but we have absolutely no tolerance when it comes our turn to listen to the causes and concerns of the younger generation. As a result, our children spend most of their time trying to patch the remnant-memories of their innocence back together again in order to yield some semblance of personal stability for themselves, while we continue to brow-beat them into growing-up and standing both emotionally and materially independent on their own. By all means, this is why they have learned from us that most human feelings and inward emotions are all-but expendable in these modern times. Then, we sit across the dinner table from them in the evening, wondering with the broadest hypocrisy laden clearly across our eyebrows why they just do not seem to understand what it means to be fully mature. God must surely be looking down upon us from His lofty perch in Paradise knowing that we cannot blister their emotions much more than we already have because they have grown calluses where we have so harshly aggravated their hunger for tenderness before.

Our children, and everyone else for that matter, who are fated to learn about mortal life and destiny from us should know that mutual trust begets faith; faith instills purity; purity nourishes our Love; and Love is the basis for all Christian holiness. It is in these things that we discover human excellence and a desire to reach for new spiritual horizons, ascending the mountains of fresh beginnings, and leaving the flatlands of our stubborn reticence behind. If we decline to embark upon this journey of perfection very soon, we will thereafter be required to subtly envision the lingering crowds of mourners gathered beside the bier where the remains of our legacies shall lay deceased, praying to God that He will bestow His Divine Mercy upon us, even though we recklessly abandoned the best of what might have been in Him. They will be stately dressed in the hopes we failed to pursue, grieving the wonders we allowed to escape, and eulogizing the uncultivated aspirations that we are now suffocating beneath the heap of our obstinate pride. It has been said that life often swirls and glistens around us, but we seem to not be too affected by the commotion because the forgotten heroes inside us are too timid to rediscover what we've lost. Indeed, we are the cowards who are letting the generations of tomorrow down—and their God as well—when we fail to elevate them to a better understanding of the Life and teachings of Jesus Christ. And, simply directing them where to go to learn it is nowhere near enough. Why would they ever attend Church if they have never even seen us darken the doorway on any given Sunday morning? We often mention these things in passing or draw references to the nobility of our genuflections, the gritty perils of spiritual enmity, and the rewarding experiences of brave conquests and highly profitable enterprises. However, this will never teach them that the Final Frontier *cannot* be the undefined limits of outer-space, but a lasting inner-peace found at the nucleus of the human heart. Why does it seem so painfully obvious to God that most of us lack the foresight to recognize this without being prompted by our encounter with the awful depravity of those who are suffering in our midst? If we are aspiring Saints-to-be, how do we explain our lack of inner-vision, inept progress, and poor record of alleviating such agony and our tangible results in achieving true justice for everyone? While in the process of researching such questions, why do we feel it necessary to impress upon our little ones that flashy blue ribbons, three-tiered trophies, World Cups, pennants, and checkered flags are more important than receiving the Seven Sacraments of the Roman Catholic Church? Why do we rarely take our desire for eclipsing such excellence into the charismatic part of Creation that is found at the center of the heart, where our final victories live and righteous romance reigns? The great composer J.S. Bach (1685-1750) once penned the musical score entitled, *Jesus, Joy of Man's Desiring*; and here we are now, well over 250 years later, still trying to capture the hidden message he lauded for the advancement of humankind—his artistic effort to imbue his portion of pious wisdom upon our deposit of knowledge about what God really intends for the human race to accomplish. Jesus Christ is the "Holy Child" because He is the only Man who was born without sin; the only Woman being His Immaculate Mother, Mary. In His Sacred Heart lives more than a clarion to summon us to look outside the universe and rediscover the Paradise we lost in the Garden of Eden that day. It is He who quietly calls from *within* to teach our children that they are born to seek the same Divine Absolution that He has wrought for all humankind upon the "Old Rugged Cross." Every yearning of intelligent men and accomplished academic doctors is placed into deeper perspective according to their relationship with Christ's Paschal Sacrifice; and this is why we must yield to Him in every extraordinary way and in all contemporary things—so that we can hear His symphony of immeasurable girth anew.

Wouldn't it be a statement for the history books if someone in the Fourth Grade walked up to a U.S. president and said that too many broken men and women are laying in abject poverty in the streets, thousands are out-of-commission in neighborhood hospice beds, countless numbers are on drunken binges and laying unconscious in the gutter, and the unluckiest ones are they whose cold corpses are laid-out on our medical examiners' stainless-steel slabs and in the dark corners of our city morgues? Anyone, regardless of their stature, would be taken aback to see a little boy ten or eleven years old so concerned about the plight of the poor, the dying, the destitute, and the desperate. So, why are they not speaking-up in throngs and staging protests about how their older counterparts are being allowed to suffer such grievous lives? Because we do not teach them about these things in our public and private schools. They are subjected only to the test of being forced to become the brightest in all social matters that have little in common with the aching heart, and altogether to do with being the best in mathematics, analytical thinking, and contextual calculation. We are far too quick to cremate our children's chances for knowing the agonizing side of the decadent lives of their impoverished friends long before they are ever allowed to discover for themselves the lack of interest and egregious neglect of their elder counterparts who are commissioned by Jesus Christ to rescue them from despair. And, in this, our morality and lasting vestige are lying beside those same blue corpses in our stark mortuaries, too; at the brink of their premature graves, having been killed by our wanton lack of Love for the anonymous family of man. Our shuddering children are often forced to take cover from the hailing ordnance of the cruelty and malignance of the world as it is; much too afraid to realize that all of it can be displaced by the resounding renaissance of Christ's orchestrated Plan for our human re-creation. What components comprise this beginning? None other than hope, charity, prayer, penance, peace, confession, and wilful reconciliation. These are the trebles, bases, crescendoes, and delicate pianissimos that have made the great works of Bach and his ingenious peers so revealing to the human spirit. What we really hear in the spiraling tunes of their violins and the melodies of their woodwind oboes is the reprisal, regeneration, and resurrection of protracted human Love. This is the reason why millions at home and abroad attend the performances of their harmonic orchestras and symphonies—because they remind us of the beauty that is inherent in each and every man and woman who is playing their part in human life to help the whole world culminate in an Evensong of peaceful propriety under the Masterful direction of the Sacrificed Son of God.

If we make the actions of our daily lives seem to our children to be as beautiful as the sounds we hear from our auditoria and chamber choirs, they will again say to us, *Would you repeat that, please?*, not because they do not understand us or are harboring a tint of disbelief, but because they cannot get enough of the placid hope that swells from within their hearts to know that, by our Love, humankind can be united once again. Most all of us sat in a wooden high-chair when we were little children, trying our best to swallow our morning pudding in time for the next bite to arrive on a silvery spoon passing through the air like a tiny airplane being guided by our mother's arm. Whatever you wish to call it—innocuous, innocent—or anything else that may apply; what we really were back then speaks to the core of everything we must become both here and now. Our souls must be sealed with new spiritual goodness, embossed with revived integrity, and affixed in character to Christian righteousness in ways that many of us cannot yet quite understand. We may not remember having breakfast when we were only a year old or two, but we have seen the photographs from which we still cringe in unwarranted shame. Why? Because we lived well, learned plenty, giggled foolishly, and had our being from our mothers and fathers, and the Holy Spirit of God who guided them. We trusted them in our early years because we were too helpless to know anything else or to ever fend for ourselves. Recapturing this "old-fashioned" Love again will make us stronger in our weakest moments and give us pause to realize that we are letting our own little children down. Indeed, we are not sufficiently addressing their struggles to know the human heart in the way that God would have it done. Can we instruct them without seeming too inconsistent in what we have heretofore taught them to believe as being the reason for their birth? After all the discipline we have imposed upon them to gain a better footing in the material world, and all the bitter warring they have seen us prosecute against those who have dared to step foot on our private paths, it is going to require a great deal more than a robust amount of diplomacy to get them to believe us now. Let us not be surprised to hear them proclaim, *What was all that propaganda about being the smartest in the class?*, as they look at us with dismay. Therein, we must be humble enough to admit that we were wrong, that we did not take their spiritual well-being as seriously as we should; and we must implore them not to make the same mistakes when God sees fit to bless them with children of their own. We should confess that we did not know it all, that our conduct has been tainted by our reluctance to pray together and listen to the sacred admonishments of our Savior on the Cross. Then, when we hear a student in elementary school laying the facts straight-out about how the neighbor's front porch roof is leaking onto the broken concrete steps below, we can tell him that it is because we did not care enough about them to go with hammer and nails to repair it before the damage was already done. And, above all, we must remind ourselves that our Divine Creator is the Original Light, and that every source of goodness ultimately comes from Him. All remaking, evolution, transformation, convalescence, and purification are products of our having chosen Him; listening to His Holy Will with the intensity of our allegiance, and accepting the sacrifices which belong to each and every one of us that were laid upon the foundation of the Earth billions of years ago. This is our time to learn simultaneously with our offspring that God was never manufactured, but that He has always been here, forever existing; and that His Holy and Divine Light is both alive and working through us when we make the Salvation of humankind the purpose of our days. And, such noble emphases should be directed not only toward our Salvation, but to our full redemption from all forms of human suffering, eradicating our grudges, and by every soul on the Earth being liberated from the confining vices of aggressive imperialism, corporeal impurity, and materialistic greed. These are the echoes of the Triumph of the Cross and an irrevocable death knell to anyone who is foolish enough to stand-out in opposition or ever get in our way.

So, rather than to cower in resignation that the world will always be as repugnant as it seems, we should continue striving to comprehend the intentions of God to guide us back to Him. What is the most distinguishing attribute to His Grace to which we are being called? *Love*! We must not allow our children to languish any longer in the confusion, desperation, and decadence of modern America just because we are too slothful to teach them the meaning of this achievable human intuition. Their perception of life right now has them on a collision course with Satan, and neither their innocence nor dignity will survive the mangled wreckage that will ensue if we do not alter their spiritual direction. How can we help them to see better? By ensuring that everyone alive understands that Divine Love is the sky-faring arbor under which all mutual friendship, brotherhood, fraternity, and conjugal interrelations reside. The key to the perspective of every affection, impulsive infatuation, and emotional stimulation is found in our acceptance that Jesus Christ wishes to preside over them all, so that every facet of our personal commitments is centered in Him. When we pronounce the words, *I love you*, do we really understand all the implicit effects which accompany such a promise? There is no doubt that Christ wishes to make clear that our Love must be directed toward His created beings and very little for anything that has been synthesized by our expertise in displaying our artistic expression. It is wholly inappropriate for us to assert that we love "something" unless such objects directly enhance our relationship with the Creator of the universe. Even the phenomena we believe to be supernatural in origin have nothing in common with the *Eternal Divine* unless they espouse the sacred miracle of our ultimate reunion with God through the Crucifixion of Jesus Christ in the Glory of Paradise. If our children begin to understand this, they will become less distracted by the diversions of the material world and well on their way to growing into spiritually-responsive people. Only our embracing of the supremacy of the Triune Deity of Christianity can lead us into a concise and complete perception of the Living Truth. When we write "love letters" to our soul-mates and spouses, they have no inherently Divine purpose unless our intentions are to include God as the Patriarch of our fruitful future. I once wrote in a personal diary of mine that,...*it is beyond shame how human actions can become so separated from the soothing ecstasy of the heart. Somehow, we seem terrified to engage the deep-reaches of each other's souls.* Therefore, we must ensure for the sake and preservation of our union in Heaven that our hearts remain inside the perfection of Divine human Love—sown with great care beneath the fertility of the spiritual power by which we are lifted above the physical world aboard the wings of the Holy Spirit. Contrary to popular beliefs, other people around us are *not* objects for us to manipulate with our hands or to psychologically batter for awhile and place back onto a shelf. Likewise, our emotions are much more than a mere culmination of sentimental journeys; and our speech and actions clearly define our motivations if we allow them to, being extremely careful to sculpt our temperament and choose our words so as not to arbitrarily or intentionally scandalize the dignity of those with whom we choose to interact.

We often assume with a measured degree of probability that other people will respond to us within a certain set of prefigured parameters when we confront them or communicate on a reasonably responsive level. We are often disappointed when we fail to meet the criteria others have established as being acceptable and appropriate for those they deign as being "worthy" of sharing their valuable time. Thus, many people have become no longer spontaneous in their interpersonal approach; and rarely do they anticipate that we will ever be transfigured beyond the blase prototype by which they have us defined. This circuit becomes complete once we surrender our dignity to the status quo and they decline to search any farther for our creative Christian genius that is silently begging to spring from within the chambers of our hearts. And, once we have done this, we have fully stifled the sacred originality and unique identity that the Holy Spirit is trying to evoke from us at the offerance of our concession that He is a portion of us inside *His* Sacred Heart. Only by reversing this trend will our children, our peers, the secular world, and rigidly orthodox clergy accept the fact that Jesus Christ is trying to work unprecedented miracles through everyone on Earth at this precise moment in time. Once we finally understand that our imperial reluctance is one of His worst enemies, we will be open to receive His manifest miracles as they are abundantly raining from Heaven upon us now. Again, it all refers to *Love* as a living presence within us that makes God the reason for our *being*; and also our motivations, our Wisdom, our extractions from the prayerful thoughts of pious men, our participation in the spiritual aspects of civil human conduct, and our anticipation of the exchange of our imperfections for the fully incorrupt excellence that we find only in our trust and faith in the Divine Providence of our consummate Savior. We too often utter wisecrack slogans and pithy remarks in order to sidestep a more sincere interaction with those who really need us; and we sometimes underestimate the malignance of the seductive responses of the opposite sex—too often mistaking their gentleness and affections as being a genuine interest in leading us into a closer relationship with each other in Christ. Beware the voice and actions of those who claim to be so dear to our hearts! Indeed, we are almost minced into pathetic little pieces because we have been misled and betrayed so many times before by people who do not know that such *affected allegiance* and sensual emotions are not the same as Divine human Love. We exhaust our thoughts while pondering why our hapless societies seem to be embroiled in so much debauchery; and when we speak about it to those who should care, they tell us that we are only pesky little gadflies who are too eccentric for our own good in this mainstream modern life. However, it is this same stuffed-shirted majority who is lost inside their own blind self-adulation! If only we would begin to see human existence through the purview of Roman Catholic Christianity, we would recognize that secular opinions are only illusions which distort our perception of the Gospel Truth—much like a weatherman and his meteorological map are superimposed onto a "green screen" in a television studio somewhere. And, this is the virtual titillation that Satan is trying to dangle before us now to get us to follow his imaginary world of power, lust, and lies instead of the *real* one of Christian goodness which lives just beyond the realms of our faith. Again, beware the deception of his lurid promises and subliminal designs, for they are the devious shadows of our post-modern age of high-tech fabrication, the false sense of security we feel inside worldly prosperity, and the baseless promises of instant euphoria we are asked to believe by those who are trying to steer us onto the road of final perdition! There is always something fishy to a story about attaining sudden personal fame or overnight financial wealth; and what often seems to be a benign physical attraction is actually attached to a hidden hook that is suspended from a bobber on Satan's nylon lines.

Only our concise understanding of the Fruits and Virtues of Divine Love as it is defined by Jesus Christ will allow us to discern whether we have strayed from His fold of faithful disciples. The present condition of the mortal world mandates our careful scrutiny of what we see and hear, and dictates the courses of action which warrant and determine what attention we should give certain timely affairs. It is Satan's evil deception that has brought us to believe that there are only a few scattered pockets of righteousness on the Earth which are only thinly cast across the surface of two otherwise very malevolent hemispheres. He seems to be succeeding in convincing most people that what he says is true because human error and sinfulness are the only issues that appear to be dominating our media broadcasts nowadays, or the scuttlebutt at our workplaces around the water cooler and at the lunch tables inside our street-corner cafeterias. The truth, however, is that Jesus Christ has fully reclaimed the Earth as a portion of His Kingdom inside the Eternal Justice of God. Our refusal to realize our Victory in Him, the efforts of His enemies who own our newspapers and television networks, and the reluctance of our ecclesiastical pastors to be better evangelists have all combined to give humanity the false impression that modern Christianity has failed. The indifference that has engulfed our material world would have us retreat into the Earth's darkest valleys and cold ravines to shiver helplessly on our bellies with the worms, snakes, and salamanders because we are much too cowardly to stand-up to outright evil; while Jesus Christ, the Sacrificed and Resurrected Son of God, is calling us to bear arms for Him at the spiritual mountaintops of human holiness to revel His Love among the soaring eagles and caroling Angels. Indeed, *this* is the 21st century message that we should begin in earnest to communicate to our children who will succeed us in bearing new life into the decades to come. The purpose of falling to our knees in humble prayer is to invoke the heartfelt aid of our loyal God and never to show submission or reverence before any secular man. Let Creation be on notice that there is no such thing as a "rookie" Christian in the game of life because a new convert carries all the power, dignity, and dynamism of every Saint to ever accept the Cross as the source of their Eternal Salvation. If we would only realize that such supernatural power resides inside us, too, we would move forward in haste with greater confidence as productively as the first Apostles, and with the full expectation that we have already secured the Divine Triumph which the Pentecostal Paraclete promises the world in the unblemished leaflets of the Sacred Scriptures. This is the real meaning of proceeding to our Redemption with childlike abandonment at the foot of the Cross of the Savior of the world. When it comes time for the Final Judgement, our souls will be located ...*either in or out!* because God has made no provision for their perpetual existence beyond Heaven or Hell.

*He that hath a talent,*
*let him see that he hide it not;*
*he that hath abundance,*
*let him quicken himself to mercy and generosity;*
*he that hath art and skill,*
*let him do his best to share the use and*
*the utility thereof with his neighbor.*

– Pope St. Gregory I
Pontificate AD 590-604

# Chapter IV
## *What a Wonderful World*
### *I Think I Saw This on Television*

The news just keeps getting worse for those who take an agnostic approach to daily life. It is true that we are stationed on a spherical rock in the vacuum of the solar system; and what we see through telescopes and with the naked eye is often referenced for purposes of complicity through the raw atheism that many realists, philosophers, scientists, and naturalists choose to espouse regarding the purpose of mortal human life. Perhaps it would be better understood in simpler terms. Both time and space are by-products of the same forces which keep the galaxies in check; but our *souls* are never subject to them. What seems like solid ground beneath our feet has little to do with the higher realms of incalculable perpetuity to which our faith in God must lead us. In fact, His Love is both the catalyst and the result that makes Creation complete. If we deny Him in any way therein, we are diminishing the multiply-arrayed dimensions of ourselves. The vast geographical aspects of the globe and other universal properties represent an ever-changing and mutating procession of alternating events, with the exception of the natural laws of physics that remain unchanged—at least until they, too, are occasionally suspended by the Son of God. If we focus upon the surface of a rubber-band that is wrapped tightly around a large envelope, we can understand how unstable we really are as we stand on the ground. God determines the tension of the Earth's surface in accordance with the influences of the elements of gravity and centrifugal force; and it is He who owns the right to amend them at the exercise of His own discretion. If it ever suits His Divine purposes, we can expect that the world might be suddenly ripped from under us like a strand of elastic in a latex stocking snapping in half. Is this possibility too metaphysical to be true? No matter how we perceive it, we have yet to truly comprehend the overall measure of our helplessness alongside the omniscience of the God and Maker of all things. And, for as long as history can remember, we have been trying to discover, retrieve, and explicate the designs of human life inside these chasms of our weakness since the early days of man. Satellites and voyagers have allowed us to peer well-beyond our atmospheres and back again; detailing the cosmos with the accuracy of a pinpoint; but there still seems to be a creepy dead silence from the heavens in response to what we really wish to know. So, we continue living as if to deny God the right to even exist because, if He was actually there, He would surely have said something audible by now that could be detected with our normal hearing or become visible in signs other than the appearance of random landfalls and melting glaciers for us to measure those pesky passages of time and the celestial clusters we examine in outer-space.

We train our thoughts on expedient human existence in other ways as a reaction to our lack of willingness to communicate with anyone from above. And, oh! what an egregious lot of inventions we have crafted for ourselves! There is certainly no doubt that our curiosity, intelligence, and ingenuity have borne the fruit of the elimination of untold manual labors, the curing of crippling and fatal diseases, and unprecedented improvements in our modes of communication and high-speed travel around the globe. Doctors, technicians, and practitioners have been the blessing of many agonizing souls; but does having such immense and innovative prowess not render us as counterproductive as if we were injuriously ignorant? What examples are to be cited? Let us recall what America looked like at the turn of the 20th century, into the decades of the grisly World Wars, to the rush for modern industry in the early 1950s, and how we have perverted the purpose of our inventions for reasons quite other than benign. Indeed, left to our own devices, we have created an atmosphere of living that devalues the articles of sound social propriety, individual dignity, public decency, and spiritual consecration. Let there be no mistake about it; *the modern use of television has been the principle tool by which the enemies of Jesus Christ have lured untold millions of lost souls away from the Holy Cross.* What began as a medium for the productive exchange of crucial information, a venue for the personal development and education of our children, and a means to understand the inner-workings of our civil democracy has now deteriorated into another new weapon for Satan to spread his evil works. Seriously—this is not an exaggeration. There is not a soul alive who can justify becoming addicted to an audio-visual electronic device that glorifies extramarital sex, innuendo, domestic violence, premeditated murder, drug-abuse, deception, thievery, gluttony, blasphemy and other such sordid and baneful discharges of the Antichrist. It doesn't matter if we have heard the excuse that the TV can be equated with the use of firearms. *Guns don't kill people,* they defiantly say, *people kill people!* Following this same illogical impudence, they also tell us that only corrupt program producers cause the television to be an undesirable medium, and that anyone watching is free to simply turn-off their set. Such an argument might be tenable if everyone who stands by it would protect their children and those who answer to no responsible adults so as to make sure they are never exposed to the horrid graphics that are spewing forth from the screen. Even in this, there is an errant assumption that every grown-up who watches the lust, vandalism, and malicious mischief on TV will not be influenced to imitate it in some dysfunctional way. There are too many unknown variables, impressionable citizens, and an uncontrollable desire for the public to be free to do as they wish for us to allow the broadcast media to continue pummeling our nation with their abusive and licentious programming. What might Jesus Christ say about such liberty inside the oldest democracy on the face of the Earth? *To Hell with the First Amendment of the U.S. Constitution!*

Perhaps there is some saving grace in the World Wide Web since getting on-line requires a little more effort than pressing a knob on a remote control; but even the Internet has its draw-backs since there are so many sites that exist for the same reason Satan is employing to convince our TV executives that dramas and sitcoms about social revenge and homosexual lifestyles are somehow alright by God. I have tried to counter this problem by placing my own nonprofit organization on the Internet, too. Its address is www.ImmaculateMary.org. I have even sent Email to various people I thought might benefit from knowing about Christianity. Unfortunately, the following are among the sentiments I have received in return.

> *—Where did you get my Email address? It would take far more than one stupid Email to get me to believe in a god. I have to laugh at you people.*

> *—I see nothing to change the status of the atheist argument. I feel sorry for you, wasting so much of your short life—your only life—that you actually have. Until you have some real, scientific evidence of your supposed god, do not waste my time! I have better things to do than listen to the ravings of someone who hasn't done any real research.*

> *—I don't see this suffering broken world in need of the balm that you appear to believe in. I have good friends, eat well, and have a roof over my head. What do I need God's help with again? Am I to fear his Eternal Wrath? Beg for Eternal Bliss? No thanks—he's your God. You play to his every whim if that's how you choose to lead your life. But, I have better things to do.*

Perhaps I digress a little. Anyway, it would not be very difficult to make the case that our child psychoanalysts and behavioral therapists can trace the root of the delinquency of their clients and patients back to their exposure to the influences of television programming; for this is the key method of conveyance that Satan seems to like the most in coercing their smug attitudes on his behalf, especially in defining the standards of their rogue personal conduct. The questions that now remain to be answered are what to do about it, how to reverse it, and why are children so captivated by the things they see on TV? There is a television set pictured on the cover of this book to the left of my two nephews as they posed so innocently for a spontaneous snapshot that day. There they stand, poised into history at the convenience of modern photography—two little icons of untarnished human life. What power and recourse humanity owns in the souls of these little children; for they represent the very essence of the pure, unprejudiced, blameless, and unimpeachable spotlessness that Jesus Christ has come seeking from us; procured through the endowment of His forgiveness upon humanity from the Cross, and entirely retrievable through the contrition of our hearts and the amendment of our lives! One can see the origin of the Divine amelioration of the ills of the world in the eyes of such little children, the pleading gazes on their little faces, and in the humility of their physical posture before a reality that they truly do not yet understand. And, this is why the Son of God wishes us to abandon our indulgence in the forces that fill us with such crass sarcasm and lead us into sin. Indeed, the knob on the television behind my nephews is in the *off* position; for they have turned their backs to its scurrilous gossip and have shone their faces upon us who should be pleading with the presence of the vision of God in them to mend the world through His Love for their souls. I once saw a motion picture in which the great entertainer and comedian Robin Williams portrayed a disc jockey who had traveled abroad in the 1960s to lift the spirits of our military troops in Southeast Asia. I think it was entitled *Good Morning, Viet Nam!* I was quite capable of recognizing the dignified power of theatrical art in such an improvised setting; and I learned that there is no question that our hearts can be consoled if we will simply stop fighting and become like little children again as Jesus would have us do. There was a particular scene in the film that appeared to be rather poetic, ironic, and surrealistic—all at the same time. The screenplay images provided a glimpse of the horrendous explosions that occurred during the heat of battle and the dark campaigns of its violent mortality. The director allowed us to envision the agony on the faces of the American soldiers, our allies, the Communist troops, and the brow-wrenching scowls and tears of the indigenous South-Vietnamese civilians—men, women, and children, whose homeland was so decimated by the scourges of that war. Thundering black clouds of flaming fuel were bellowing into the air. Soldiers lay dead in undignified positions atop the ground. Armored cars and personnel carriers were overturned, burning, and toppling into the swamps of the subterranean rice fields.

And, yet, the musical score playing during the scene seemed to hold all the irrational imagery and unforeseen effects that might possibly be experienced by the mind of man—bar none—as the soundtrack, entitled *What A Wonderful World* by Louis Armstrong (1900-1971) could be heard outplaying the stark poignancy of the sad slow-motion photographs. The bloodshed, agony, horror, and mayhem unfolded in awful sequences as we listened to the lyrics, *I see trees of green, red roses, too. I see them bloom for me and you. And, I think to myself, 'what a wonderful world.' I see skies of blue and clouds of white; the bright blessed day, the dark sacred night. And, I think to myself, 'what a wonderful world.' The colors of the rainbow, so pretty in the sky, are also on the faces of people going by. I see friends shaking hands, saying 'how do you do?' They're really saying, 'I love you.' I hear babies crying. I watch them grow. They'll learn much more than I'll ever know. And, I think to myself, 'what a wonderful world.'* (George Weiss and Bob Thiele). And, with the familiarly quaint sound of the gravelly resignation in his voice, old Satchmo sang about the world that was supposed to be, but had somehow been corrupted by the unwillingness of contemporary men to bear restraint upon their own naked aggression, or to favor the voices of the many over the totalitarianism of a few, and the outright reluctance of sovereign states to settle their disputes peacefully around the negotiating table instead of warring so painfully against one another upon hellish battlegrounds. This is exactly the irony that makes Louis Armstrong's song so appropriate in our day, too; not only for the movie in which it was positioned, but for the ongoing lives of humankind at large. If it is true that trees, roses, rainbows, handshakes, and babies' cries can instill in us that elusive new beginning which is the core of the reconciliation of all the Earth, then should we not refocus our attention upon them now? Are they not all manifestations of the presence of the Love of Almighty God in us, His glorious reflections, His matchless reprieve for the condemned, an antidote for the world's betraying kiss of inevitable death, and everything remedial that makes the culmination of human life all that Jesus Christ has proposed it to be since He first set foot in the Womb of His Immaculate Mother? Here we are again: it all reverts back to the blamelessness of a tiny Child. There were certainly no televisions, motion pictures, or soundtracks in Bethlehem when Jesus Christ was born; and it is a good thing because the jubilant voices of the Cherubim and Seraphim would have assuredly drown-them-out anyway. They are still singing as we speak to this day, but we decline to hear them; just as we never really understood the significance of the lyrics of Louis Armstrong's song until it was awkwardly situated with such diametrical opposition alongside the gory fate of the troops who fought so boldly and courageously in the South Viet Nam War.

Does anyone wish to know what God really thinks when He sees us watching television these days? I know for reasons that are nothing-less than miraculously revealed that His Sacred Heart feels the same pain that we do when we search for such peace inside; and yet, we watch the battles and skirmishes in *Good Morning, Viet Nam!* and wonder what in the world could have possibly gone wrong. He knows the adversities we face in the ravaged paths of evil that those who are the most susceptible among us now refuse to fight head-on. He is aware of the plight of millions of Christians who struggle to hold their heads aloft as they walk through their workplaces everyday and see their colleagues scurrying through life as though He is the last person they would ever call upon for help when their troubles begin to multiply. Yes. Jesus has seen nearly every opportunity He ever put within the reach of our hands to make the world a better place being dismissed as a figment of someone's zealous imagination, and thereby left on the table of the Earth like scraps to fall over its edge so as to light within the grasp of those who really care. Do our little children beg for riches or wares that will set them apart as more celebrated people among their peers or in the social elite? It goes without saying that they wish only to be loved; taken by hope and spirit to their stationed perches of dignity and given a chance to grow in faith and honesty alongside those red roses that made the heart of Louis Armstrong declare that this is, indeed, a wonderful world. The garishness of our neighbors' pride need not be reason for us to relinquish our desire to alter the face of humanity amidst the ostentatious productions that come from our God-forsaken Hollywood studios, world news network desks in New York, Atlanta, and Washington D.C., and even from the pretentious exclamations of the giddy fortune-seekers who hound us all the time to take-hold of the latest fads and fashions or to ensure that we secure our allotted portion of the American Dream. Believe me, these people are not true dreamers; they are exacters of exorbitant profits for their own personal gain, setting themselves high above the weakest in their midst, after which they devour their prey and retreat into the parlours of their ivy-covered palaces to sit for seemingly endless hours in front of—you guessed it—their big-screen surround-sound digitally-enhanced color TVs. Truly, the cycle is now complete. And, for all the wrong reasons, they poke their heads out again in the morning under the guise that they wish to set us free from rampant global terrorism, poverty, and human suffering; so the more photogenic hosts among us cover themselves in pounds of make-up, broad-search for guests to tantalize the scandalous curiosity of domestic partners who stay at home, vilify the sacredness of God's spiritual Truth, and proclaim that personal discretion in the face of mortal temptation is a characteristic of ignorance, weakness, and mediocrity in this undefinable procession called the human experience.

The producers of our television programming of today would have us believe that we own some type of unwarranted prosecutorial authority over those we perceive to be our enemies. As strange as it might seem, early shows celebrated the decades of American life wherein the characters portrayed by the actors and actresses owned no television sets—they had yet to be invented in the context of their written scripts. The old spaghetti Westerns, various early nature programming, and staged comedies depicted the simplicity of the middle and late 19th, and first half of the 20th centuries as if to say we were then adequately entertained by the artifice of ourselves. Does it seem ironic that the television industry utilized its own product to persuade Americans that life without one was somehow deficient; that no one in touch with reality would want to live in the "void" of the radio-age which gave us only our imagination to determine the facts? Indeed, were not those fancy wooden TV consoles a temptation to those whose goal was to also own a flashy, fish-finned black Cadillac? Perhaps the evolution of the content of staged programming might tell us what signs or symptoms have led us to such dependency upon it. No doubt, the earliest black and white broadcasts were blameless enough; shows like the Red Skelton and Jack Benny comedy hours; or perhaps the antics of The Little Rascals, The Three Stooges, and Jackie Gleason and Art Carney on *The Honeymooners*. Lest we forget, without all those "B movies" that were aired on TV, would the world have ever heard of the Screen Actors Guild whose upper echelon consisted of a supporting actor by the name of Ronald Wilson Reagan from Tampico, Illinois? But, with what subtly did the television medium begin to decay through the passing of time? Do we recall those daytime game shows that seemed to be so harmless when we were all still quite young? Surely the Gary Moores and Gene Rayburns of the world did not know that their careers would beget the slow metamorphosis of good old-fashioned entertainment into an electronic medium with a much more detrimental influence on the American psyche. What was the underlying incentive for their contestants to do well in the various skills and talents to which they were challenged? The answer is simply their desire to acquire modern appliances, the best in housewares, and to fatten their wallets with as much hard cash that they could stuff inside the pockets of their trousers. Was this not made perfectly clear on *The $64,000 Question*, and by Monte Hall on *Let's Make A Deal*, and by Bob Barker on *The Price is Right*? Yes. It was their corrupt appetite for material wealth that has made the United States so despised by paupers around the globe, and our not yet realizing that it is our perverse possessionism that is still making them starve. And, it is not as though we have not had plentiful time to see the errors of our ways. Dick Clark hosted the *$25,000 Pyramid* program, then another boasting a purse of $100,000. Shortly thereafter, Americans and the rest of the world were slapped in the face with *Wheel of Fortune, Who Wants to be a Millionaire?, Greed*, and dozens of other such programs with materialistic themes. What makes this so overly egregious is that the U.S. population watches these shows by the millions of viewers per broadcast, proving that we as a people have centered our lives around the drive for personal profit and financial gain.

Is it any wonder why our impressionable children resort to crime and deception when they do not have such assets in their possession nor a means to get them? Where did they learn the need for being surrounded and comforted by physical objects and national fame? From us! And, let us cast-away the argument that educational game programs like *Jeopardy!* are innocent venues for the advancement of modern intelligence. What do the players get if they succeed? Cash on the barrel head! We have somehow equated victory and triumph with personal financial gain; and this is one of the most grave consequences of the information age. I have spoken about this issue in an earlier book, *When Legends Rise Again: The Convergence of Capitalism and Christianity*; wherein I have delineated how we as a religious nation are moving with almost warp-speed away from spiritualism toward the blind rationality which accompanies the influences of American politics, sensationalism, and cultural idolatry. What does this have to do with the phenomenon of modern television programming? Does it seem odd for the greatest democratic superpower in the history of the world that we often discover who will be the next President of the United States based upon the projections of national television networks within minutes after the polling places close on the eastern seaboard? Where in the world did such arrogant media producers and executives get the idea that they have the right to subvert the American system of democracy in action? Because they are the medium that is bilking billions of dollars in advertising money every year from our candidates; and they keep us all addicted to the latest fads, fashions, foods, computers, and automobiles. It is not that big a leap for them to presume the outcome of certain state and national elections by allegedly speaking on behalf of the electorate before we ever exercise our right to vote. Is there not something terribly wrong about an unsuccessful presidential candidate running for the White House sitting-down to write his concession speech before the Electoral College votes have ever been tallied from every state and commonwealth that lies west of the Mississippi River? Why has this been done? Because the American broadcast media believe it necessary to be the first to announce the winner by conducting "exit surveys" consisting of voters' opinions as they are emerging from the polls, thereby preempting the natural progression of our democratic process before the outcome of a certain election has ever been determined. In other words, time is not a sufficient element to satisfy the curiosity of America's news organizations. They believe that they must be the first to make the announcement of a particular winner before their counterparts and peers so more people will become dependent upon them as a source of information. And, into what does this translate? Their ability to charge audacious prices for commercial air time based upon the number of viewers they have, which is reflected on the bottom-line of their financial balance worksheets. Here we go again. It is all about money! They subject the Truth to the trial of *their* error so they can be the wealthiest networks in the world.

Rather than to permit the United States electorate to vote according to the way in which their particular schedules will allow in any given time zone, TV reporters and pundits take it upon themselves to adopt as their *illegitimate* civic duty to subvert the process by telling potential voters in western states that, based upon their networks' early projections, their votes will probably not count. Even though they might sheepishly add, "...if the polls are still open in your area, please go and vote," such propaganda is only their disclaimer to get us to believe that they are not influencing the final outcome. There are many political races farther down the ballot in the western Mountain and Pacific time zones that are adversely affected by the irresponsible gossip of the broadcast media; such as key elections for the U.S. Senate, gubernatorial contests, and hundreds of individual state and local offices that are regularly up for grabs. What a mockery and laughing-stock the U.S. television media made of the November 2000 presidential election! In all their high-minded mightiness, they decided to arbitrarily "award" the 25 Electoral College votes from the State of Florida to the Democratic candidate, Vice-President Albert Gore, and then suddenly took them away because they had not done their homework as accurately as they thought. Subsequently, after another period of unsubstantiated pondering, they later placed Florida in the column of the Republican nominee, Texas Governor George W. Bush. It then seemed like we could finally go to bed; but just before we hit the button on the TV remote, our not-so-prescient television networks decided that Governor Bush had not won Florida either. The four major news anchors were thereafter forced to admit that they were wrong during their commission of these separate erroneous projections; and they were almost forced to use jack-hammers to get the eggs off their faces as a result of their wanton error and lack of professionalism. Just in case anyone may have been living under a rock since the November 2000 election, the U.S. presidency was finally decided some 36 days later by a majority of the Republican-appointed Justices on the Supreme Court, who voted 5-4 to appoint George W. Bush as the 43rd President of the United States, although Vice-President Gore had out-polled him by well over a half-million votes. And, through all of this, many of our young men and women who had just turned 18 years of age had exercised their franchise for the very first time in their lives and were left to wonder about the role of the television industry in our American democracy, knowing all along that the rest of the world was looking at us with a collective heave of social disdain and practical disbelief.

The absolute debacle that our television news anchors made of that election-night coverage, their tantalizing stories over the next five weeks, and their reluctance to admit that they had caused much of the confusion that made such a scam of the 2000 presidential election have left most of us without any trust in their word, and quite skeptical about their purpose in the evolution of our postmodern republic.   Indeed, what began years before in the simple confines of *Ozzie and Harriet* and *My Three Sons* back in the 1950s culminated in November 2000 by exposing the television industry as being nothing more than another financial opportunist in a nation that is already filled to the gills with its share of corporate thieves, and is much too fraught with division, cynicism, apathy, low productivity, and fraudulent deceit.   What must our children be thinking about the present status of the democracy that their grandparents bequeathed to us, and the one we shall eventually entrust to them?   The electronic window around which we once gathered to watch the Ingalls on *Little House on the Prairie* and those time-honored Christmas broadcasts with Burl Ives, Bing Crosby, Andy Williams, and Lawrence Welk has now deteriorated into an absolute monster that spews-out rancorous venom such as the countless violent virtual-reality programs, survival of the fittest and vanquishing of the weak formats; and, of all things, legitimized sexual exploitation, bold displays of verbal abuse and physical aggression, and unabashed extramarital erotica on daytime programs such as the now-defunct *Geraldo Rivera Show*, which has left deep scars on our nation, and the still popular *Jerry Springer Show*.   It does not take a genius to figure-out that the video-taped ambush of an unwary  man who was lured onto the set of the *Jenny Jones Show* under the pretense that he was going to meet someone there he thought to be a female secret admirer who turned-out to be a male, instead, was what caused him to snap into a violent rage against the man who made a scurrilous attempt to claim his affection.  This is evidence enough to prove that the systemic deception of a given venue can often cause malevolent harm and even death.  Why?  Because Jenny Jones wanted to secure the best ratings she could possibly achieve, knowing well in advance that such sensationalist programming was her means to do it, and that her ratings would translate into higher financial profit.  One of the things that Satan is trying to convince us is that these types of television programs are inevitable in America because they somehow represent another inalienable faction of our citizens' right to free speech.  He tries through grossly evil works to get us to believe that we are victims of something that our estranged family members and the enemies in our midst have committed by some kind of premeditated stratagem that is completely unbeknownst to us. Such fear-mongering has been the origin of the terrible paranoia of many less-stable people who live in the social margins of

American cultural life; they who are most apt to respond erratically and without sound judgement to the unrecognizable things they see and hear everyday.

The essence of what I am saying is that the invention and evolution of modern television programming has too-long been a saga about missed opportunities. For all the talk we hear about being the greatest debating society on the face of the Earth; and certainly the best informed, it is what we are *not* told that is hurting us the most. It has been reported that our children watch TV between three and five hours on any given day; and we may never know whether Gilligan and the Skipper had any lasting effect toward making us like little children again or if the righteous determination of Walter Brennan in *The Guns of Will Sonnet,* as he searched on horseback for his lost son, brought us any closer to understanding the love of a father or the longing in his heart. But, it is quite obvious that what we see on the TV screen today can do absolutely nothing to make our younger generation seek the peace of the Holy Spirit over the hatred of the vengeful world. We are sometimes more inspired by the legacies of the dead than we are by the living prophets in our age because everyone knows that bygone heroes can do no wrong. Even in this, we must direct our children forward once again, evoking from them all the cumulatively sincere, constructive, and modest aspects of their personalities they can muster. While the wind blows where it wills, it does not infer that we are to be equally as haphazard in our goals of protecting the priceless value of human life or preventing its decadence from taking hold of our deep roots in Christianity. For all their breadth and latitude, we must employ our contemporary tools of communication as a means of mending society's ills and bridging the dark breaches that keep our generations so far apart. Perhaps we are much too timid and afraid, or we may lack the proper motivations because we simply do not understand one another that well. But, there must be a sliver of hope in our hearts that, someday, our grandchildren will crawl upon our laps with a broad smile on their faces and say with an intonation that only their virtuous innocence can effect,...*what a wonderful world!* Our trust in the goodness of the human spirit, our determination to be the best in all noble things, and our collective desire to seek change for the better should instill in us the courage to take our country back from the lurid forces that are almost ruining our children's early years. Television networks could be like princely stars, themselves, if only they would realize the devastating impact they are having on the consciousness of our young. We value our capacity to make things such as this come true because *we* are the people, not the media executives who are stationed in New York's Rockefeller Center or in their bureaus and outlets in Chicago and Detroit. *We the common people* are the proprietors of this nation on behalf of our little children; and ours is the sacred commission from God to lead them back to Him.

# Section II
## *Return the Age of Innocence*

### Chapter V
### *An American Immoral Revolution*
### *The Western Cultural Divide*

If we stopped to think about all the men and women who have taken-up military arms throughout the annals of history and fought until untold millions of them died so the rest of us could live free from the chains of totalitarianism, Communism, Fascism, and unadulterated slavery, we would always remember such suffering as an almost unimaginable price to pay for human freedom. With what independence do we really declare that we are autonomous from other men? How long must we wait before we conclude that "community" is as important to civil progress as personal liberty, itself? The phrases we turn, the whining claptrap that has become the tone of our speeches and public oratories today, and the value we place on individualism would have the whole world believe that there are no two people inside the continental United States who think alike. We sometimes try to hide our inner priorities; and our reluctance to agree with the social prospectus of the "majority rule" can make us look an awfully lot like utter outcasts sometimes. On the other hand, however, this is often the same cost of standing by the Truth of Jesus Christ in a land which is absolutely engulfed by the landslide of error we see everyday. Americans claim to be free to espouse their individual religion; or perhaps none at all, to the extent by which their spiritual inquisitiveness gives them that long sought-after inner peace. The question that God is putting before us now is whether we believe that our power of persuasion on His behalf should stop at the fence gate of our neighbors' property. Is there any reason for us to conclude that anyone who disagrees with our Christian philosophies can ever really be as happy as us?—even though Jesus says, ...*he who loves his life will lose it.* While there seems to be far too many questions and insufficient answers, the period during which we are procrastinating has become the perilous void in which our little children are being raised. If we do not appear to be aggressive in our trust that God is completely in control of His Kingdom here and now, they will assuredly be just as doubtful, too. It has been said that there is a crisis in confidence in America today because so few of us are willing to think in terms of the *paranormal* as it works in tandem with the ordinary to reshape our existence behind the scenes.

I remember during the summer of 1979 before the beginning of my senior year in high school in the village of Ashland, Illinois seeing then-President Jimmy Carter on the news speaking about a certain "malaise" that had overcome the citizens of the United States. The purported basis of his speech that hot July 15th was to talk about the nation's oil shortage, but I believe to this day that his true purpose was to address the lack of concern for faith and religion in the greatest democracy in the world. Mr. Carter was mocked, ridiculed, reproached, and verbally assaulted by the media, other isolationist Americans, and by members of the opposition party. I read another assessment of that speech in a column written by Bill Bishop of the Lexington (KY) *Herald-Leader* about twelve years later. In his article, Mr. Bishop indicated that the President's legislative agenda had been stalled by horrible economic indicators, and Americans everywhere were under the influence of public apathy and social doldrums. Carter began his speech that day by saying that our country's political interaction had ...*become increasingly narrow, focused more and more on what the isolated world of Washington thinks is important.* The President came to believe that ...*all the legislation in the world can't fix what's wrong with America.* He referred to the crisis of confidence that I have mentioned heretofore, saying that ...*our people are losing that faith, not only in government, itself, but in the ability as citizens to serve as the ultimate rulers and shapers of our democracy.* Bill Bishop continued by recalling that President Carter admonished an indifferent American nation for...*worshiping self-indulgence and consumption,* and for ...*a growing disrespect for government and religion.* Carter had the thoughtfulness, foresight, and fortitude to reprimand each and every U.S. citizen by saying that...*this is not a message of happiness or reassurance. But, it is the truth, and it is a warning.*

It is the conclusion of Bill Bishop's newspaper article that says all that needs to be recorded in history about why the United States has taken such a perilous turn away from God. Said he in July 1991, ...*recent history tells us that Carter's warning was wasted. The 1980s were a decade of self-indulgence and consumption for which our children will pay. The scandal of the savings and loan industry (a $500 billion due bill), the Wall Street rip-offs, the takeover mania that ruined ongoing businesses—this is what Carter was warning of in 1979. Meanwhile, the 'narrow' debate Carter complained of in 1979 has been reduced to a sliver. Congress' troubles in passing a budget last year and a civil rights bill this year—two pieces of compromise legislation with no direction and little meaning—have convinced citizens that the national government is irresponsible when it is not irrelevant. And, the energy crisis has gone around and come around in a terrible and wasteful war in Iraq that is not over now and, it appears, never will be. Much of the blame for Carter's defeat in 1980 traces back to this speech. The* *cock-sureness of Reagan stood in such high and enviable contrast to the brooding and searching Carter. We picked the happy ending of Hollywood over the heat and dust of Plains, Georgia. The defeat, however, was ours. We ridiculed a man who spoke the truth. We laughed at his piousness. And, to our shame, we ignored his prophecy.*

We are now beyond the beginning of the 21st century, long-passed the years when President Jimmy Carter held office and the pen strokes of Bill Bishop who so fondly remembered him, too. The 1990s saw more of the same greed, incivility, recklessness, lawlessness, lewd social conduct, and material selfishness that the 39th President of the United States knew was destroying us. It was as though we needed no foreign enemies to take us down the drain—we were doing quite sufficiently on our own. But, then, on September 11, 2001, the unthinkable finally occurred. Radical terrorists felled the World Trade Center, destroyed a portion of the U.S. Pentagon, and God-knows what else they would have done with the jet airliner that crashed prematurely in a grassy field in Pennsylvania. And, what was their reasoning for taking so many innocent lives? That we Americans are a bunch of self-indulgent consumers who care little about the plight of the rest of the world. The George W. Bush White House established a task-force to study America's image in the summer of 2002, the Office on Global Communications, whose purpose is to try to tell the rest of humanity that we are not the selfish war-mongers that they perceive us to be. The Council on Foreign Relations, another task force whose goal is to persuade foreign countries that we are not really that bad, indicated that the United States of America is seen as ...*arrogant, hypocritical, self-absorbed, self-indulgent, and contemptuous of others.* (Sonya Ross, Associated Press, July 31, 2002). While we continued to pursue the profits of our secular lifestyles after President Carter's speech in July 1979, who could have guessed that our ignoring his words would have had such catastrophic consequences 22 years later? He returned to private life after leaving office in January 1981; but he certainly did not give-up the goals of spiritual goodness about which he had spoken with such ominous overtones a couple of years before. He traveled the globe on what (the late) television news commentator, John Chancellor, described from the NBC booth at the 1992 Democratic Convention as being a *Franciscan mission* to alleviate human suffering, ensure fair elections in fledgling democracies, teach global self-sufficiency through The Carter Center at Emory University in Atlanta, write prolifically about the nobler aspects of human nature, preach the Gospel of Jesus Christ from the pulpit in his tiny Baptist Church in Plains, and prove to humanity that negotiation is always a better tool to effect change than war. God created Jimmy Carter as a man; America shaped him to be an international leader; and the world praised him as a prince among paupers by awarding him the Nobel Peace Prize in Oslo, Norway on October 11, 2002.

We have learned from our own experiences that President Jimmy Carter did not invent the things that made him so great among the many historical heroes we have known, but that he reveled the knowledge of the goodness and justice that was written into Creation by virtue of God having been born as a sinless Man in the person of Jesus Christ. And, if Mr. Carter could mend so many millions of lives by being simply honest, why can we not each and all imitate his own emulation of the Savior of the world? The things that affluent nations sometimes celebrate as being ultimate personal success are quite the opposite of the Christian Truth that men like him extol. The deviancy and backlashing against our selfishness by the people we have allowed to suffer, and the millions more we shamelessly force into the harshness of poverty and indigence everyday is the real reason why the red, white, and blue of Old Glory are so despised by people around the world. We have proclaimed ourselves to be free from the responsibility of tending to them because America is under the false impression that she has somehow been blessed by God to be a land full of endless wealth. The dearth of isolated societies and secluded tribes in the nations of Africa, for example, is not just some imaginary agony that we believe to be untrue. The fact is, many American capitalists, including our citizens living abroad, have become ungodly rich at the expense of such poor and neglected individuals. Is it true that there could be anybody alive who is so coldly-calculating when it comes to the almighty dollar? Do we remember the great America hero, Todd Beamer, who was flying aboard United Airlines Flight 93 that had been commandeered by the terrorists on September 11, 2001? He thought of a plan to recapture control of the plane with some of his fellow passengers and, upon attempting to do so, exclaimed the words *Let's Roll!* over an in-flight telephone. After the plane crashed, this became a catch-phrase that was used to muster the fighting spirit of Americans everywhere. Even President George W. Bush quoted him in various rally addresses. Soon, the race was on by U.S. merchants and private companies to obtain a trademark on the phrase *Let's Roll!* so they could market T-shirts and hats with these words inscribed on them for their own financial gain. According to Michael Rubinkam, also of the Associated Press, the Todd M. Beamer Foundation set-out in court to stop anyone else from trademarking the phrase unless the profits were given to the families of the victims of the crash. According to Rubinkam in an article dated February 2, 2002, a man named Jack L. Williams from Grosse Pointe Park, Michigan, whose intention was to sell T-shirts and sweatshirts bearing the catch-phrase, applied for a trademark on September 24, 2001, two days before the Todd Beamer Foundation. He ignored letters from the foundation's lawyers and responded to them by saying ...*I don't care what your name is, it's first in, first swim. It's all about good old American capitalism.*

Perhaps that's all that needs to be said about this. The point is, we see a common thread which connects and complements the lives of Former President Jimmy Carter and the American martyr Todd Beamer of mutual self-sacrifice that makes the rest of humanity more free. And, in union with the life of Jesus Christ, they have both made the interrelation between the natural and the paranormal seem quite obvious to those who are inclined to believe in Him. Hence, the entirety of the ages has been reapportioned in a beneficial way through the sacrifices of men like these; and also their wives and children, and the distant admirers who encapsulate what made them such gentle giants among men. We should always remember that this same potential and generative capacity are present inside us all when we are confronted by the throes of necessity or other decisive circumstances which warrant their being divulged. Living deep within every man, woman, and child today is an anonymous healer, teacher, benefactor, and friend. And, it seems that each of these becomes a product of the social attributes which are apparent on any given day—someone who suddenly aspires to be a president, or another person like Todd Beamer who got out of bed on that fateful September 2001 morning not knowing that it would be his last. But, through his indivisible courage, and that of his martyred friends, he saved countless lives at the destination where the terrorists had intended Flight 93 to fall aground. His heroism, although probably never before known to be so intense, became the salvation of an entire group of unwary citizens. So, what does this say about all the wallet-thumping capitalists who slouch behind the tinted glass windows of their streamline limousines? There is not a whit of doubt that God is asking them to come to a halt, get out of their cars, and greet reality head-on as servants in the same way that Jimmy Carter surprised America by walking courageously down the center-line of Pennsylvania Avenue on his inauguration day. He once said that it was a moment in time when everything in the world seemed absolutely right. Thank you, Mr. President. So did we. However, what are we to tell our children when they ask about the assets of the world's billionaires? How do little Sally and Tommy reconcile the life stories of our popular leaders and public heroes against those of wealthy entrepreneurs? Let's take a look at some of Forbes magazine's 400 most wealthy Americans as recorded in the Fall of 2001 as a case in point.

## The Wealthiest of the Wealthy

| | | | |
|---|---|---|---|
| 1. | William H. Gates, III | Microsoft | $43.0 Billion |
| 2. | Warren E. Buffet | Berkshire Hathaway | $36.0 Billion |
| 3. | Paul Gardner Allen | Microsoft | $21.0 Billion |
| 4. | Alice L. Walton | Wal-Mart | $18.8 Billion |
| 5. | Helen R. Walton | Wal-Mart | $18.8 Billion |
| 6. | Jim C. Walton | Wal-Mart | $18.8 Billion |
| 7. | John T. Walton | Wal-Mart | $18.8 Billion |
| 8. | S. Robson Walton | Wal-Mart | $18.8 Billion |
| 9. | Lawrence J. Ellison | Oracle | $15.2 Billion |
| 10. | Steven A. Ballmer | Microsoft | $11.9 Billion |
| 11. | Michael Dell | Dell Computer | $11.2 Billion |
| 12. | John Kluge | Metromedia | $10.5 Billion |
| 13. | Forrest E. Mars, Jr. | (candy) | $10.0 Billion |
| 14. | Jacqueline Mars | (candy) | $10.0 Billion |
| 15. | John Franklyn Mars | (candy) | $10.0 Billion |

*Source:  AP*

It would appear that most all of these people are fearful of human life to the degree that they will not surrender their material wealth to get any closer to really living in temporal terms with its purpose. Being a hero in America today, or anywhere else in the world, does not require tangible acquisition—indeed, it often mandates quite the opposite. Champions and conquerors are not necessarily those of great eloquence or private citizens who live in luxurious homes with exquisite appointments. The essence of true greatness rests not in what one holds, or even has access to; but what he gives away, even if it means relinquishing one's own impending and inevitable achievements and sources of comfort so that those in his midst can share more broadly in the fullness of the vast commonwealth. I am not advocating a world that is based upon some structured socialism, but one whose principles are defined by those things that enrich the lot of the multitudes everywhere, given outwardly and freely by those who have been duly resourceful and enterprising in a completely legitimate way. This is the meaning of true kindness and civility; and it is to these noble effects that God responds in-kind. Above all else, we must succeed in conquering our enviousness and jealousies, refraining from comparing ourselves with the upper-crust societies who live in gated communities and in sequestered condominiums. If any one of them says that he is happy with the world he sees on the news and along the public thoroughfares everyday, we can rest assured that he is lying through his teeth. People like this are short on miracles and long on apprehension. Their security rests in their artifacts, and never in their spirit. Even though they are adorned by fine threads and jewelry, they are a miserable people; lost, lonely and abandoned by God, at least for now, until they finally accept Him for who He is and react by making themselves poorer for the sake of the Redemption of their souls. Every mortal being who walks the face of the Earth ultimately discovers that there can be no grace in a life that only searches for fame, money, food, and sexual gratification. God must become the reason why they live. By all means, do most of us really understand the amount of assets that these billionaires have amassed? It is like trying to comprehend the chemical consistency of a pharmaceutical compound. One of the more popularly prescribed medicines to treat high blood pressure is erythritol, which is known in the laboratory as $CH2OHCHOHCHOHCH2OH$. Most ordinary people have no way of grasping what this really means; and such is the confusion that surrounds us when we try to calculate just how much money someone like Bill Gates has. He announced on November 11, 2002 that he and his wife had pledged $100 million through the Bill & Melinda Gates Foundation to help fight AIDS in India, a dramatic initiative that he says will help women protect themselves from getting the disease.

Let's take a closer look at this whopping $100 million that Bill Gates has decided to give to our foreign friends who are suffering such a grievous and fatal demise. Forty-three billion dollars is the estimated amount of his assets; that's $43,000,000,000; and he has decided to sacrifice a portion of it because, *...I realized about ten years ago that my wealth has to go back to society. A fortune the size of which is hard to imagine is best not passed-on to one's children*, he is quoted as saying. Oh, really, Mr. Gates? Let's see if we have this right. Someone who is a self-proclaimed billionaire has at least "a thousand times a million dollars" in material assets because 1,000 times $1 million equals $1 billion. According to Steve Forbes' magazine, Bill Gates has forty-three times that much, or 43,000 million-dollars, for a total personal worth of $43 billion. He has chosen to make 100 of these 43,000 millions available to the women of India, which is the grand sum of only a .0023 fraction of his recorded assets as of September 2001. This is equivalent to someone having a hundred-dollars on their person and pulling 23 cents from their change pocket to give to a gaunt-looking pauper sitting in rags on a street corner in front of the local post office. Who in the world with a hundred-dollars to spend is going to miss a measly twenty-three cents? I have always maintained that selfless charity is defined *not* by what someone gives to a certain needy cause, but by how much they retain for themselves. The example I have used here, Bill Gates, could give an entire billion dollars to the poor people of India and still have 97.6% of his money left in the bank. And, yet, we picked-up our newspapers on Tuesday, November 12, 2002 and read the headlines, *Gates pledges $100 Million to fight AIDS in India.* His household name is being hailed around the globe for giving such an unprecedented amount of money, the sum total of which he can probably offset against his taxes for interest income somewhere. Please do not get me wrong! Anyone who says they are going to give millions of dollars to the poor has a definitive concern for the suffering of others. But, Jesus Christ tells us the parable about the elderly woman who laid her last two pennies in a collection box at a temple many centuries ago. Indeed, I am not singling-out Bill Gates because he is one of the richest men on the planet. After all, his Microsoft Corporation has left an indelible mark on the progress of our western democracy in the fields of science and health care, advanced social redevelopment and public policy administration, and management information systems all around the world. However, if I had $43 billion in assets in the bank and in viable market shares, and decided to give an almost minuscule percentage of it away, I would cringe to think that it might make the newspaper headlines somewhere and the rest of humanity would realize just how stingy I am.

Nonetheless, we continue to envy such people like the ones we find listed in *Forbes* magazine as being the most wealthy Americans because we errantly assume that they have somehow been subliminally blessed by God to live so affluently. However, Jesus Christ will never stop broadcasting His overtures across our rural plains and fancy prairies, on the street corners of our busiest cities, and throughout every village and hamlet until we finally understand the right perspective of owning material things. Only after He has won our worship to the exclusion of all human infatuation with any tangible goods will His Kingdom be assured of arresting every last human heart. We are all sinners against Creation; and perhaps we do not own the right to reprimand anyone else for hoarding billions of dollars in assets in their private coffers. But, are we not obliged to live by one code of conduct in accordance with the Holy Gospel? I am convinced that every man alive should humble himself before the Throne of God, and thereafter squire Lady Wisdom to the opening dance of Redemption once Jesus comes again in Glory. We cannot do this if we believe by brash assumption that to be inordinately rich is to also be acceptable in His Holy sight. What does He say regarding such profiteering? *Thou Shalt Not Steal!* The Catechism of the Catholic Church cites it rather tersely.

2404   *In his use of things, man should regard the external goods he legitimately*
       *owns not merely as exclusive to himself, but common to others also, in the*
       *sense that they can benefit others as well as himself. The ownership of any*
       *property makes its holder a steward of Providence with the task of making*
       *it fruitful and communicating its benefits to others, first of all his family.*

2405   *Goods of production, either material or immaterial—such as land,*
       *factories, practical or artistic skills—oblige their possessors to employ*
       *them in ways that will benefit the greatest number. Those who hold goods*
       *for use and consumption should use them with moderation, reserving the*
       *better part for guests, for the sick and the poor.*

I have always believed that our windows are our best friends in the daytime, and can be our worst enemies late at night. We are living hours of tremendous over-exposure right now; ones during which it is veritably impossible to hide our riches from other people because of the homes in which we choose to reside and the sporty cars our children drive. When it is broadly daylight outdoors, we can peer through the vast expanse of our picture windows and see the rushing traffic passing on the neighborhood boulevards. Our assets are concealed inside our castles, where neither our motivations nor actions are discernable by anonymous passers-by. But, whenever the inevitable darkness looms, as it does in America today, it is us who become the targets of the curious underworld. We are then forced to hang tapestries before our wooden panes in order to shutter ourselves from sight through those same window glasses that, by day, we feel the warming of the sun. And, so it is with our struggle to hold onto our material things. We install padlocks and deadbolts on our door jams to keep potential burglars out; but, do we not realize that we are locking our own freedom there within? Our possessions have become the reason for our paranoia—too afraid are we that someone might take a liking to the things we consider as belonging only to ourselves. Such secrecy is a parable for our hearts! In the darkness of this world, we should decline to fear the raiders of the night by opening our spirits wide; giving the entire of Creation the fullness of vision as to who we really are. Invite one another in!—I say! And, thereafter, we will not look so much like hypocrites when we attend Church on Sunday morning and ask God why His presence does not seem to be so prevalent anymore. We rue the violation of His Sacred Commandments by others in our midst, but rarely take an introspective view as to whether we are really pursuing them ourselves. This is what the United States of America has become! And, it is altogether the reason why there is a phenomenon in the world today known as *private billionaires.* The cultural divide that separates us from indigent nations is more than a cloistered breach between the peoples of the Earth because, by default, we are providing God ample evidence to prosecute us as the very isolationists whom He sent His Son onto the globe to cultivate, scold, harvest, discard, and annihilate at His destined whim!

Our western-American immoral revolution has never really been about personal freedom, but of our conquest of the galaxy for the purpose of binding us in chains. How ironic it has become that the east meets west according to the details and particulars of the face-value of a copper coin. We do not need any foreign nationals to subvert us into death to spite our Christianity because we are already committing outright spiritual suicide before Jesus' weeping eyes. And, what enhances the intelligence of our children about the Kingdom of His Love has very little to do with what we are asking them to learn. The U.S. market system and private corporate structures are operating in the wide-open spaces of the outer-universe and in direct contradiction to the tenets of our Apostolic faith which relate to the Judeo-Christian Seventh Commandment. Our capitalistic democracy is an aberration in the history of humankind because we are slowly extracting ourselves from the common good that Jesus Christ holds so dearly inside the cynosure of His Most Sacred Heart. The very righteousness He extols demands that we share, and share alike; but there is nary a man or woman alive who would not proclaim, ...*what I would give to be as rich as the five Wal-Mart billionaires!* Why? Because we would own the right to make decisions that we could never have been able to ponder before. It is beyond conceivability for most of us what it would mean to not have to retire for the day at 9:00 o'clock p.m., toss and turn through the midnight hours and wonder what our boss will complain about tomorrow, and what necessities we will purchase with the residual receipts of next week's payroll check. Will we remit only the minimum amount that is due on our credit card bills so we can ensure that the utility companies do not send us a past-due notice again, threatening to shut-off our heat and lights on the 15th of the month? Can we afford that new drill for the workshop in our garage and pay for our daughter's piano lessons, too? Good Heavens! What would life be like to never again have to pay another installment on the mortgage of our home or on our family automobiles? Is it any wonder why so many people play the Power Ball Lottery in droves around America today? Indeed, all they want to secure is certain peace-of-mind, freedom from the burdens of their contracted financial debts, and the opportunity to decide when and where they will spend their idle time or the remainder of their lives. We see an occasional half-hour TV "infomercial" that tells us how to become wealthy almost overnight by investing what little we have in begetting our own personal real-estate business.

Where will all this end? What will bring this onslaught against the Seventh Commandment to a halt? I must confess to everyone that I cannot even pretend to know.

I penned this chapter on Tuesday, November 19, 2002, the day after the *Abraham Lincoln Presidential Library* was dedicated in my home town of Springfield, Illinois; and the 139th anniversary of his Gettysburg Address in 1863. While I did not attend the ceremony because I chose, instead, to receive the Most Blessed Sacrament at the Holy Sacrifice of the Mass at the Cathedral of the Immaculate Conception a few blocks away from there; it became clear to me that our perception has been skewed by what we think certain individuals would say if they were still alive. The new Presidential Library and Museum came at a price-tag of about $120 million; and I keep wondering whether Abraham Lincoln, himself; who was not a wealthy man; would rather the funds have been spent in accordance with the wishes of the very Son of God in whom he placed the trust of his entire life, his public career, his family, and the legacy of his abbreviated presidency. While he fought with candle, book, and bell to keep America indivisible during the War Between the States, we contrastingly dedicated a facility in his memory in late 2002 for the sole purpose of garnering a greater portion of money in our local merchants' banks. The first article on the city's television news that night was to regale the financial benefits that the nearby vendors were reaping from the opening of Mr. Lincoln's new hall of liberty. This is the same error that has foddered the drive for Americans to be free—not from slavery or the perils of civil war, but the right to proclaim that the accumulation of personal wealth should be the reason for our encounter within the public domain. Sadly, this is also the legacy we shall leave to the generations to come; beyond the hollow thud of our shiny coffins impacting the bottom of our darkened graves, awaiting the death-rattle of our limp and abandoned skeletons. We are wantonly destroying the innocence that is reminiscent of our children's street-side lemonade stands by plucking them from their wooden stools behind their awkwardly-handwritten dime marquees and putting them in front of computer screens before they ever turn the age of six. We have stripped them of their fine denim blue-jeans and pretty plaid dinner-skirts; and have clad them in gunnysack britches, fluorescent-colored racing jackets, and blinking white tennis shoes. Quite affiantly! They are like little tape-recorders, alright!—Too quick to learn what's wrong, sharper than upholsterers' tacks, and fully prepared to snap-back with clever retorts as soon as the opportunities arise; and we have become the enablers of this strange adolescent arrogance!

It sometimes appears as though our little children would have our knowledge of their lives become limited only to what they think we should know. All they wish to hear from us is that we are confident that the fossil fuel *coal* from a mineshaft is black and that cooking flour is powdery white. Every other shade and hue in between, it seems, they reserve under the economy of their own private interpretations. And, it is in this leverage that they have gained an entirely fallacious sense of security because they are completely unaware that their choices and preferences have little to do with Divine Truth. Rarely do they adhere to the admonishment of responsible proverbial human instinct; but rather they make decisions on the fly and ignore the insight and intrigue that have made the rest of the world an organized macrocosm of logical thinking. When we were all very young, we studied bacteria and other invisible organisms by growing them in a petri dish, after which we placed the cultures under magnifying lenses to see an entire form of life we never previously knew existed. As unbelievable as it may sound, adults are oftentimes taken for granted by their offspring in much the same way. One of their peers could defy gravity by riding on a skateboard in midair for the longest "hang time" on public record, but most of them would not be slightly interested in watching a single termite devour an entire giant redwood tree in three minutes' time. Or, perhaps we could try some historical proverbs on them for size. *The lazy is a brother of the beggar,* to which they are apt to respond, *What?* Maybe we could lay a little Sino-Tibetan logic on them. *It is not the knowing that is difficult, but the doing;* so say the Chinese. This one would surely earn us their version of a free pass into a modern-day Bellevue. They are apt to turn to us with their bellicose exasperation and remind us that they are free to say, choose, and do anything they want to by virtue of their heritage as natural-born American citizens. If all else fails, it would do no harm to hand them some literature that they might read during their own precious time; and a favorite of many is a weekly flyer called *The Faith Connection,* which is published by Resources for Christian Living in Allen, Texas. Their edition for the 33rd Sunday in Ordinary Time for 2002 bore the following quotation that I think is very profound regarding the symbolic ways we can teach our children right from wrong without their always believing that we are brow-beating them. *Parables and proverbs are many layered words of wisdom intended to teach us how to live in this world—a world that God continuously creates and whose resources humanity manages with varying degrees of justice and mercy. We are not to be enslaved by Creation's natural cycles and seasons, but bound to them by God's Plan of Creation and Salvation revealed to us by Jesus Christ and the Holy Spirit. We exist in a world in which pain, darkness, and death have their due time and season—but not the last word. The wise live acknowledging and trusting that only God has the last word.* We can assure our younger generation that we, too, are subject to the same principles of Divine Revelation by which they will ultimately be judged and to which each of us who is mortal must eventually succumb. Leading them to this eternally-sustainable Truth is about all we can do for now.

As everyone with any semblance of conscience in America knows, our 21$^{st}$ century western culture is hanging like a great albatross around our children's necks, choking the life-blood of piety from their daily existence. The incessant pummeling they receive from the entertainment industry is as malevolent as the things they see on TV. While I devoted the previous chapter of this book to castigating the programming on the "idiot box," it does not even scratch the surface of the pornographic themes, violence, terrorism, and bloodshed they see in home videos and on motion picture screens. Who in their right mind would allow their children to watch the outright evil that is manifested by such human vermin as the producers of *Night of the Living Dead, Halloween, Friday the 13$^{th}$, The Texas Chain Saw Massacre, Deep Throat, Behind the Green Door,* and *Debbie Does Dallas?* It surely must not be enough, according to them, that Satan is having a field day in real life by luring people everywhere into despicable acts of sexual perversion, rampant murder and suicide by the thousands every day; gluttony, sloth, and adultery every time the clock ticks another second, and their uncontested declaration of independence from anything whatsoever to do with the Love of God in our public schools, government buildings, and renderings from our courts of law. Somehow, such devious people believe that these same grotesque images are also fit to play on our movie projectors, in slide-shows and magazines, and across the entire globe on the world-wide Internet. We have turned to our daily newspapers for some sense of balance in the past, still reeling from the tabloid mentality that comes from behind the scenes in Hollywood, and seen paid advertising in their classified section for such molten crud from the stench-filled bowels of Hell as movies like *The Exorcist* and *The Last House on the Left.* What do the American media do about this continuous deterioration of the moral fiber that their foregone predecessors once espoused? They profit from it and shamelessly take their blood-money to the bank! Are we to blame them for intentionally wreaking havoc upon the psychological stability of our adolescent children, or is their awareness of what our progeny wish to see the true reasoning behind their assault against the individual discretion of every impressionable youth in the United States today? Has the cart finally outrun the horse; and has the egg now come before the chicken? Indeed, this is not to say that there have been no "morality plays" to give us pause to think about the plight of the underclass whom we have defined as being anyone who cannot afford to pay $8.00 apiece to buy a seat inside a motion-picture theatre, not to mention the $22.95 it costs for four boxes of popcorn and a round of soft-drinks. *Oh! But, you are able to* *get free refills!*—they exclaim while they are robbing us blind at the confectionary counter after selling us a half-gallon container of Coke for ten times the price we might pay in a restaurant or at the nearby Schnuck's grocery store.

Now, our nation's favorite pastime has become international war. Wow! There's a way to teach our young adults how to effect change for the better with their neighbors! Are we subject to the fate of always fighting for what's right with smart-bombs and bullets instead of intellectual logic and sealed peace treaties? Will our children learn that military aggression is the reward they will receive for our having amassed the most lethal arsenal in the history of the world? What about the noble legacies of U.S. Presidents John F. Kennedy and Ronald Reagan who taught us that having weapons of endless capabilities helps maintain the peace through strength? And yet, we should refrain from using them; not by cowardice, but because no one will win if such an international Armageddon should ever ensue. I am not convinced that our upcoming American leaders who are now in preparatory institutions and Ivy League schools are really certain as to the true dangers of the decisions they might have to make someday. And, yet, we allow them to learn about the uncertain future by exposing them to such visual images as *Independence Day, Terminator 2, Rambo First Blood, A Time to Kill,* and the *Lethal Weapon* sequels. Why don't we just ask them to put blinders over their eyes and walk across the Adriatic Sea in a fog as thick as pea soup to try to get them to tell us why they cannot see any goodness in human history anymore? Every last one of us is guilty as charged by Jesus Christ as having committed sins of omission by not prohibiting our children from being exposed to the satanic verses that broadside their consciousness everyday. And, yet, we label their reactions as reprehensible, their excuses deserving of reproof, and their attitudes galled with total disdain. In the meantime, they realize that they learned all of this from us!—that we have allowed modern America to become so corrupted by crime and impurity that they falsely believe that it is an acceptable way to live. They come home with new piercings in places that only their doctors should be allowed to see, green hair that is molded into spikes jutting straight-up into the air, and tattoos of serial killers and punk-rockers on their chests, arms, and legs. They get involved in fatal skirmishes between street gangs and rap-star gun fights; but our admonishment of them rings rather hollow when they look us in the eyes and say they learned about such conduct from military action in the Viet Nam War, Desert Storm, and the offensive operations Just Cause and Enduring Freedom. All of a sudden, the American body politick has the word—*h-y-p-o-c-r-i-t-e*—spelled-out in bold graffiti across our collective brow! I opened this chapter speaking about the perils of totalitarianism, Communism, and Fascism; and I am confident that most of our children today are not aware of the global circumstances that have led us to sending U.S. troops onto foreign soil to try to preserve their democratic freedoms. They seem to take it for granted *not* because they hold a definitive adversity against it, but because they do not know what human life is like in many parts of the world. Why? Because we have fooled them with our immoral western materialism and "anything goes" cache of false moral choices. We might think we are doing them a favor by allowing them to believe that America's billionaires are some kind of heroes; but the effect has been only to steep them more deeply in the very materialism that, in the absence of its shared abundance, has been the origin of their erotic lifestyles and debased artworks; and is the new collusion of our deeply sinister reptilian age which they have somehow seen fit to exalt.

# Fears

*At five we were afraid of the dark,*
*Afraid of all the animals in the park,*
*Afraid to leave our safe home,*
*And, so afraid of being left alone.*
*At ten we learned to fear dying,*
*And, to fear the thought of crying,*
*And, we were afraid of new faces,*
*And, the moves to new places.*
*At fifteen we feared not making the team,*
*Not mastering the skateboard,*                                    10
*or the pinball machine.*
*We feared not being one of the crowd,*
*And, we feared prospective dates*
*would say 'no' much too loud.*
*At twenty we were afraid no more,*
*Though in front of us was the threat of war.*
*We got by and took it all in stride,*
*And, then came the fear of losing our pride.*
*Thirty gave us new fears, and many,*
*With the new family, we counted every penny.*          20
*Economic stability was fear number one,*
*And, by now, our children's fears had begun.*
*At fifty we began fears for our health,*
*The medical bills took all of our wealth,*
*And, we feared our grandchildren's colds,*
*And, we so feared growing old.*
*At seventy, we are accustomed to the dark,*
*And, we see daily, all the animals in the park,*
*But, again, we're afraid to leave our safe home,*
*And, so afraid of being left alone.*                              30

F. P. Dufer
Published in *The State Journal-Register*
Springfield, Illinois
November 25, 1983

# Chapter VI
## *Awesome, Dude!  Did I Already Say That?*
## *A New Mode of Communication*

It has long been known that the key to any form of psychological understanding and the origin of human accomplishment is whether we are successful communicators.  No matter how we accomplish it, the meeting of the minds for the purpose of mutual interaction is always necessary for any world of societies to progress and survive.  If we take a moment to think about it—ancient hieroglyphics, smoke signals, handwritten letters, the telegraph, radio, telephone, and Email—all of these have been the tangible extensions of our desire to relay messages to one another.  While they have never been true substitutes for interfacial conversation, they have augmented and facilitated our word-of-mouth communication.  Indeed, braille for the visually impaired and sign-language for the deaf are their auxiliary means of keeping in contact with the rest of the world.  We enter campaigns of war and likewise avoid them by declarations of animosity or negotiating peace through every form of human interaction; making the things we relate by direct reference or implication often as important as the physical motions we undertake.  The parameters existing in this vast field of extemporaneous exchange are almost mind-boggling.  If we could see all the radio waves that are generated by cellular telephones and TVs, or the millions of miles of electrical cord that connect land-line phones all around the globe, we might wonder how there can be any room atop the ground or beneath it for anything else.  On the intangible level, our discourse takes us from such conversations as superfluous palaver between customers sitting on cigarette-burned bar stools sipping cold Lager beer and Scotch whiskey at the neighborhood bar to the altruistic poise and eloquence of presidential inaugural addresses being delivered on the bunting-adorned west steps of the U.S. Capitol that are transmitted by relay satellite to every nation in the world.  What we say, the tone in which we deliver it, and the intentional and accidental effects of our words tell a great deal more about us than we really know.  How many times have we heard somebody counter a statement with the phrase, *That's not true*, or *I don't have to believe that!*  On far too many occasions, we are forced to retract our disconcerting expressions and clarify what we mean because we are too inept in communicating what we actually want to say.  It is sometimes even difficult to formulate accurate thoughts of what we are feeling inside, let alone place them into sensible sentences.  We can be clever and witty; or obnoxious, maudlin, sarcastic, critical, and complimentary in sequential moments by the nouns, verbs, adjectives, and adverbs we randomly select to describe our sentiments.  Having referenced President John F. Kennedy in the previous chapter, I recall having studied a portion of world history whose purpose was to evaluate the effectiveness of certain public speakers.  When it comes to those who have made a great difference in shaping global opinion with their powers of persuasion, highly visionary civic leaders have always enjoyed an opportune venue to amend the course of human events.  The likes of Sir Winston Churchill of Great Britain, Charles de Gaulle of France; and the American statesmen Abraham Lincoln, Franklin Delano Roosevelt, Thomas E. Dewey, Adlai Stevenson, Ronald Reagan, and Bill Clinton all perfected the art of espousing effective oratory and persuasive communication.

We are all best known for the kindness of the words we employ, or the ones that serve to ameliorate difficult circumstances, to diffuse potential conflicts, and provide assurance and perspective during times of personal crisis and national tragedy.  The unprecedented consolation that the world's poets and lyricists have brought to the collective human spirit is nothing-less than another blessing from God, Himself.   Are not the statutes of His Commandments, His Wisdom and prophecies of the eternal ages, and the implications that each of these has on the final destiny of human history all explicated by the written Word and the intonation of the Will of Almighty God through the potent presence of the Holy Spirit in the hearts of all who fear Him?  If it is true that laughter is the best medicine, do we not receive it in plentiful doses through the oral humor of our jesters and comedians?  Do not the playwrights of our tragedies, dramas, and parodies own a parcel of the genius which has shaped the landscape of our dreams and fashioned the architecture of what little contentment we discover in the stressfulness of mortal life?  And, what seems to be the most admired of all is a speaker's capacity to remain calm under pressure, even exhibiting a sense of levity in the face of outright rejection.  Who could possibly speak about this subject, therefore, without mentioning President Kennedy and the wit that became a trademark of his public conversations?  Why?  Was it because he was the first occupant of the White House to be born in the 20th century; for all the charm and grace that this meant for our changing American democracy that had finally evolved from the dirt main streets of the old west into the progressive and industrious republic we have become today?  President Kennedy was the first of his peers to conduct live press conferences in front of the entire nation.  Previously, questions from reporters and other media operatives had to be written-out so a particular president could prepare his remarks in advance; but John F. Kennedy changed that.  At the rostrum in the public auditorium of the old State Department press room, President Kennedy spoke without a script on sixty-one different occasions, fielding questions whose answers were not always so easy to render.  The air in the arena became somewhat thick during the tense and heady moments of the Cuban Missile Crisis, the violence surrounding the Civil Rights movement, the Viet Nam War, and his struggle to procure the Nuclear Test Ban Treaty to curb the aggression of adversarial states half-way around the globe. But, for all of this, humor best describes the legacy of JFK to interact effectively with the American people. One of his witty remarks is still known to this day as a bold shot of raw intelligence that was heard around the world. A reporter he had formally recognized stood to put a question before him that was somewhat argumentative in nature. *Mr. President, you have said, and I think more than once, that heads of government should not go to a summit to negotiate agreements, but only to approve agreements negotiated at a lower level. Now, it's being said and written that you're gonna eat those words and go to a summit without any agreement at a lower level. Has your position changed, sir?* As we looked into the face of President Kennedy while he was intently listening to this particular query, we could detect by his expression and body posture that he was not about to allow anyone to imply that he would be eating his words anytime soon. When the reporter finished articulating his question, it seemed as though President Kennedy was prepared for such a verbal pot-shot from a member of the media. He never hesitated for so much as a brief second before he responded, *Well, I'm going to have a dinner for all the people who have written it, and we'll see who eats what!* Of course, JFK said this with a rather uncanny presence of cool confidence and reassurance resonating from his voice while he, the inquiring reporter, and the usually stoic White House press corps broke into uncontrollable laughter; as he simultaneously pointed his right index finger in the direction of another questioner in the back of the room to beckon a subsequent inquiry. This was President John Fitzgerald Kennedy's subtle means of verbally disarming his opposition—by a mild disposition and able intelligence, convincing those around him that life need not appear to be as serious as it oftentimes is, and implying that our broad public discourse should be accompanied by a greater sense of decency, commitment, shared values, and with the ultimate goal of lifting oppressed peoples into dignity once again; all of this with the same larger-than-life identity that allowed his aforementioned predecessor, Franklin Roosevelt, to become the only U.S. president to be elected to four consecutive terms and to be remembered as the premier *happy warrior* for the cause of advancing western democracy in the chronology of modern civilization.

My friends—that was then, and this is now. What our grandfathers and their sons and daughters spoke about, the terms they used to describe the particular conditions of their age, and the purpose for their expressions were all focused upon legitimate, reasoned, and comprehensible linguistic temperance. Unfortunately, there is more nonsense involved in our public debate now than there was forty years ago; or even ten or twenty. I am not necessarily referring only to matters of government and political science, but the interchange of opinions that are butted in common places across broadway streets, at truck stops along our interstate expressways, and in billiard parlors and gambling casinos all around America. We have survived the trite cliches that have come from these places, causing most of them to become obsolete by the sheer nature of our reluctance to be defined by any previous generation. Thank God Almighty we wore-out the exclamation that anything that is satisfying to us is known as being *groovy!* And, people who rarely exceed the dimensions of what we believe to be well-rounded individuals are no longer *square.* However, things that are agreeable to our sense of purpose or set of personal standards are still *cool!* Conversely, anyone who is regarded as physically or sexually attractive is complimented as being *hot!* We have even decided to add more flavor to the proclamation when the object of our infatuation is a rather petite female. Someone in this category is referred to as being a *little hottie!* The door has been ripped completely off its hinges in this new century for the introduction of an entirely different set of criteria for human interaction, manifested mainly by our adolescent children who wish not to concede to the way their parents are disciplining them or anyone else who otherwise bosses them around. The litany of street slogans and phraseologies is almost too much for us to believe sometimes. For lack of a better way of saying it, let's delve into the previously unexplored deposit of these extraordinary passages to see what makes our young people tick.

I do not think it would be too broad a stretch if we compared our children's approach to verbal interaction with the commercial that began airing on television in March 2000 about a certain laundry fabric softener. It begins not unlike most others, telling us about the great benefits of the product and that everyone should purchase it for use in their own home. Then, all of a sudden, a huge cockroach begins to crawl across the surface of the viewer's TV screen that appears to be a living creature on the glass. As it turns out, the commercial is not to market a fabric softener at all, but the Orkin Pest Control company. Thousands of television viewers across America were fooled into believing that the pesky roach had come from somewhere inside their homes and had made its way onto the surface of their TV picture tube. The commercial was created by J. Walter Thompson Incorporated, an advertising agency based in Atlanta, Georgia. Orkin, their client, reported that they received dozens of phone calls from people who were either frightened out of their wits or rather amused by the ad. In other cases, the reaction was somewhat more aggravated. A couple of watchers asked the pest control company to replace their TV sets after they were provoked into throwing such objects as dishes and shoes at them; and a woman in Tampa, Florida even hurled a motorcycle helmet at the screen to try to kill the imaginary bug. Anyway, I believe to the depths of my soul that this is the same kind of "shock reality" that most of our young people try to exploit in relating with their parents, friends, and peers everyday. For whatever reason, they avoid exposing their real inner-identities by creating a makeshift mode of communication in an attempt to become a part of the cultural fad of novelty seekers and social movers and shakers. In essence, they want to be like that fake cockroach on the TV screen that seemed so ingrained in the daily lives of the rest of the world in an almost intangible way; and yet, like the creepy bug, they cannot really be touched, harmed, or exterminated. This seems to be the *coupe de theatre* of most of the trite expressions and modern cliches they are using these days. While no list could ever be exhaustive or as contemporary as it need be, here are some that have been heard recently, alongside their accompanying translations. To Wit: the new American lexicon.

| | |
|---|---|
| *I was really stoked!* | I was very excited. |
| *Straight up!* | Definitely! |
| *This place is a real dive!* | This is an unseemly location. |
| *Get legs!* | Move more quickly. |
| *This band is hip!* | This band plays well. |
| *Whassup?* | What is going on? |
| *Let's bop around.* | Let's take a casual drive. |
| *Float me some cheese.* | Loan me some money. |
| *This is a drag.* | This is no fun. |
| *Nerve city* | A tense moment |
| *That's a big 10-4* | I agree. |
| *Hanging-out* | Loitering |
| *Shoot the bull.* | Have a casual conversation. |
| *Get my ears lowered.* | Get a haircut. |
| *Gag me with a spoon!* | Surprise me. |
| *He's got issues.* | He has personal problems. |
| *Everything's Jake.* | Everything is alright. |
| *Up your nose!* | I dislike you. |
| *Inna' your face!* | Verbally assault you. |
| *Go postal!* | Become outraged. |
| *Get Borked.* | Get lost. |
| *Chill, dude!* | Calm down, sir! |
| *Flip-out.* | Throw a tantrum. |
| *He's takin' on water!* | He is confused or deluded. |

| | |
|---|---|
| *Duh?* | That is rather obvious! |
| *Smack'em and jack'em.* | To be arrested by the police. |
| *Gives me the creeps.* | Makes me feel uncomfortable. |
| *You da' man!* | You are an important person. |
| *Homeys* | Friends |
| *That's butter!* | That is nice! |
| *Get crunked up.* | Get intoxicated. |
| *Slammin' tight!* | It is a good thing. |
| *The illest threads!* | Very stylish clothes. |
| *Happen'n!* | In vogue. |
| *There you go!* | Thank you! |
| *Bogus!* | Fake or falsified. |
| *Pushing the envelope.* | At the extreme. |
| *Been there, done that!* | I have already experienced it. |
| *Go figure!* | Ponder the evidence. |
| *Connect the dots!* | Decide for yourself. |
| *Yadda, Yadda, Yadda.* | I know, I understand. |
| *Deal with it.* | Accept it. |
| *Don't even go there!* | Do not broach the subject. |
| *24/7* | All day, every day. |
| *Same difference.* | You are correct. |
| *That dog'll hunt!* | This will definitely work. |

There have been various ways to record the unrecognized terms and expressions of the English language, including the unabridged print of the CNN Book of Slang and other such publications. One of many favorites was one reported on by Buford Green in the Springfield Journal-Register which was written by an English professor at MacMurray College in Jacksonville, Illinois by the name of Allan Metcalf, PhD. The studious doctor released another new book in November 1997 entitled *America in So Many Words: Words that have Shaped America* (Houghton Mifflin, Inc.). Dr. Metcalf began teaching at MacMurray College in the early 1970s as an instructor of English literature and journalism, and later became the executive secretary for the American Dialect Society in 1981. Another lexicographer, David Barnhart, assisted Dr. Metcalf in writing *America in So Many Words* to more formally explore when and how certain terms were included in the customary daily speech of the American public. Believe it or not, many words that we assume to be commonplace today were actually regarded as being slang when they were first introduced into our Western style of speaking and writing. The research of Dr. Metcalf's extraordinary book extends back some 500 years, according to Barnhart and him. They make the claim that it was on July 24, 1497 when Captain John Cabot and his 18-member crew stepped off the ship *Matthew* onto the east coast of Canada and spoke the first English syllables to be heard on the North American side of the Atlantic Ocean. While Dr. Metcalf concedes that some of his citations might be subject to further scrutiny, discussion, and interpretation, some of his noteworthy entries are older than most of us really know. Examples of certain western-oriented words that he lists and the years they were favored are nouns like: canoe 1555, Indian 1602, turkey 1607, corn 1608, Manhattan 1614, and pumpkin pie in 1654. Other articles of food include: chowder 1751, hamburger 1884, and hot dog in 1895. Political terms have been equally as interesting, most of them conjured and associated with rather negative connotations: logrolling 1792, gerrymander 1812, filibuster 1852, pork barrel 1909, and Watergate in 1972. Nowadays, anything bearing the slightest implication of impropriety around the Washington DC area is known as something-*gate*. We can thank the Richard M. Nixon administration for this accusatory curse upon our native language. As for the derivation of other commonly used words, even those that our adolescents falsely believe they invented, Dr. Metcalf cites examples like: bogus 1797, OK 1839, nifty 1866, dude 1877, cool 1949, duh! 1963, couch potato 1976, yuppie 1984, PC 1990, Not! 1992, go postal 1994, and soccer mom in 1996. As surprising at it might seem, these and other words were introduced into our daily speech much earlier than we may have otherwise thought, even though they did not appear in most printed dictionaries in their particular period. Examples are terms like: mileage 1753, cowboy 1779, airline 1813, lipstick 1880, commuter 1865, skyscraper 1883, credit card 1888, yellow journalism 1898, media 1921, supermarket 1933, teenager 1938, babysit 1947, hotline 1955, sound bite 1973, and stealth in 1979; the latter word being thrust into more prominence in the American vernacular when it was used to describe the U.S. military's strange new B2 flying bomber that is purported to be undetectable by enemy radar.

There seems to be a strange set of circumstances that exists as an almost duplicitous reflection of our own personalities when we perceive our enemies who are reluctant to act in accordance with our wishes as being stubbornly obstinate, but the same conduct coming from those we admire as an air of careful discernment. There is a great deal to be said about our discriminatory thinking; that we somehow see the younger generation as not having yet earned their stripes well enough to be heard amidst a crowd of learned thinkers. Our respect for them should be greater than this; and our lack of it has caused them to feel outright rejected. Perhaps it is the older generation that is paranoid—afraid that we will never be intelligent enough to compete with the panoramic genius of our children's insights. After all, youthfulness is not necessarily a sign of ignorance; and old-age is not always a presumption of wisdom. The essence of their speech is often derived from an evocative system of personal attributes they rarely allow us to see. Their diatribes of verbosity are internal and deceptive disguises to distract us from their unaddressed miscalculations, uncultivated eagerness, mental confusion, collective rebellion, and an inherent desire to be even greater participants in the evolution of human life. We have no reason to fear them just because they are different or to assume that their purposes are to construct an invisible scaffold around our time-honored traditions and sacred tenets upon which they will someday ascend to the summit of modern civility and dismantle it one piece at a time. They often appear to us as being just a pugnacious group of mischief seekers whose agenda is to eliminate most common logic and organized religion; but their internal works are usually no greater than an unplanned, day-to-day interaction with the brash realities of human existence as they fly by the seat of their pants in an effort to come to plausible grips with the Truth. Most of the arrows they aim at the forehead of our timely traditions and established morality have suction-cups on their tips rather than flaming flints and razored edges. Our own reticence is often mirrored by what we see our children do; so we should never be that surprised by the unorthodox ways they try to get their more subversive messages across. Whether we know it or not, the young people of America are quite direct and intense in explaining the grandeur of our lives more clearly than us because adults have already settled-in to their ritualistic themes of living-out their days as a function of thoughtless habits. Our children possess a broader sense of awe, power, inspiration, and a higher veneration for the value of being free. This is the seed in them that we must always cultivate to allow their mark on Creation to be one of individual distinction in the likeness of no other age! It is not to say that they should ever stray from the Christian principles and spiritual values that will lead a nation toward the greater blessings from God, but that they can turn to their own children someday in the next twenty years and instill in them that same thirst for knowledge, purpose, freedom, and inspiration that we are impressing upon them now through the Paschal Resurrection of the Sacrificed Christ. It is in this prophetic goodness that the entire continuum of humanity must eventually succeed.

When we approach our sixteen-year-old son to ask if he recites his prayers everyday, are we too surprised if he looks back at us as he turns to walk away and says, *Gees Louise, what planet are you from?* We might be amazed to know how many of our adolescent children would lend a better ear if we communicated with them in a manner that is not condescending to the tone or marked with a certain sense of verbal disdain. Our young people wish to love us; they want to learn about the makings of our success, to be asked by their schoolteachers how they are really feeling inside, rather than wasting their time studying something so freakish as an Einstein shift. We cast their attention span into orbit with abstract lessons about spheres and astronomy while they are really looking for any way they can discover to alleviate the heaviness of their depression and the aching in their hearts. Am I again indicting the fosters of our children for the way their offspring appear to be so resentful of their parental advice? Well, it is not beyond reason to believe that we share a great deal of the blame for their new fads and fetishes by which they conceal themselves from the proverbial sound of the disciplinary whip they hear cracking at their feet almost everyday. *Get up by six o'clock. Comb your hair! Clean your room! Take out the garbage! Walk your little sister to the school bus. Bring in the mail. Put your dirty sweatshirts in the laundry!* None of these nonessential requests seems too unreasonable; and our dependent children should be expected to perform them without being prompted by their parents, siblings, and guardians. The point is, however, that their minds are trapped inside an invasive vacuum called unbridled curiosity! They sometimes see living within a nuclear family as being a sentence of social imprisonment because mothers and fathers rarely spare their disciplinary rods, female siblings are constantly hogging the mirror in the upstairs bathroom when their brothers need to get in, their younger counterparts are always nosing through their "stuff," and all the grandparents seem to be interested in doing is pinching them on the cheek, ruing what little in wages they earned 50 years ago, and remarking about how much the grandchildren have grown in the last few months. But, what is happening in the minds of our frustrated teenagers? *When will I get my drivers license; which girl will I take to the prom; where is this weekend's beer bash; will Dad advance me twenty-bucks on my allowance; and how much longer can I put-off writing that stinking English paper?* As I have indicated before, they are not posturing some organized coup against the values of family life, they are simply trying to find their niche in the expanse of our shared mortality and usually questioning the motivations of anyone in their midst who wishes to amend the status quo. While we compare their conduct in gradations like breezes, gales, storms, and hurricanes; they seem not to care whether there is any consistency in their emotions or outward behavior. That is why they can take a swipe at their best-friend's reputation at the lunch table at noon, and chuckle heartily thereafter about some off-color joke while dressing in the locker room for an intramural basketball game. It all comes down to the dimensions of communication; whether we guard our feelings as though they are as fragile as icicles on an outdoor Christmas tree, or if we are resilient in trusting that the exhortations and opinions of others cannot really affect any honest assessment we might make of ourselves.

Concepts of reality are sometimes defined quite differently by our offspring because they do not yet own the benefit of the perspective of the years in making their own decisions. This does not make them incapable of knowing right from wrong or strip them of the capacity to choose wisely in matters of personal safety, cleanliness, morality, and spiritualism. The face-value of their youthfulness might infer that most of them have yet to suffer the true consequences of any egregious error. While this will surely pass in time, as it has for us; the process of growing toward maturity is the parenthetic conduct we are seeing in them now. Some choose to call it a counter-cultural phenomenon of irrepressible bliss; others see it as an arrogant assault against the dignity of man; while still more are wondering when the bottom is going to fall from under them and finally cast them into Hell. However, we must set-out to rescue them all! It requires the fuller comprehension which comes from the clerical nature of our hopes; to stoop to reach the suffering who are disillusioned about the meaning of human life; to lift the physically and emotionally abused back to their feet once again; and to make it crystal clear that our children represent the future success of every form of social etiquette in the world. Communication! The imparting of knowledge, the transmission of mutual understanding, the interchange of thoughts conducive to self-expression, the revelation of the secrets of the heart, the extermination of the myths surrounding our darkest fears, and the exposing of the intimate emotions that are haunting the insecure sides of people unto themselves. Insofar as it is humanly possible, we must not let our little children languish any longer beneath the burdens of their transgressions or their feelings of remorse, uselessness, or the wrong impression that we do not care what they have to say. The whole tirade of expletives they often use in public is not the real problem we are facing now, but is a symptom of the adversity they hold against established hierarchies and such elitist snobs as people who operate certain fast-food restaurants and chain stores, the ones who believe that the labors of our teenage children are not worth any more than the minimum wage the federal government requires them to pay. Even in this, our merchants and wealthy retirees are saying that our young adults should consider enlisting in the armed forces to learn a little respect for the nation that has given them so much lateral freedom and the capacity to achieve success on their own. Excuse me? It may be true that former U.S. President George H. W. Bush declared that the Viet Nam era had ended by the date of his inauguration on January 20, 1989; but the haunting dirges of its 58,000+ dead soldiers, many of whom were conscripted, are still echoing rather loudly in the opening days of our new millennium, the ones they sang in their personnel carriers on their way to the front lines in Southeast Asia. *What are we fighting for? I don't know; and I don't give a damn!*

*Our next stop is Viet Nam! So, it's one, two, three—Open-up the Pearly Gates; oh, yea!—there ain't no time to wonder why! Whoopie! We're all gonna die!* Instead of being honored as the heroes they truly are after having given their mortal lives for a grotesque political bloodbath, our federal government has had to be prodded like neutered bulls by veteran's organizations everywhere to finally recognize them as being dedicated martyrs for our American democracy. And, yet, we wonder why the surviving offspring of these heroic soldiers and the rest of our children are having so much difficulty identifying with the mainstream world. We question why they have unilaterally invented an entirely different dialect for speaking their minds when all they ever hear from our nation's Capitol is an incessant drumbeat of war-talk and breathy saber-rattling; threatening the categorical annihilation of a whole segment of young people from our national census at the hands of our enemies who regularly take their own lives by blowing themselves up and anybody else in their immediate vicinity in the name of justifiable terrorism. Do we still wonder why our children do not communicate so well with us anymore?

The futuristic ideals of our computer techies and Star Trek groupies who are taking the constant pulse of Generation X seem not too directed toward the spiritual health of the everyday world. Despite all their logical thinking about globular reasoning and complex impulses, they are no closer to discovering the basis behind human Love than their more casual peers who spend their spare time spray-painting fatso images of their prep-school teachers on the sides of their Blue Bird buses in the middle of the night. It is in complying with one set of standards that we will finally discover what it means to be free—not in the challenges of the world's highest peaks; not in the Gravity Games that follow the NASCAR Winston Cup race on NBC-TV nearly every Sunday afternoon; and definitely light-years away from the psychosexual dysfunction that has trained millions of dead consciences upon America's peep shows wherein such promiscuous activities seem to be almost free for the taking. When we finally look upon the Holy Sacrifice of the Mass with a collective allegiance to Christ Jesus in our hearts and turn outwardly with compassion to the suffering in our midst, we will truly understand what interacting with God is all about. When our young people begin to envision the Crown of Thorns impaled upon Our Savior's head and the nail-scarred palms of His hands, and thereafter exclaim with a genuine sincerity in their souls, *Awesome, Dude!,* we will know that Creation-entire has trekked into a higher relationship with the Kingdom of the Angels and Saints. Everything that is trying to distract them from the Truth of Divine Absolution will fade-to-black once they are fully committed to His Blood on the Cross in good faith. It is true that we can take them to the water's edge, but we cannot yet make them drink. Our admonishments ring rather hollow in the face of such things as the organized crime of our labor unions, the financial corruption of corporate executives, and men in tasseled velvet hats with swords across their facades who demand to be called such things as benevolent high priests, exalted rulers, and grand potentates in phoney organizations as the Shriners and other orders of Free Masonry which stand in crass contradiction to the Holy Gospel of the Son of God. Our children's social conscience has finally been ruptured by the arrogant misgivings of adults; and their uncivilized conduct is another casualty that is not really of their own making. What would we have them say? None of them has ever bribed a jury or bought-off a witness with laundered money to be acquitted of a white-collar crime. Is it possible that the morality of the entire western hemisphere has gone bust at the hands of affluent Americans; and are we using our children as unwary scapegoats to hide our own culpability? By all means, let their nonsensical bosh proceed!

# Chapter VII
## *Youthful Indiscretions*
## *What Will They Think of Next?*

While many of our little children are wandering blindly, helplessly, aimlessly, and seemingly adrift, their lives represent much more than just God's time-honored purpose of the multiplication of the human species. They own a significance that is almost greater than life itself; reserving their future for the eruptive and molten restlessness of the ages to come. And, yet, they are also our peace-bond for tomorrow, the progression of modern history, catalysts for enhancing our collective social dignity, and the doers and dreamers of advancements in science, technology, and medicine that are so profound and great in magnitude that we can scarcely imagine them now. Let all of Creation perceive our younger generation in these same romantic terms, and they shall live harmoniously with their predecessors once again!—yesterday, today, tomorrow—all united in that unique purpose that is known to every new universe as the inexplicable grandeur of human exploration. Whatever affections, joy, suffering, gladness, revelation, and sacred mysteries that are hereafter revealed to the world as we continue to live-out our days, we must accept them as the Will of the Almighty Father. Should our offspring subsequently be inclined to depose us in search of any evidence of our having been the benefactors of their future success, we can boast in gleeful confidence that we have given them all in our faith in Jesus Christ through the Holy Spirit who has deigned to reveal it to them. When we ponder the thought of "...what will they think of next?" we might infer that some of their decisions might have been counter-productive, lacking in proper form, and even the cause of downright malevolent deeds and accidental evil works. What do we stand to lose by elevating our children for no other reason than for them to know that they have been elevated? Would they not be taken by surprise to see that we honor and respect them by the singular virtue that they are who they are? If they never said another consoling word or lifted a pinky finger to toss a branch from the pathway of a beggar crawling on his belly to his grave, should we not believe that they are just as inherently blessed to be alive as anyone else within the destined Providence of God's immortal plan? If we pleaded for their eyes to fall upon the Holy Scriptures for the atonement of their sins and expected Jesus to take them at the utterance of our prayers, would He not conquer their brazen indifference against the destiny of the human soul in the same way He did His Original Twelve? Indeed, when Saint Paul was still known as sinful Saul, did he not persecute the very Church of Christ for whom He later gave his entire life and being? He wrote untold reams of testimonies, persuasive monographs, and spiritual pastorals for the purpose of assuring humanity long-passed his age that the New Covenant of the Messiah is true.  Speaking about our fulfillment through Jesus Christ and our unity as His Mystical Body, Saint Paul wrote to the Ephesians,

> *In Him, we have Redemption by His Blood, the forgiveness of transgressions, in accord with the riches of His Grace that He lavished upon us.  In all Wisdom and insight, He has made known to us the Mystery of His Will in accord with His favor that He set forth in Him as a plan for the fullness of times; to sum up all things in Christ, in Heaven, and on Earth.  In Him, we were also chosen, destined in accord with the purpose of the One who accomplishes all things according to the intention of His Will, so that we might exist for the praise of His Glory, we who first hoped in Christ.  In Him, you also who have heard the Word of Truth, the Gospel of your Salvation, and have believed in Him, were sealed with the promised Holy Spirit, which is the first installment of our inheritance toward Redemption as God's possession, to the praise of His Glory....May the eyes of your hearts be enlightened, that you may know what is the hope that belongs to His call, what are the riches of Glory in His inheritance among the holy ones, and what is the surpassing greatness of His power for us who believe, in accord with the exercise of His great might, which He worked in Christ, raising Him from the dead and seating Him at His right hand in the Heavens; far above every principality, authority, power, and dominion, and every name that is named not only in this age, but also in the one to come.*
>
> (Eph. 1:7-14, 18-21).

Hence, this same Jesus Christ is the essence of our Divine nature; our predestined formation, freedom, conscience, evolution, and meticulous counsel. What brighter dawn could our young people ever anticipate than the morning Resurrection of their very souls past the error of the ways of all humanity—youngster, adolescent, teenager, adult, the middle-aged, and the elderly—all carefully and simultaneously recaptured and laid back into the Womb of God's Justice as it was in the beginning, and ever shall be, world without end?  The endless vestiges of our elegant recessionals, harkening toward the homeland of Eternal Truth by which the Divine Nature of God has always been illuminated, explicated, sustained, dignified, evangelized, ordained, and blessed; we are led not only by Him, but through the pious faith of one another to put-away the false distinctions that make us enemies so all peoples from every age can live as one Mystical Body in Christ Jesus, for the God who pines to regain us in the Paradisial Light of Heaven.  From now on, when we ponder what our children might think of next, we should anticipate that it will be another way to make us *all* holy and acceptable in the presence of the God of all life.  In this is the never-ending expansion of the fullness of His peace and

Grace, and the continuing perpetuation of all supernatural revelation. And, it is in the unconstrained power of God that our Love is never diminished and our hearts stand protected against any dismemberment because it is He who seeks us as one people again; He who has always sought us from the start, even before any of us ever knew we were alive or that we might once dream of coming to life; and even prior to our realizing that there has always been a place prepared for us in the dawning hours of Eternity; put there, fashioned, and positioned therewith and alongside the Holy of Holies with a conclusive surety that our mortal souls would, beyond any doubt, make it there someday soon.

So, in honor of Saint Paul, let our younger generation know that we cannot foretell what they might think of next, but that we *can* become the amaranth, the undying flower of trustworthy allegiance to the restoration of their piety in Christ Jesus. Why? Because He is the sublime Face of our Creator's Creation: established both permanently and miraculously in the realms of the Holy Paraclete and in all the pious little spirits of everyone living on the Earth who are humble enough to respond to His beck and call for submissive servitude in the image of Himself. Jesus Christ is the beauty of the Easter Lily and the perpetual crimson velvet love-lies-bleeding in one Paschal Garden; the immortal blossom of Eternal rest in whose bountiful presence the world will lastly be put to bed. This is what our adolescent children and the youth of all the nations need to know, and is what we must implore them with the power of Christ in our hearts to think of next! How? Our first priority at the present time is to defuse the ticking time-bomb which has evolved from their lack of spiritual direction—to eradicate their fears of an uncertain future, to seek-out and conquer the maculate enemies of their preeminent virginity, and to eliminate every source of distraction that is preventing their focus upon human Salvation in the Blood of Jesus Christ from being both clear and precise. They may never be completely blameless in the material noncompliance we see and hear them do, but the most grave consequences of their future really belong to us. What they will eventually know and understand, how they will approach the perils of the upcoming ages; be it with courage or cowardice, are ultimately defined by how well we prepare them in advance. Sooner or later, we will be forced to come to grips with the fact that our smiles, handshakes, pats on the back, and false promises are all insufficient in satisfying their curiosity of who they are and why they were born. As I have indicated earlier, the heart of a five-year-old child can be touched in as many soul-searching ways as someone ten times his age. Before he became known as someone else, the popular-music singer and lyricist Cat Stevens recorded a hit ballad entitled *Oh, Very Young*. While many of his releases were visionary oracles about the prospects of growing old, he was a man of only twenty-five years in 1973 when he penned these words, *Oh, very young, what will you leave us this time? You're only dancing on this Earth for a short while. And, though your dreams may toss and turn you now, they will vanish away like your daddy's best jeans, denim blue, fading up to the sky. And, though you want him to last forever, you know he never will; and the patches make the goodbye harder still. Oh, very young, what will you leave us this time? There'll never be a better chance to change your mind. And, if you want this world to see a better day, will you carry the words of love with you? Will you ride the great White Bird into Heaven? And, though you want to last forever, you know you never will. And, the goodbye makes the journey harder still.* While these lyrics have an aura of finality about them, they give us great hope coming from a man whose Earthly tenure at the time was but a quarter-century long; requiting, imploring, and admonishing the peers of his age about the uncertainty of the future, the finitude of our fathers' years, and our transformation from this life into the next.

There are too many dimensions, massive numbers of unanswered questions, an overwhelming deposit of unresolved enigmas, and an entire gamut of reasons why we should stress the most spiritually renowned issues among us and file-away the rest as being less important for now. Just like us, our children will grow old someday and ask, *where have all the people gone with whom I used to intone our most favorite musical renditions and subscribe to the innocence of daily human life?* And, then, they will turn to God not knowing otherwise where to procure the answer and beseech Him to tear-open the Heavens and come down because no ear has ever heard and no eye ever seen any God but Him doing such deeds for those who wait for Him! Would that He might meet us doing what is right, that we were fully mindful of Him in our ways! (Isaiah 64:3-4). Here, we recognize the full anticipation, poignance, relevance, and the dignified purpose of the existence of our children of the future—hope in the knowledge that the best of all possible worlds is yet to come; and this is also what they will think of next! Some of them will die much too precipitously, while others' health will slowly fade-away; but this is no reason for them to stop thinking about the Kingdom that lies beyond. Our revealed religion and our present hours were never meant to cease upon our wakes, but to transcend them in far-greater measure than we have the faculties to realize. Life is changed, but not ended when we die; and so death is never the point—but that we might overcome dying to the extent that we do not care anymore when it shall arrive at last. For all of our adolescents and teens who believe themselves to be immortal and lead lives of recklessness as a result, let them be warned that there is nary a smidgeon of truth in the proposition that the malignance of human mortality will not suck them into its viscid tentacles despite their obvious youthfulness; and that it will grant them no passage to escape their graves and retract their heedless indiscretions! The Grim Reaper shall own them permanently if we refuse to commend them to Christ before; and only God can know when we have done enough to woo His blessed affirmations and preclude our commiserating posthumous exhortations and eulogies yet to be divulged! What we do now, however, to prepare both our progeny and ourselves for such an ominous instigation seems to be all in everything that ever matters to His Son. He knows that the rite of passage of any age of mortal hosts need not be a cataclysmic one, but rather a fruitful declaration from the Halls of Paradise that we have been regained, that the Child of Mary has fulfilled His promise from the Cross. Too many of our youngsters are dying needlessly from drug overdoses, pratfalls and intentional plunges from penthouses of sky-scraping buildings in headlong leaps, automobile accidents with cars bouncing through midair like giant rubber balls, and the gruesome dogbane of homicide spiraling out of control.

While none among us is ever prepared for the end of human life, our potential must lean in that direction like a shining horizon of anticipation arching across our souls to the origin of Love, toward God Almighty, and in the vicinity of wilful absolution. Then, when our children die too quickly and needlessly in such catastrophic events, at least they will awaken on the other side and know that they have made it back to the forest greens where the essence of their souls began. *This is what we shall all think of next!* No matter who we are, sometimes our inner-spirits feel as decrepit and rickety as a thousand-year-old toothpick-fence in the vortex of a hurricane, and we stumble around trying to regain our bearings when Jesus Christ calls us by the heart, asking us to sit down with Him and take it easy for awhile. To all the world!—once this occurs, He will own us forever and eternally! Perhaps now, we can make our reassessment of the Earth somewhat more delicate to the tone and our acknowledgment of the necessity of faith more appealing before the omnipotence of Our Father Who Art in Heaven who dispenses all mortal life and deals death equally to each and everyone! And, maybe our parables and metaphors will bear new meaning about the arrival of the Truth which has come to us in the Baby Child on Christmas, birthed from the Womb of Mary, the Beloved Spouse of both Saint Joseph and the prophetic Holy Spirit! Would She not ask us to imagine what our world would be like if the clouds above were made of sulfide lead, rather than the puffy likeness of the woolen fleece that was shorn from the Lamb of God who Lent them to the universe to hover in our midst? Would they not sweat bullets to execute us for our arrogance instead of little raindrops to keep our tongues from being so parched as we engage the Orders of the Angels in singing His praises both now and forevermore? What do we do instead? We babble with ambidextrous ignorance that we know our right hand from our left in belching-forth our flippant wryness and rampant deceit which runs completely contrary to the teachings of Her Son. Indeed, would such leaden boulders be as courteous as the dew-filled snow banks in the skyline tier in allowing humankind to parlay our hopes into dreams-come-true at the mere utterance of *I concur with you!* from our Triune God who resides far and above them in the celestial heights?

We may never know in this life, but suffice it to say that our hopes for Redemption are not made of such an impermeable heavy metal; and this is why our recitations should always be of greater Light than the solar spires which cast such beautiful rays upon the ground to camouflage the air we breathe throughout the day. We are to believe with an almost subservient disposition that every imagining we hold so dear having anything to do with Love will eventually come to be. It is somewhat difficult for us to convince our children that the unconfessed transgressions they commit under the cover of darkness will be laid-bare by Jesus Christ in the blinding brightness of Judgement Day when we allow an unbelievable 37,000 homeless people to sleep in gutters and beneath underpasses in New York City every night, and another 600+ to be murdered either in cold-blooded premeditation or in the flames of envy and outrage in places like Chicago, Illinois during any given year—all in the broody exposition of the broad daylight hours. It is equally beyond credibility that local newspaper publishers conduct holiday fund-raising drives to assist the poor during the Christmas season when their posh editorial boards endorse candidates for public office at every election cycle whose last act on Earth *might* be to provide health-care coverage and medical benefits to the 60 million Americans who cannot afford it now. Why do they do it anyway? Because some publications believe that huge pharmaceutical companies and Health Maintenance Organizations ought to be able to reap as unlimited profits as the free-market will allow. It may surprise humanity to discover someday that all the impoverished offspring of God's Creation already recognize such profiteers as being enemies of human Love; and that the self-proclaimed purpose of the wealthiest people in the world is to concoct new ways to increase the values of their estates. Is it not true that little children suffering in cold orphanages and homeless babies huddled in the back-seats of their parents' automobiles are somehow looking through their minds' eyes at the affluent executives of such solvent corporations with the conscience of God in their gaze and asking Him beneath their soft breath, *...what will they think of next?* What about the manager/owner of the local Subway sandwich shop who is seen driving his $40,000 Lincoln Navigator SUV down the street on his way to the corner bank that, itself, has passed ownership four times in the past five years because new corporate conglomerates keep purchasing its assets on behalf of another set of stock-market shareholders? Indeed, what *will* they think of next? Have we adults not become the world's new gold-diggers and opportunists upon whom our younger children are looking these days and wondering whether we have ever really abandoned or relinquished our own youthful indiscretions? Perhaps America should redefine the meaning of personal irresponsibility to include anyone that is aged nine to 99 who is lacking the Christian insight to know that the rest of the world is suffering; that those who hold the greatest compilation of wealth are not only selfishly juvenile in their conduct, but blatantly delinquent as well.

It is an almost unimaginable prospect for us to know that about 95% of the American people do not see reality this way; but that they instead blame their juniors for everything that has gone wrong in their lives. This is simply more of the same arrogance from people who are thirty, forty, and fifty-something who believe that their children should worship the very ground upon which they walk. When we adults start treating the legacy of The Son of God with the same charitable respect that we demand from our own adolescents, He will probably work a miracle and finally give us what we want. Our Almighty Father lives as an independent Sovereign, meaning that our praises or the lack of them have no bearing upon how glorious He really is. He is our Divine Creator, and we are freed from the imprisonment of sin in Him and gain our liberty above all mortality; but we cannot boast too soon because no man can yield his own independence who is lacking in God's Grace. The record of history has proved this to be true, as we have failed before; and if we continue to ignore His dominion over all the world, we shall surely fail again. Many of us are still living-out the misery of our earlier misgivings; and we will continue to fall through endless time if we further decline His invitation to immerse our souls in His life-giving Blood. All the guile and intuition in Creation cannot prepare us for the missive warning from Jesus Christ that He is about to pronounce the mortal ages closed, whether we are ready to greet Him or not. There is no doubt that we assume that our souls are prepared in advance like sleek new stainless steel ovens that have not yet taken the opportunity to devour the leaven of the afterlife. I'm almost afraid to admit it, however, that Jesus sometimes sees us more like a parade of rusty jalopies being towed-away for recycling into something He is more likely to recognize. What will we tell Him once we see His Heavenly Face? If He asks what could possibly have taken our little children from sitting inside their high-chairs with their thumbs in their mouths to being splayed as young adults across psychedelic rugs behind doorways adorned with string-beads, passing one-hitters of fresh marijuana around, what will we say in response? There is probably enough blame to share between all of us: the parents who decided that the Wednesday night Bridge game was as important as teaching their children the virtues of right versus wrong in the family room at home; the brother who chose a baseball game over helping his sister with her homework; the tutor who canceled class with his student because he did not want to miss his second wife's Bingo party; or the mentor who became intoxicated after his son's wedding and was killed at a railroad crossing on his way back home in the burbs. What a shame it has been, too, for our youngsters whose parents have made criminal mistakes and are serving hard time behind bars, or their court-appointed guardians who have suddenly become among the chronically unemployed. Someone does not have to be a minor child to make such unfortunate decisions—big ones that can alter the fate of an entire family or the welfare of the poorest of the poor in any given state. It cannot really be true that our youthful indiscretions ever escape us in America these days because there are still too many circuit clerks, probation officers, and police departments who maintain our profiles in their permanent records and are more than willing to remind the rest of the world about them anytime they get the chance. If ever we have reason to come into contact with them again, regardless of whether it is initiated by us, all they have to do is look into their lap-top computer data base to see if our name and birth date are there, or if they have ever dealt with us before.

    This must never be the way we conduct our private lives with our friends, next-door neighbors, or even the strangers who live down the block. Paranoiac people have to stop logging-on to the State's sex-offender Web site every time a new renter moves into a vacant house around the corner to see if they should issue an unofficial all-points bulletin about him. Such overreaction is geared more toward sensational vengeance on a societal scale than about the personal safety of their children. Whatever happened to the neighborhood welcome wagon we used to pull-up to their porches to try our hand at good will in initiating new relationships, or the May baskets we used to leave on their front steps, ring the chimes, and be gone by the time they answered the door? For once in my life, I feel sorry for America not because our enemies are anywhere close to taking us over, but because we are slowly defeating ourselves by the fear which has displaced our trust. We take disingenuous steps in controlling the lives of the weak, turning our backs on the personally afflicted, pretending that in a country as poised in riches as ours that everyone should be capable of fending for themselves. It is time we made a critical statement about the plundering of lives that has become our new national pastime! What could rally the rejuvenation of a democracy better than an old-fashioned resurrection of the moral civility that gave us such things as baby-buggies with rubber bumpers, holiday greeting cards, florists who deliver door-to-door, vacuum cleaners that roll on wheels, beds that unfold out of the closet, the electric steam iron, silk petticoats, polka-dot shirts and bow-ties, and wing-tip shoes? What about the innocence of the flashing neon age when we used to steer our coupes, sedans, and convertibles into the local drive-in restaurant and be served by waitresses sporting pony tails and wearing roller-skates? If we think about the decades after World War II: the rumble-seat automobiles of the early 1940s, the era of Rock & Roll and Wolfman Jack in the '50s and '60s, and the black-light posters, discotheques, and platform shoes of the mid- 1970s, haven't we left a huge portion of our creative culture behind in our struggle to become the only ones left standing at the conclusion of any game of *Kill or Die* that we see in almost every storefront today? This is proof enough that modern America has never really matured! We are less discreet in the 21$^{st}$ century than we have ever been before!—what with the raw nudity in the streets instead of behind closed doors, the drive-by random shootings of people the perpetrators do not even know, parents getting into fisticuffs at their children's sporting events, girls who are barely entering puberty who dress-up like high-fashion models in an attempt to date men three times their age, and the outright frontal assault on the dignity of our traditional family values in nearly every metropolitan area in the United States. It may be true that our churches are failing to get their message of reconciliation across, but there is no law on the books that mandates anyone to ever darken their doors. Did someone say hypocrisy again? If we take our message of Christianity into the suburbs and to the downtown boardwalks, we are heckled, treated like freaks and scoundrels, and greeted with doors slamming in our faces so loudly that it sounds like our U.S. Air Force B-52s carpet-bombing Viet Nam, Kosova, Afghanistan, and Iraq all over again. We may not be forever young, and may never outlive every indiscretion, but this does not mean that we cannot be bold in reveling the love of the human heart among the citizens of the world in every bluff and borough, from the tallest mountains to the deepest valleys, inside seedy taverns and ornate museums; from ostentatious braggart to social introvert, athlete to invalid, horseman to pilot, and stockyard to showroom. Wishing that our reputation will be spared in defense of Christianity is a vain thing. Imagine the day when our young sons seize the moment to evangelize for Jesus, approach their friends who have boom-boxes in their ears, and say with the courage of saints, *Yo! Dudes! We wanna tell ya' something!* This is when we will know that the Earth has changed for good, that our children have finally gotten the message about the Holy Gospel of the Resurrected Christ from centuries ago, realizing that their youthful indiscretions can be wiped clean from the face of the globe by His powerful Blood on the Cross, and that anyone—no matter who they are, the color of their skin, their place in the deposit of human history, or where they choose to live—can become new creatures and a portion of the nobler part of the family of man. This is God's hope; and like Him, it has never changed. He'll never commission a different Savior into Creation than the One He sent before. His mind is made-up and time is on His side. What is left to be revealed is whether we will ever take it to our own advantage as well.

# Section III
## *The Rite of Passage*

---

# Chapter VIII
## *Spirituality in a Tortured Adolescence*
## *Driving Out the Demons*

    I knew an acquaintance one time who was—well, I wouldn't say he was obesely fat, but he required a rather large berth when he got up to walk anywhere. Additionally, to put it gingerly, if the perfume industry had to depend on his patronage in order to survive in the marketplace, they would have gone bankrupt a long time ago. It is patently incredible that there are these kinds of people in America today with the commercial availability of things like bar-soap and open public baths. Toiletries such as Dove, Lever, Ivory, and Old Spice really do have an important place alongside the deluge of medicines that are available to the ailing nowadays. Anyway, my friend also had a genuine heart of gold. He was gentle as a lamb, willing to listen to anyone's story; generous, amicable, unassuming, and always fair. I can only imagine what life must have been like when he was younger; for all the teasing, fun-poking, and sour jokes that were aimed toward his overweight stature and the grease in his hair that, on any given day, might be sufficient to lubricate a tractor-trailer fifth wheel for a trip across the entire breadth of Texas and Louisiana. Therefore, I always wondered why he was not personally callous as an older man; and I have arrived at the conclusion that he never allowed any insecurity, jealousy, adversity, or offense to create any spiritual demons to infiltrate his bountiful disposition, either in his mental stability or outgoing personality. Within the context of another set of circumstances—if he would have brashly pushed himself on others or tried to eclipse his lack of proper grooming with the same overbearing attitude that usually accompanies people who are antisocially or psychologically scarred—his approach to daily life might have been less secure than it finally turned-out to be. I have come to remember my friend not only as a gentleman who was kind and affable, but like a parable about how we often perceive other people who seem to be "lesser" than us because of attributes that place them onto a lower rung of our socioeconomic trellis. There is too much emphasis at the present time in defining human devotion as being anything which is not beyond the parameters of the secular culture, or that which is only peculiar to our hometown standards. In other words, "...if they ain't like us, they must be our enemy." It is obvious that this can never be acceptable; but neither can the converse be true regarding our religious practices when an individual or group hails a proposition about some new dogmatic revelation by which God has allegedly presented Himself before humanity in a previously unknown doctrine of Deific visitation. The New Age philosophy that has been so damaging to established Christianity by drawing millions of people away from the Ecclesiastical Sacraments is one such deviant example. Just because they recognize the supremacy of an idolatrous god in the universe does not imply that they always direct their subscribers and followers to the Truth of Jesus Christ, who is Our Savior, Emmanuel: God, Himself, who was born of the Blessed Virgin Mary, suffered and Died on the Holy Cross, entombed in the Sepulcher, and was Resurrected by His Father on Easter Morning.

There are demons aplenty that are haunting us as we enter this new millennium; but generating a fanatical approach to theocratic spiritualism which fosters the "any god you wish to please" mentality is not going to save anyone else's soul. Only the Crucifixion of Jesus Christ on the Cross of Mt. Calvary can do that. Any religion that is not in alignment with or in obedience to the Apostolic Church of Christianity will do nothing to destroy the evil that is keeping humanity divided. Why is there war on the face of the globe? Because not everyone is putting their faith and the practice of it in the Sacred Heart of Christ. While there have been countless miraculous manifestations, inexplicable healings, supernatural apparitions, and private revelations throughout history, many of which I have discussed in detail in Section V of this book, we must remember that the proper discernment of unseen spirits is to require evidence from them to declare their compliance with and allegiance to the Blessed Trinity of Christianity—Father, Son, and Holy Spirit—from the other side of life. We don't have to be body builders, prom queens, or Harvard graduates to be a part of that beauty which comes from within because, just like the pudgy friend I spoke about earlier, the religious Truth and the pristine nature of the human spirit shines from the heart. And, more to the point, embracing the New Age philosophy solely for the sake of being metaphysical does not imply that our efforts are poised to enhance the Divine Kingdom of our Crucified Savior or to evangelize the Christian Doctrine of the absolution of mortal sinners in the Blood of Jesus Christ. Too many of our young people are torturing themselves trying to decide which "god" the New Age movement wants them to worship—their inner karma, mother earth and her forests, summits and rains, the moon and constellations, their recollection of some mysterious instinct, or the principles behind the mysterious cosmic effects of a life in some previous incarnation (whatever that means.) The whole world would be better off if New Age activists would give-up the fight against

Messianic Christendom, receive the Rite of Reconciliation, get in line with the rest of us who have happily taken the plunge into the Chalice of Our Lord's Sacrificed Blood, and stop distracting our impressionable youth from accepting their Divine Salvation in Him.   The whole idea about lateral prophets and trance-channeling may be alright for agnostics and atheists, but they are utterly useless, invalid, and illegitimate in leading their following into a deeper relationship with the Slain Redeemer of the world.   There is also too much emphasis placed upon the relevance of dreams in the transpiring evolution of our religious faith and the movement of the universe, as well.   Assuming what they might imply can sometimes place new demons in the minds of our agonizing children because they are only searching for the Truth; and it is the Gospel Truth of Christianity that we must give them.   Disagreeing with the metaphysics of other people does not infer that we are intolerant of their viewpoints, however; but it is a way to liberate them from their error before it is too late for them to learn.

    This discussion revolves around the unique potential that everybody owns to eventually become a part of the *Divine* through their acceptance and emulation of Jesus Christ.   There is a great deal to be said about each individual in this process and how we, as a united people under the Cross, preserve our personal dignity.   We must never allow our pursuit for justice-delayed to embitter our passion or the call for more patience; nor should we arrive at premature conclusions about anything as important as our Godly justification solely because we have grown too weary from thinking about the transcendent nature of the facts or why a lasting peace seems so elusive to harvest sometimes.   We employ the use of parodies, satires, spoofs, spin-offs, hoaxes, practical charades, and even summoning poltergeists to try to capture the remnants of the Truth which the evil in the world has tried to blow apart in the dividing of nations and inciting of wars between dissimilar peoples.   However, the constant drum-beat of Holy Love and the persistent ratta-tat-tat of the Truth are much too formidable to suppress or conquer for anyone whose soul will eventually live in Heaven with the Holy Trinity, the Immaculate Mother of God, and the Hosts of Angels and Saints.   Moreover, residing in a country such as the United States where our little children are constantly forced to fight against the temptations of lust, the pathologies of depression, and the competition of capitalism imposes an almost perpetual assault of heinous battery against the delicate fabric of their yet-to-be unveiled mortal souls.   This is why they clamor so loudly, and sometimes in rather obnoxious tones.   The mind-boggling ways they find to vent their anger and frustrations is almost too much for older generations to take.   Unfortunately, it is not something whose attribution is known only to them.   The middle-aged and elderly, alike, are always looking for new ways to let their inner-glory shine through. I have learned that it is one thing to get someone's thoughts published onto a printed page, but quite another to ask anybody to read them. I attended an Authors' Fair in November 2002 at the Illinois State Library in Springfield at the invitation of Secretary of State Jesse White where I met about three dozen other writers who were trying to induce the world into sharing their work. Many of them seemed not unlike our young children who wish someone would pay more attention to the priceless expressions of the call of their hearts. I remember the vast diversity which was present that day as I sat directly to the right of former U.S. Representative Paul Findley of Jacksonville at the book-signing table who had just penned a new volume, *Silent No More: Confronting America's False Images of Islam,* an elderly gentleman, Kazimir Ladny, who authored an autobiography, *It Was Worth It: The Adventures of a Polish POW in WWII,* and numerous other writers who had been invited by Secretary White to share their new poetry, personal advice, novels, and instructional manuals of all kinds. And, while their masterful works were a sight to behold, what I remember most is the child-like eagerness on their faces which reflected the fact that they had something unique to share with the rest of Creation. It almost seemed to me as though they wanted to expel the demons of their own youth, to tap one another's genius, and to alter history by getting their manuscripts on record not only for their future legacies, but to provide the generations to come a means to understand what it was like to live in the first slice of the third millennium. Is this not also the same record of distinction that our children are seeking from us now?

I know beyond any shadow of doubt that Satan tries to taunt us into surrendering our vitality in becoming one with the victorious signs of high relief that we enjoy in our self-expression, especially when our great works serve to familiarize humanity at large with the promised New Jerusalem we are ultimate seeking. Let's face it, when our great economists, physicists, philosophers, physicians, composers, musicians, painters, vocalists, actors, peacemakers, politicians, educators, meteorologists, scientists, engineers, laureates, judges, athletes, presidents, ministers, historians; and everyone else who ever claimed an avocation under the stars first aspired to place a hallmark in the corridor of human excellence, their talents and declarations came from the unblemished hope that they could all make a difference in reshaping the galaxies into a panoramic procession of the accomplishments of humankind. This is the dynamic courage and imbedded trust that kept them all going one minute to the next, for days and months on end; and ultimately to the satisfaction of their years; and it is the same glow I saw emanating from the visages of the humble authors at the State Library that day. They comprise an intermingled web of consecration to the greatness of the human spirit; to the proposition that, as nobler men than me have always said, "we are created equal under God." And, this is the dignity we must give back to our children who have been so scandalized and neglected by our lack of remembrance that we were all once in their shoes, too. To remember the premonition of our Divine Creator:

> *A strong city have we;*
> *He sets up walls and ramparts to protect us.*
> *Open up the gates to let in a nation that is just,*
> *one that keeps faith.*
> *A nation of firm purpose you keep in peace;*
> *in peace for its trust in you.*
> *Trust in the Lord forever!*
> *For the Lord is an Eternal Rock!*
> *He humbles those in high places,*
> *and the lofty city He brings down;*
> *He tumbles it to the ground,*
> *levels it with the dust.*
> *It is trampled underfoot by the needy,*
> *by the footsteps of the poor.*

Isaiah 26: 1-6

Herein, the Holy Spirit reminds the world about protection, faith, peace, and trust. Are not these a wholesale portion of the Sacred Beatitudes that were taught by Christ in reflection of the Mosaic Ten Commandments? And, did He not add Divine human Love in His own likeness as being the greatest of them all? So, when we think of marked geniuses like the poet William Shakespeare, the sculptor Michelangelo Buonarroti, the astronaut John Glenn, the great French novelist Jules Verne, devoted American servants like James Madison and Monroe, Thomas Jefferson, Abraham Lincoln, and the Roosevelts; cultural icons like Samuel Adams and John Hancock; the revered Negro educators and social activists Mary Bethune and Martin Luther King, Jr; and the entire arpeggio of Supreme Pontiffs of the Roman Catholic Church, we cannot resist believing that a world of peaceful justice lives in the aftermath of their undying love for the legacy of the rekindled human spirit. And, whether we choose to recognize it or not, they all began as novices!—gifted ones, perhaps; but each and all with no more than their willingness to conquer the fears and drive-out the demons that might have otherwise kept them from becoming true giants among the world that not even the Pacific-Californian redwood trees could ever overshadow. These were the offspring of the children of the God of their fathers who never once surrendered to the perils of poverty, disease, pestilence, anarchy, insurrections, civil wars, the environmental elements, or personal hopelessness. They became living legends because they never allowed the spirit of youth to die in them, even unto their own deaths. And, our stubbornness in refusing to adhere to their same allegiance to the God they could not see is the reason why our world is failing so miserably in everything having whatsoever to do with unbridled valor! Our search is for new ways to continue to be lazy, for avenues of ideals that have little to do with blind faith, and for anything that will allow us to procrastinate in our good works because we are waiting for someone else to pull-in the slack that, unwitting to us now, will only bind us more deeply into the bondage and slavery of the vainly coveted material world.

Are we too naive to know that our younger generations see through the facade that we have built before them, that our actions rarely agree with our intentions, and that our want of veracity is keeping us from detecting the world undergoing a great meltdown of international cooperation; even to the point that the threat of nuclear holocaust has never been any higher since the days of the Cuban Missile Crisis? The United States of America supposedly stands as the Earth's lone superpower right now, and conditions have never been worse in the history of man. Not even during the great World Wars were the nations of the globe as divided by racism, political partisanship, pandemic diseases, economic disparities, religious wars, acts of terrorism, the breakdown of the nuclear family, paranoia, intimidation, and outright Satanic seduction. We wanted to be the great city left shining on a hill; and we indeed became just that; but look at what it cost the rest of humanity for us to be able to brag that we are number one! We created more demons to haunt our little children and grandchildren in the last two decades of the 20th century than were generated by any threat of war or its collective list of casualties. How? By defying God, Himself, to the degree that we have become anything except that shining city; and nowhere close to the one He spoke about in that passage from the Book of Isaiah. If we could only close our eyes for moment and think of the world that the likes of (the late) Bobby Kennedy warned us about, we would probably crown him posthumously as one of the greatest prophets of Christianity to have ever lived. His own worst nightmares are coming-to-pass right now; and all we have to say to the God in whom we claim to believe is that such is the cost of democratic freedom. Demons? It would appear by the conduct of the contemporary world that *they* are doing the driving! Perhaps we ought to take another look at those legends I mentioned a few paragraphs ago to discover why their names are scribed in our history books and biographical anthologies.

We cannot imitate them if we continue our seemingly endless search for personal wealth. Most all of these larger-than-life contributors to the grandiose successes of the human experience were *paupers* who garnered the power of their improvisational genius from the Holy Spirit of God! Please allow me to utter it again: the origin of their creative intellect and extraordinary inclinations were given to them because they quit the world and gave their talents to the Divine Creator who gave them life. They challenged the heartstrings instead of the lifeless world. It should come as no surprise to us, therefore, that they achieved what they set-out to do when God ratified their trust in Him by commissioning His Grace upon their good works. Call it a mirrored supernatural intuition, but most of us know that everything we will ever accomplish that has anything to do with lasting prosperity must be done through the intercession of Jesus Christ because the kind of success that He implants in us is one of perpetual regeneration. The genesis of continuing the masterworks of the greatest people who have ever lived on the Earth is to humble ourselves before Him and beg for His eternal blessing. He hears our prayers; His presence is within us; and He already knows the sad history we are about to bequeath to the disheveled world we will someday leave behind.

However, we do not have to be masters of the English language to become great spiritual heroes in the United States and around the globe, or be willing to be blasted-off far into outer-space in oxygenated airships, or acquire the education and prominence of renowned architects, financiers, or honorary statesmen. Our struggle to become the true people of Light is always a work in progress; and we may already be closer to getting it right than we originally thought we were. If we pictured an old barn sitting at a distance from a superhighway upon which we are traveling that appears to be under repair, and we see that about three-quarters of it is a color of green and the rest a bright shade of red, it might be difficult for us to determine from our vantage-point which of the coats of paint is the old, and which is the new. In other words, we cannot decide whether the painters' labors are almost finished or if their work has only just begun. This is the same misconception we often have of one another, too. There is really no way we can tell how well someone else is connected to the power of the Holy Spirit unless we cease our own motion, call our souls into a peaceful poise of solemnity, and get much closer to them. Thereafter, if they try to fight us off with a brick and a broom, it would be appropriate to conclude that their Christian conversion is barely underway. We should admire the tenacity of our spiritual advisors, preachers, and evangelists who seem not to mind how poorly they are treated while working in God's vineyards to seek new followers for Christ. And, even though someone may not react to them right away, the seed of hope will always be planted in them.

The pastoral nature of the Mystical Body of Christ, which is the people of the Church, is an immortal meadow of free-flowing nourishment for the lacking in our hearts; ours for the taking, always in plentiful supply, and willing to wait until the cows come home and Hell freezes over before they surrender a single lost soul to the damned. We can pretty much tell when someone else is in need of anger-management counseling if he threatens to kick us in the teeth when we dare to raise an image of the Holy Cross before his eyes. Any such hesitation, reticence, opposition to, or rejection of the messengers of Jesus Christ is a sure indication that not all the demons have been driven from our ill-intentioned friend. Humble submission before God and Divine obedience to the Holy Spirit were never meant to draw honor or attention to ourselves, but to the Blessed Savior who is calling us; and this seems to be the main point that most enemies of Christianity seem to be mistaking. However, if our opposition is waiting for any sinless mortals to come speak to them about the prophecies of God, they would also be waiting for the return of the meandering kine and the air temperatures in the fires of Hades to plummet to well below zero. The Kingdom of human Salvation, itself, would be hamstrung into near paralysis if Jesus Christ waited for the first person without sin to stand-up for His Death on the Cross. He knows that we are prone to every weakness He ever warned us about; but His Father in Heaven is also aware of our power to overcome them in Him. We cannot cast a pall of eery dead silence over the conversion of the multitudes of millions who inhabit the Earth just because we somehow believe that we are unworthy of pronouncing His Name. We are all transgressors against our God who are searching for sinners in the lineage of our previous selves. What we sometimes fail to recognize is that our mission has already been perfected by the Son of Man in us; and it is His unsilenced Spirit that is actually speaking the Truth.

It is not enough, it would seem, that our benign defense of modern Christianity would appear to be as contentious and controversial as it is, but recent attacks against our religion have often been to the point of becoming disconcerting, at best. And, this is not really the issue in how we go about transmitting our faith to the rest of the world; but rather how we deal with the unsightly darkness that begins to creep-up on our souls when we see that not very many people are listening. We could imagine standing before masses of strangers wearing our humbler shoes one day, simply trying to explain as best as the Holy Spirit can evoke from us the afterlife of majesty that we shall all inherit come the end of time. And, then, we appropriately make the case that humanity does not really have to wait until then to know what true peace and goodness are if we would only take to heart the tenets of Christian Love which Jesus has spread over the minutes of the ages, past our present difficulties, into the boundless future. We struggle for words to lead our brothers and sisters into the ornate reality of comprehending our hopes and dreams so they, too, will be born again in Christ. But, when the only thing we hear from them revels the material world—what homes or automobiles they are considering purchasing, or about a new book that has absolutely no relevance to the eternal Salvation of souls, or where the latest fads and fashions can be procured—our hearts seem to drop with a thud against the earthen floor. We can somehow feel our numbness sinking like a foundering ship slipping beneath the surface of the whitecaps, slowly but surely falling downward into the fathomed depths of human despair. The greatest Saints who ever lived on the Earth left their personal diaries and manuscripts about how they were forced to confront such depression; and there is really no good solution in any of them about how to prevent it from occurring to us, too. It seems to be a natural part of being a Christian; that to become one with the Light, God shows us the darkness so as to reveal Himself with such stark contrast. When we look around the globe and see that only about one-fifth of its entire population has claimed the Holy Cross as the origin of their Salvation, it gives us pause to wonder what we are doing wrong in failing to spread the Good News about the expiation of human sinfulness in the Son of God. Our Lord would have us believe that we can do no more than He gives us the power and providence to attest, a gift without which no Christian can succeed. He seems to be telling us that the Holy Roman Catholic Church of Christianity is, indeed, His Original Apostolic Church; and that it is the suffering borne by it and within it that is making reparation for the other religions. How do I know this to be true? Because the recorded history of the first sixteen centuries A.D. proves it beyond any doubt. If only we would consider what has happened since then by Satan to fracture the delicate fibers that are binding all living saints together, we would know that such misgivings as the edicts of one Martin Luther and the Protestant Reformation comprise a giant leap away from the Sacramental Grace that God has intended for the entire human race. If there are people in Creation who feel as though they have been rejected or otherwise hard-done by the Roman Catholic Church, it is because their own arrogant lack of faith will not permit their return to the fold at the very Seat of Christianity that Jesus Christ, Himself, commissioned upon Saint Peter for the mortal world on the Day of Pentecost 2000 years ago.

The ultimate demise of evil works, therefore, requires that we never concede to the darkness that is trying to chase our own faith in God away, no matter how many factions and divisions develop before the lapse of the years is complete. No one knows the degree to which other people suffer the sadness that is now engulfing the world through ruthless secularism. Christians may live in perpetual hope for the destination of their eternal souls when they deliver them over to God in death, but this can sometimes be only sparse consolation for the gruesome task of living on the Earth day after painstaking day. Christians point to the innumerable blessings of God in paramount ways with the hope that those who do not yet believe in Him will accept Him to the joy and enamoring of all higher revelations. But, for whatever reason, many of our most intelligent men and women continue to resist. It is as though some of them are passengers in our automobile as we pass along the motorway and ask them to focus their attention on that barn I mentioned a few paragraphs ago; and they turn toward us with a look of confusion on their faces and say, *what barn?* It is at this moment that we have lost their perception about what color it might be and are forced to grapple with the prospect that our travel together will never be long enough for us to explain to them everything we really want them to know. It makes us wonder at times why God gives such great leeway for the mitigation of their transgressions and why we feel so helpless in leading them to Him for their spiritual reward. Everything that is exculpating is dispensed from Heaven through Jesus Christ; and we know it, but our tongues seem to be too heavy to speak because of the darkness which overcomes our spirits when we see other people who seem to be so blatantly blind. We accept the fact that Jesus loves them anyway, even in their ignorance, and that He will give them the benefit of the doubt at the end of time that it was us who could not communicate the facts about His reign over Creation well enough when we had the opportunity to. This, also, is one of the reasons why our darkness and depression about the ineffectiveness of our works seems to be so pronounced. All we hear from theologians these days are such things as extenuating factors like the typical effects of feelings and passions, forces of acquired habits, pathological disorders, and external pressures as being blameworthy for the lack of moral decency in the world today. And, this is probably alright by God; but the rest of us can only admit that we are not loving one another sufficiently, which appears to me to be the very core of what Christ has been saying all along. We should evangelize the necessity of growing our faith in Him for the purpose of Divine Love and allow Him to sort-out the reasons why other people are failing on His own. He knows that we are all strapped by human sinfulness, some of which is not always of our own choosing if we are coerced into aberrant conduct by others; and that we live in a world filled with deception and corruption.

The negative influences of the countless demonic forces we must battle everyday is oftentimes difficult enough for the holiest people alive, let alone those who have never professed or espoused a desire to discover who Jesus Christ really is. The world can be wicked, cruel, and evil; and many of us are not equipped to fight against it with the vision of the Angels quite yet. It is for this reason that our mutual compassion and forgiveness are so important if the coalescence of our human interdependence is ever going to succeed. We have fought against foreign enemies around the globe that have been detectible with the human eye, and have been victorious on any number of occasions. But, the question remains whether we are prepared to take-on the evil thugs and legions which continue to haunt millions of people everyday at the center of their souls. Jesus laid-out our battle plans when the Roman soldiers impaled His Holy Body to a tree on Good Friday. That Cross is the secret weapon of mass-destruction against the adversaries of a world which has become civilized through the Virtues of the Life of Christ and the resonance of the Sacred Scriptures. Understanding that our temporal environment and the unseen Kingdom of God in Heaven are not mutually exclusive helps us to understand how the Holy Spirit became an Incarnate Child in the Womb of Mary. Jesus was born on Christmas Day  because His Father deigned that the fullness of time had arrived for the remaking of the Earth into the likeness of the Garden of Eden once again; and it cannot be told any simpler than this. Indeed, if anyone riding in our car says that this is not really true, we would probably have the right to put on the brakes and tell them to get out to wait for the next bus to come-by that is on a one-way trip to the bowels of Hell. We do not need people like them tempting us to surrender our weapons against the very indifference that has made such a travesty of their own better judgement. Whether they choose to believe it or not, Christianity is not some visual masquerade that should be left to those with enhanced theatrical talents or people whose aspirations are to foster the portrayal of an artifice about something that does not really exist. Our faith in Jesus is a function of the factual Truth by which we are sustained, healed, protected, and saved. It is believing in the practical absolution of the departed human soul without having seen the evidence in advance. And, this is the face of justice that the likes of Martin Luther King, Jr. went back to the Deep South with after his speech by the reflecting pool in Washington DC on August 28, 1963; and it is the same integrity which keeps our hopes alive; and it is the absolute Truth that will lead our little children beyond the throes of the world's rampant horrors and discontent. Not all of them are misspent, misguided, maligned, ignored, or misunderstood. But, too many of them are; and we must invest more of our time in them before the seeping deposit of the mortal ages takes its last gasp and it becomes too late. They belong alongside us in every form of dignity—not to the spiritual demons, not to our plagues of hypocrisy and procrastination, and certainly not to the darkness of the netherworld. All in all, it is incumbent upon us to retrace our steps where we have failed them in the past, implore Our Divine Lord to ameliorate the suffering that is too protracted in them now, to seek in their bounty what is lacking in us, make amends to God for our egregious ignorance of their needs, and honor them as equal brethren in the briny tears that Christ Jesus has shed for all of us. Time may have its way of exacting its price upon our best intentions, our advice at the dinner table, and from the eloquent speeches of our nation's patriarchs. But, we must never allow it to steal the sacred Love that is ultimately to be shared between our children and ourselves.

# Chapter IX
## *Friendship Conversions*
## *The Factual Nature of Brotherhood*

Alright, I am not a wagering man, but I lost a bet to a friend and had to put another chapter in this manuscript that was a little lighter to the tone. And, with today's relationships the way they are, what better one to choose than the subject of friendship—for all the jesting, jousting, joking, and revelry we do with one another in America today? Let's see—according to the American Heritage Dictionary, a friend is defined as "...a person whom one knows, likes, and trusts; any close associate or acquaintance, a favored companion, a boyfriend or girlfriend, one with whom one is allied in a struggle or cause, or a comrade." And, according to Random House, it means, "...a person attached to another by feelings of affection or personal regards, a patron or supporter, a person who is on good terms with another, and one who is not hostile." The latter also advises that we take a look at the meaning of, "chum, confidant, ally, confrere, and compatriot." Perhaps our modern use of "friend" is something with far-less commitment than its literal meaning requires. Well, before we become too closely associated with other people, we usually run them through the mill of our own set of standards to see if they at least think like we do in any way that would keep them on the short-list of those we might bother to contact on a moment's notice every day. So, if anybody is thinking about sizing me up, I will offer a brief, quite varying, mostly irrelevant, and not necessarily interconnected synopsis of the dos and don'ts that appear on my laundry list of subtle priorities. *To Wit:* the television commercial that asks where we might be when our laxative kicks-in really irks me. Who in the world would board an airplane and get ready to take a seat after having just swallowed a physic? Has anyone on the battlefield ever sneezed while they were pulling the pin on a live grenade and accidently blown himself up? Let's try some more funnies on for size, like a mother allowing her 3-year-old daughter to carry a Grade A carton of chicken eggs from the check-out counter to their car in the parking lot, or walking a dachshund across a freshly plowed field, seeing President Gerald Ford falling down the steps of Air Force One, the grand poopah of the Scottish Rite Cathedral getting caught by the police in an XXX peep-show in Peoria, Elton John shoving a baby-grand piano off the stage into the audience, and a wedding groom's first wife standing awkwardly out-of-place catching the bouquet that has just been tossed by his new bride over her left shoulder. Let's not forget the man that ran for mayor in a small city in Illinois who created a new government position for economic development, resigned his office, and appointed himself to the job that paid almost twice as much as the salary for mayor; and then had his majority party on the city council select his best friend as the new mayor to complete his term as his successor at City Hall. I know it is said that every keen eye has its blind spot. Perhaps some of the following random tongue-in-cheek peeves and preferences could fill the void in mine.

I would choose cantaloupe over coconut-cream pie any day; I will not eat raisins straight from the box; and I have never bought a lava lamp. I don't know how to braid someone's hair—correct that—I don't *want* to know how to braid anyone's hair; I never got to meet John Wayne; getting a physical examination is demoralizing; I have never understood what it means to be star-struck; animal pets do not belong in the house; I don't know why veterinarians think pigs are so intelligent; people who constantly giggle confuse me; show me a guy with an obnoxious mouth, and I will show you an idiot; I would never buy a used 1956 Buick or a Guy Lombardo Christmas album; I have always liked priestly vestments better than military uniforms; I would rather win a cash jackpot than a trophy; not everyone who claims to be a victim really is one; I am afraid to go down into a coal mineshaft a mile beneath the ground; the founders of the State of Florida are Jeb and George W. Bush; I have never seen a bird fly backwards; a cold beer once in awhile never hurt anybody; I like loaves of bread that have never been sliced; most district attorneys are right-wing bigots; a strong libido is often a curse; Dick Cheney is really Peewee Herman in disguise; school buses ought to have seat belts; dead presidents should be forced to pay taxes; I wish I could start and stop my beard from growing at-will; it should be against the law for anyone's necktie to be more than four inches wide; getting a fishing license should be optional; somebody should invent a light bulb that never burns out; tickets to a major-league baseball game should cost fifty-cents apiece; I have conceded the fact that angels probably don't wear glasses; someone needs to track-down the guy who said that it is seven-years' bad luck to break a mirror, and break a mirror over his head; black socks make nice gifts (I like this one because it makes a nifty tongue twister); telephone solicitors should be required to give us their own home phone numbers before being allowed to say anything else; and free peanuts, out of the shell, should be given-away at the entrance of every public office building in town. Hey!—I'm no David Letterman; and this is no Top Ten list, but at least you get my point. Levity. We base our friendships upon it because it gets us through the terrible years of tragedy that fall between our briefer moments of personal triumph. I have often wondered whether many people seek the friendship of others because they really understand the purpose of human interaction, or if they are just too tired of speaking to themselves, or if they are extroverts who have some transcendental message to share by reaching-out to other people to make the world a better place. I have never been known to be one; but neither do I understand why some people become hermits by enclosing themselves behind the walls of their houses, rarely to be seen in open public or on the street. Perhaps they are pondering what life would be like living on another planet, far from the chiming hypocrisy of the people on Earth.

I have always been an admirer of the world's astronauts who were either brave or reckless enough to be shot like balls out of cannons into the vacuum of the upper atmosphere. I followed the American space program like clockwork when I was a child, collecting as many of the arm-patches of the various flights as I could. And, like most everyone else, the first Moon landing in July 1969 left a mark as much on me as it did the rest of the globe to know that we had become something larger than mere mortals whose feet were planted helplessly atop the ground like birds caught in invisible snares. Even though we had achieved the conquest of flying in midair through private and commercial aviation, the space program seemed so much different because we made physical contact with another cosmic sphere that has a separate gravity from our own. The inheritors of future human history should never forget the words of Neil Armstrong when he first planted his feet on the Moon's surface from the ladder of Apollo 11's lunar module, ...*that's one small step for a man, one giant leap for mankind.* And, he was brought safely back home, along with Edwin "Buzz" Aldrin and Michael Collins, to the welcome of cheering crowds as national heroes. We returned to the Moon again that year in November, in February and July 1971, and April and December 1972 with Apollo missions 12, 14, 15, 16, and 17. Of course, everyone in America remembers the ill-fated Apollo 13 flight that endangered the lives of James A. Lovell, John L. Swigert, and Fred W. Haise; and with equal poignance, the very first of the program, Apollo 1, that resulted in an unfortunate launchpad fire on January 27, 1967, killing Virgil "Gus" Grissom, Edward Higgins White, and Roger Bruce Chaffee. Indeed, not nearly the number of mass-viewers watched the other five lunar landings as did the first; and even the television programming was not interrupted like it was for Apollo 11. This is the same way we often take for granted the regular launches by NASA of the space shuttles in our modern times; with the possible exception of the often-viewed film footage of the Space Shuttle Challenger on the 25$^{th}$ mission that exploded 73 seconds after lift-off at an altitude of 46,000 feet, taking the lives of fellow astronauts Francis R. Scobee, Michael J. Smith, Judith A. Resnik, Ellison S. Onizuka, Ronald E. McNair, Gregory B. Jarvis, and the first civilian school-teacher to try to enter the darkness of outer-space, Sharon Christa McAuliffe. It is a sad commentary on America that we rarely seem to remember what we accomplish before anyone else on Earth, sauntering onward to something else as though these unprecedented feats were never really that great. The names, flight numbers, glide-paths, splashdowns, and official telemetry have gotten lost in the passage of time. This phenomenon was marked with a rather obvious hollowness when the 30th anniversary of the final mission to the Moon, Apollo 17, was observed in December 2002. As I indicated before, the world will never forget the profound words of Neil Armstrong when he hopped almost gleefully with one foot off the bottom rung of the ladder of the Apollo 11 lunar-module on July 21, 1969. But, how many of us can remember the last quote ever to be uttered by any mortal man to depart the Moon's surface before returning to the Earth? It was voiced by Eugene Cernan, *...we now leave as we once came; and God willing, we shall return with peace and hope for all mankind.* And, since that day which eventually brought the splashdown of Apollo 17 on December 19, 1972—and a total 12 men having walked on the surface of the Moon, 160 hours of pedestrian exploration over a 60 mile distance, and some 30,000 photographs later—we have yet to do two things: no one has ever returned to the Moon; and the nations of Earth are still declining to discover and establish true peace and hope for all humankind. Is it not ironic, therefore, that the first U.S. citizen to orbit the Earth was the American hero, USMC Col. John Herschel Glenn, who is now a former U.S. Senator from the State of Ohio, in a nine-by-seven foot wide capsule atop an experimental rocket called—you probably already guessed it—*Friendship 7*? Hmmph! Now, there's that familiar "friendship" word again, and the beginning of a long voyage into the vastness and stark yonder that opened a whole new age of cosmic travel and medical research which will live long past our own epoch in history. Indeed, John Glenn was truly made of "...the Right Stuff," having thereafter returned to outer-space on October 29, 1998 as a humble Payload Specialist aboard the NASA Space Shuttle Discovery Flight STS-95 at the ripe-old age of 77 years.

In the meantime, the loins of all those so-called intelligent pigs are on display as fresh-cut pork steaks and link sausages in grocery stores and supermarkets all across America while life continues here on Earth, one day at a time. And, those archaic NASA command modules lay-in-state behind epitaph-like placards in our aerospace museums, all but forgotten except for references to them on certain anniversary dates and as fodder for the indexes in the back of our modern history books. Could Orville and Wilbur Wright from Dayton, Ohio have ever foretold that their achievement of defying gravity at Kitty Hawk, North Carolina on December 17, 1903 by flying midair for 12 seconds for a stretch of about 120 feet might portend so many grave disasters, continental crashes, mid-air collisions, skyjackings, and untold other treachery when they completed their lofty experiments, including civilian airplanes filled with innocent hostages being used as guided missiles by suicidal terrorists to cause such devastation as that which occurred upon our U.S. mainland on September 11, 2001? Could the Wright Brothers have predicted that their seismic work would become four-decades later the very delivery system for the first atomic weapon that the scientists of the Manhattan Project developed for use in the Second World War to destroy the Japanese cities of Hiroshima and Nagasaki to avenge their earlier air-attack against the U.S. Naval Fleet at Pearl Harbor, Hawaii? The answer is obviously to the negative, but how can we know in advance where the branches of our yearling visions will grow and the nature of the fruits they will bear? If we had utilized the products of our early inventors, scientists, and doctors more nobly, perhaps we would have seen fit to resist the bold temptation to build armaments for destroying people's lives in deference to carrying more of them to safety above our flash flooding lowlands and beyond the dangers of such natural disasters as blistering forest fires and snowy free-falling avalanches. Maybe we would have enlisted our medical research techniques more for discovering analgesic cures for crippling and fatal diseases than to produce substances which have become our aphrodisiacs to enhance the pleasure of our sexual lives, and others to prevent the conception of our children altogether, and even more to kill their fetuses already alive in their mothers' wombs, and lethal toxins to execute men and women who are sitting on death row in our state and federal prisons. Instead of growing our roots deeper in the constructive ways that people like Wilbur and Orville Wright intended their genius to be remembered, we have soured the fruits of their labors by our clandestine perversions of shameless selfishness and the mutual destruction of our foreign enemies. We might claim to be more civilized than the eastern European hate-mongers of the middle-20th century, but our antics are proving our actions to be just as malignant as theirs. We can also publicly assert that our progress has been a source of international freedom; but, for whom? God knows beyond question what we are doing! We can try to fool Him by sounding more upbeat in tempo, striking a few different chords, and stringing the melodies of life in other keys; but He knows that it is a facet of the unbridled human intellect for us to misconstrue anything that has been bequeathed to us by our forefathers, proclaim them to be amendable at our behest, rewrite recorded history to justify our prejudices, and proceed to prove to the rest of humanity that we have always been superior to them. This is the sad legacy of America that goes far beyond our having liberated every prisoner of war we could ever find, after having nearly rebuilt all four corners of the globe in the aftermath of history's military massacres, and assisting in the removal of political walls that have too-long divided family members and countrymen. It may be true that we were the best of friends to the other continents when they needed us most, but what we are doing to destroy ourselves from within by turning our backs on Jesus Christ is more than any legion of rogue nations could have ever pined to achieve in the legendary recollection of all the centuries from the past until the moment we finally die.

We look to one another everyday for the fulfillment of the spirit of the laws of friendship, if not to live them to the precise letter. However, are we attempting to launch our hopes and dreams into reality by ignoring the relevance of our past? I will always remember having attended elementary, middle-school, and high school in the small Village of Ashland in the 1970s that I referenced earlier. While the main school building was constructed in 1920 at the northern edge of town along what is now Buchanan Street, it wasn't until 1958 that a new annex of the lower grades was added at the site with several classrooms and a state-of-the-art gymnasium. Following the architectural plans, the carpenters and brick-layers connected the old and new facilities together while providing for the appearance of a smooth transition, trying their best to avoid making them look like an ancient castle connected to a TWA airport terminal. They left an open passage between the two sections which later came to be known as "the breezeway" because it allowed both fresh air and daylight to enter between the older high school rooms and the newer 8th grade. Indeed, to further keep the unit integrated, the east part of the old building served as the sixth and seventh grade home rooms on one side of the breezeway, while the eighth grade bordered the west row of windows in the new. And, the census at the high school was so minuscule that the entire student body shared one large room in which about 150 desks were located, appropriately nicknamed "the study hall." Indeed, it seemed like another giant leap for mankind when they finally installed lockers against the walls of the hallways and remodeled the old study area into a library/media center just prior to the beginning of the September 1971-1972 academic year. Anyway, this small breezeway served as somewhat of a symbol of freedom because it gave us the perception that, even though we were confined behind the dangling curtains and glass of our daily curriculum, we could still enjoy the outdoor weather through them in the hope that we would soon be released during our recesses and at the end of the day. As inanimate as it is, that paved passageway was a friend of mine because it never once moved during the entire time I attended the Ashland schools; it never required more than it gave; it never needed to be shielded from the outside elements; it had *sky-as-the-limit* for a ceiling; and it sometimes accorded us passage from the north hallway to the south. But, were we allowed to enjoy our fabricated friend with any semblance of true freedom? The doorways that opened into it were supposed to be used only in case of emergency; any students caught lingering there were quickly run-out by teachers, custodians, and administrators; and we were taught that it was entirely taboo to even think that something so inorganic could satisfy the curiosities of our inner-growth and maturity. Were we being taught at such an early age that there can be no spiritual romanticism between God, nature, and the architecture of man, and that the poetic affections we feel in our hearts cannot become a fashion of any meaningful relationships? Are we required to believe that our friends are only meant to give us the square root of 3,025 for our Algebra homework, bat-back red rubber balls during physical education period in the gym, and hold the skin on the belly of a frog ajar so we can dissect its innards in Biology class? We will never effect the conversion of our brothers and sisters to Christianity if we keep our modest persuasions of creativity, grace, and reconciliation locked inside our hearts as though they are akin to the guarded doorways in my hometown's schoolhouse breezeway that no one could really enter.

   *Friendship conversions and the factual nature of brotherhood*: these are the preferred articles of our confidence that make the human soul so endearing to the entire economy of our Redemption in Christ Jesus, to the invaluable legacies of the Proverbs, and to every grain of sand that has ever plummeted like a fallen sycamore tree in an abandoned forest through the hourglass of mortal time. God has allocated and allotted us only a certain degree of years in which to react on His behalf; and His Will is for us to incorporate our legitimacy in Him within the interpersonal forgiveness that will ultimately make friends of us all and bring lasting peace into the world. We can never be authentically converted through our faith in Christianity unless we also accept our sacred duty to take our friends there with us, to build-up Our Lord's Mystical Body through the humble diminishment of ourselves. This is the invisible interior deposit of Grace that Jesus has been calling us to accept, and the one which seems to be so often misunderstood by His enemies of the Cross. And, I dare say, there are more people that claim to be His disciples who truly do not know what this means than those who do. The manifest proclamation to which we attest is that Christ has Died, Christ is Risen, and Christ will come again. It is in this Truth that we relinquish our own deaths to the mortal ages and make ready our souls for extraction from the netherworld to reside with Him in Paradise. We have all seen the feel-good moving backgrounds that flash behind our television news anchors as they are interviewing their guests; with all their rainbow colors and network logos. What they seem to be subliminally telling us is that the world is indeed in motion, a movement over which we may have control, but refuse to master, as though it is an inevitable part of life. But, we cannot just produce electronic images on a screen while we are talking about the problems of our age because our mission is to get down into the trenches of everyday life to derive permanent solutions. We have become, instead, the evasive targets to whom our friends and children have come seeking the Truth, but we simply utter warm and fuzzy quips about some mysterious God that we do not care to know and send them on their way. The question He must be asking of us now is—what kind of advocates are we for their *souls?* Never mind that they might be linked to us by blood relation or have inherited our family traits. Every Saint who ever lived knew that convincing their siblings and arch-rivals, alike, that the Son of God Loves them to His death seemed an almost impossible thing to do. They often laid-down their own lives for them, lived without food and shelter, and walked dark and lonely pathways as they were cast from the mainstream world like eccentrics, zealots, and fanatics. However, we must continue to convince our friends that their conversion is worth this price, that the Son of God has always owned the final Word over the trials and tribulations to which He was ultimately subjected on Earth and His worthy acceptance of the authentic Diadem that His Holy Father in Heaven eventually placed atop His head to supplant His Crown of Thorns. And, in this same sense, He is both the Alpha and Omega by whom every last soul who was ever born into the world will finally be judged.

Our Lord finished our faith by allowing His Holy Spirit to descend into our hearts; as He was in the beginning and shall be evermore. It is our responsibility to convince our friends that this is not a fantasy about some symbolic parable—it is the same Divine Truth by which we were given the very breath of life; the factual record of supernatural events that transpired only a brief twenty centuries ago. We need not fear that the passing of time has either diluted or altered the meaning of these Sacred Mysteries which we celebrate to this day during the Holy Sacrifice of the Mass. Therefore, if we declare ourselves to be wise, we must have good reason; and it should be unaffected by the tests imposed upon it by the buffeting of the decades. All of the tenable principles that mankind has ever known are those which have sealed our relationship within the Preeminence of God. This is the spiritual genius that will remake the Earth into the likeness of Heaven, even before our clocks expire and the sun shall rise no more. If we are looking for a land of peaceful justice, for equal opportunity for the masses, and a genuine commitment to do it overnight, Jesus Christ is the Way. We must resolve to do things right; to plot our progress around the Cross, rectify the errors in our rotting cities and stagnant states, and regain the dignity of the hundreds-of-thousands who are yet living in abject poverty and under the oppression of partisanship and racism. Herein, our devotion to Christianity is a reciprocal one; receptive, complementary, and always interchanging from one segment of society into the next. The resulting goodness we feel inside must be given as a gift to others if we expect to receive it in return; for this is the broader foundation of all friendship conversions and the true source of international brotherhood. There are some readers of my books who pose the question, *Why must you always conclude every chapter with some kind of reprimand of people who have rejected the Holy Gospel; and why keep brow-beating us with so many references to Christ?* The reason is simply this—that the Son of God who has perched His lofty Paraclete at the center of my heart blooms from the origin of my mortal consciousness and at the core of my very being where I have recognized Him to be God since I was old enough to realize that I was given birth as a human person on the face of the globe. The Spirit He has placed in me has become a portion of His apostolic mission to recapture humankind in His network of Divine Revelation, to which I owe my life and Salvation. Therefore, it is for Him that I shall expend the remainder of my days, balancing *not* religion with the tangible, but searching for the equation that will reconcile the mortality of the entire human race with the prefigured mysteries of Eternity where the two meet as one—on the Holy Cross—which is by no means a pittance to the billions of souls of bygone eras who have already passed-away and been blessed beyond the aftermath of the world they left behind. Our sufficiency must always be a part of the invincible Domain of Truth which can only come from God. We are forever friends and brothers within it, but enemies if we choose to decline. Our Lord has visited the Earth and shone a great Light upon us; and this is the brilliance by which all friendship conversions are ultimately refined.

# Rhymes and Reasons
## 1969

*So, you speak to me of sadness and the coming of the winter,*
*Fear that is within you now; it seems to never end.*
*And, the dreams that have escaped you,*
*            and the hope that you've forgotten.*
*And, you tell me that you need me now;*
*            you want to be my friend,*
*And, you wonder where we're going,*
*            where's the rhyme,*
*            where's the reason,*
*And, it's you cannot accept it is here we must begin*
*to seek the wisdom of the children,*
*and the graceful way of flowers in the wind.*

*For the children and the flowers are my sisters and my brothers,*
*their laughter and their loveliness would clear a cloudy day.*
*Like the music of the mountains, and the colors of the rainbow,*
*they're a promise of the future and a blessing for today.*

*Though the cities start to crumble*
*            and the towers fall around us,*                    *(1)*
*The sun is slowly fading, and it's colder than the sea.*
*It is written: From the desert to the mountains*
*            they shall lead us,*                               *(2)*
*By the hand and by the heart, and they will comfort you and me.*
*In their innocence and trusting, they will teach us to be free.*

*For, the children and the flowers are my sisters and my brothers,*
*their laughter and their loveliness would clear a cloudy day.*
*And, the song that I am singing is a prayer to nonbelievers,*
*Come and stand beside us, we can find a better way.*

John Deutschendorf Denver  (1943-1997)

*(1)*  New York City, September 11, 2001
*(2)*  The Book of Isaiah 11:6

# Chapter X
## *I Pledge Allegiance to the What?*
## *Patriotism and Generation X*

The practice of American politics is the next best thing to a national plague. It is a scourge, an affliction, an aberration, and a menace to the social fabric of our advanced Western civilization. It is a mud-hole in an otherwise pristine landscape of celebrated decency in the historical annals of modernized man. And, rather than spreading our windbreakers across the surface of the muck like good little Boy Scouts would do to allow Lady Liberty to pass, we have shoved the world's greatest free republic head-first into it, soiling the dignity of our people, tarnishing our image of seemliness both at home and abroad, and setting our date with immortal destiny back hundreds of years while we wait for God to strip us to the democratic buff so He can scrub, sanitize, keel-haul, and aerate us into something He can bear to hold at least the distance of a light-year beneath His nose. What has happened to all the civility that our parents used to brag about? The United States boasts of our capacity to blast our foreign enemies completely into smithereens because we have come by it naturally—we have been trying to decimate the dignity of one another within our own country for the past twenty years. And, more than half the time, the conduct of our elected officials borders on the criminally insane; well beyond the parameters of any sound moral propriety. What can be said in defense of our patriotism, centrism, and moderation in a country with such a tawdry history of so many factions as the Ku Klux Klan, neo-Nazism, the Black Panthers, street gang-bangers, militant militias, fundamental extremists, leftist immorality, corporate embezzlement, wild-cat strikes; sit-ins, walk-outs, land-marches; blue crimes, white crimes, sexual revolutions, substance abuse, bloodshed, boredom, privatization vs. eminent domain, and the shoot-to-kill National Rifle Association? Sometimes the atrocities of life hit us in the face with such random ferocity that it is like trying to see the far horizon through a deluge of rain that is falling like translucent sheets of plastic hanging from the clouds. It might be accurate to assume that many young adults have a low threshold of tolerance for contemporary politics, but there seems to be little confusion about why this is the case. The Baby Boom generation which appears to be pretty much in control of the management of America at the opening of this new millennium is a product of the counter-culture that has become a monster of their own making. However, when anyone other than a U.S. citizen grabs us by the collar on the way by and inquires how we can claim to be so well united, we brand him as a closet conspirator against our majority-rule freedoms, an underground terrorist, a remnant of Communism, or someone from deep in the woods who has never had the opportunity to see the full light of day. And, in an attempt to disguise the disorder and divisiveness in America, we drape the U.S. flag over everything in sight, salute it at attention with four fingers smartly aligned, and point to our so-called civility—even while any casual observer who is readily trying to find it would be forced into playing the game of guessing under which nutshell he might find the pea.

Our arrogance has led us to scoff at the castigations of intelligent men, turn a deaf ear to their eloquent admonitions, bicker about who will ultimately possess our wares, cringe at the thought of public piety; and, for what it's worth, we would refuse to walk across the downtown street to see an apparition of St. Michael the Archangel if we knew in advance that he would be strung with Rosary Beads of 24 karat gold from his halo all the way past his hem. Moreover, to further denigrate our national reputation, there are tens-of-thousands of openly gay, lesbian, and bisexual men and women who are asserting their "identity" across the continent, trying to pervert the meaning of affirmative action, when good Christians everywhere ought to be telling them to drop to their knees with their faces to the skies and ask God to render them healed. There are nearly 250 of them who hold elected political office these days whose agenda is not only public service, but also to effect and amend certain laws aimed at advancing the extension of their movement and to further express their dissatisfaction with how God created their own private parts. We see them in crowds with people holding an Emmy or Oscar, a Grammy, or the Congressional Medal of Honor. But, if any one of us ever expressed our concern that their station before Christ might be in grave danger and asked them to pray with us to be changed, they would turn and say, *You hate me!* Oh, yes—let's not forget about our decision to clone pigs, then cattle, and finally even ourselves! Who said that animals don't outrank us Homo sapiens at the thin cutting-edge of genetic engineering? We have focused our attention on cyanide-laced Tylenol, the intentional spread of poisons and disease like anthrax and smallpox; SCUD missiles, box-cutters; pills that keep us awake, capsules to put us back to sleep; amphetamines, barbiturates, heroine, LSD, crack cocaine, alcohol, marijuana; and bongs, one-hitters, custom hypodermic syringes, and roach clips of every shape and size. And, let us never be fooled into believing that the use of such contraband is restricted only to addicts who are slouching in their slum-lords' tenement buildings, in backyard garages, and inside trash dumpsters behind the church. There are scores of users who hold public office and drive their fancy Volvos, MG's, and Mercedes Benz sports cars with a little stash of pot locked in their glove boxes or stuffed under the front seat. Many more Americans live this kind of dark life, with a cloud of confusion surrounding their heads; and with images of prophylactics and pyromania, beach bashes, trips to the Virgin Islands, and even ideas of self-destruction vividly permeating their thoughts.

And, when the time comes for our children to approach us to ask what we are going to do about all of this, we throw abstractions at them like the law of supply and demand, what are cause and effect, and the influences of recession and recovery. These things are our way of beating around the bush before we eventually get to the point of saying, *I don't know.* In the meantime, we continue our senseless psychobabble with certain commands and instructions like, ...*stand up straight! Clean your plate! Wipe that silly smirk off your face! And, get a job!* The hypocrisy thus continues. All of this is going on while good people, the truly righteous ones, are sitting back waiting for the Son of God to burn our nation to the ground, and shooting the first flaming arrow right-smack-dab at the United States Supreme Court Building which has allowed such awful liberalism, infanticide, the abuse of free speech, and outright public immorality to ensue. Then, Americans will hark to the opening scenes of the 1998 motion picture *Titanic* and recall what Leonardo DiCaprio, a.k.a. Jack Dawson, said at the poker-table to his counterparts Fabrizio, Olaf, and Sven while guarding a Full House in his hands, ...*Alright, the moment of truth; somebody's life's about to change!* Perhaps the writers of that script knew by premonition that such a remark would be quite applicable in America today. There is no doubt that God once shed His Grace upon us, but we blew it!—and neither the summer breezes across the University of Alabama at Birmingham nor the winter solstice above Bangor, Maine have the intercessionary moxie to get us out of this one! It is up to us whether we have what it takes to face the future with holiness and to acknowledge that we have let Jesus down with outright obsession. We forget sometimes that we grow old much too quickly; from diapers, to sunbathing suits, to Depends before we ever have the chance to discover what living Divine Love is all about. As far as our children can see, it has nothing to do with our politics and wars; it is not even close to defining the appropriate meaning of patriotism; and it cannot be referenced in any of the history books inside which we have exalted our domestic Civil War heroes, industrial and civil engineers, our larger-than-life entertainers, and award-winning laureates of the Kennedy Honors. It sometimes seems as though we gain a certain intuition about life when the cracks of darkness in our thinking begin glowing with a new light, but then our gracefulness suddenly gives-way to a heavy distress that comes with aging. Indeed, we grow from crawling on our hands and knees as little toddlers beneath our mothers' apron strings to being tied to beds in nursing homes with the sun outside our windows sinking quickly in the west. It is at that moment when we realize that the most productive of our years are gone. Should we be so fortunate that our grandchildren might visit us there, what would we tell them about having lived here in America? Under what pretense can we give them hope that the world we see from the purview of our deathbeds owns any penchant for change to the better when we—all of us—have done precious little to sustain ourselves in goodness, let alone how they will ever redress the grief of all the children they will see starving to death half-way around the globe on their $5,000 flat-screen TV when they get home? How will we eulogize the dog-eat-dog nature of American politics that they have grown accustomed to despising in their brief span of years? How can we respond to their questions about why our Nation's flag has been burned in so many native villages around the world, and that it can be seen desecrated by being stitched into curtains, on headbands, gloves, and on T-shirts; and depicted with snakes and goblins surrounding it in permanent marker on the bathroom walls, mirrors, and turnstiles of their city high schools? We must somehow convince them before it is too late that it is not unpatriotic to dream of an America in which the Gospel of Jesus Christ is accepted as the premier purifier of human life.

This is not to say that most of us have not really been trying to get that message across or that we are unable to effectively communicate the more viable aspects of our nation's Preamble. But, we have a great distance to travel to convince our progeny and our republic that God has stationed His Love and charity like sentinels in the night to guard the world against the obesity of our egos while our consciences are still trying to find their way to His threshold of Truth in the darkness of our sins. Perhaps it would not be so bad if people in political life were not so entrenched in what they are doing by making a career of living off the public dole. And, by the way they raise campaign funds over their challengers, their incumbency tends to beget their greater ability to remain steadfast in office. Indeed, what adjectives could best describe the political climate in America today? How sick and tired are we of seeing derogatory television commercials depicting the smiling face and living color of someone who is trying to get himself re-elected or chosen for a freshman term whose opponent is shown as some crass ogre in a slow-motion black and white fuzzy newsreel, bobbing his head up and down, his lips moving like molasses in a January blizzard, and wagging his index finger through the air like General Manuel Noriega, the defunct dictator of Panama, slapping an oriental sword against the top of a lectern? Not only that, the entire landscape of the country is littered with political signs while our candidates' supporters get into arguments over various issues at coffee counters, bars, and on the street waiting for a bus to arrive. Billions of dollars are raised and expended on media advertising; and, when all is said and done, less than half the eligible voters in many districts ever bother to show-up at the polls. The American electorate is simply fed up with the lies, mud-slinging, and the distortion of the facts from candidates running for office. Please allow me to cite an example of what I mean. If I were a member of the U. S. Senate and a legislative bill came across my desk proposing to allocate $50 billion to help feed, clothe, house, and extend healthcare to thousands of poor children in America, I would be inclined to vote in favor of it. However, by the time another party agrees to it only if I concede to amending the bill by adding a provision through which no private corporation in the United States would ever have to pay any income taxes again, I could not in good conscience support it on the Senate floor because I believe that the wealthy ought to pay their fair share. However, when the next election cycle comes around, my opponent takes to the airwaves with the false accusation that I am staunchly against taking care of our impoverished children, and that I refused to support a measure aimed at easing the burdens on our taxpayers. This is the same kind of outright lying, deception, and twisting of the truth that American voters are getting tired of. And, in the midst of all this distraction, there can be no doubt that the fondest imaginings of what our Founding Fathers wanted our democratic system to become have been mutated into complete oblivion by now. We tell our little children ten million times a day never to exaggerate their stature, fudge on their resume, or slip any money over the transom for a cheap political trick. We implore them to be patriotic and to embrace the red, white, and blue; but they can see for themselves by the product of our actions that there is no such decency in many people who aspire to serve faithfully in America's post-Cold War elective offices and various governmental institutions.

What would happen if a blind man approached one of us and said that he has never even seen the U.S. flag, let alone ever paused to consider whether its fibrous material is worthy of all the worship that most right-wing federalists are heaping upon it? Would we tell him that he can be no true American patriot if, in his sightlessness, he cannot determine whether his hands are touching Old Glory or an ordinary kitchen towel that has just been removed from a linen closet down the hall? Quite the contrary, the spirit of America lives inside our hearts, not in the flashy facade of secular pageantry or our oaths of office; and not in the engraved bombshells and eagles' claws on our battle caps and breast pins. The success of America is a mixture of good timing, fate, talent, opportunity, and destiny—and all of these are the fonts of our sustainable achievements. When a very young Bill Clinton visited the White House as a member of Boys Nation from Little Rock, Arkansas to meet the same John Fitzgerald Kennedy whom I quoted in Chapter VI of this book, could the 35th President of the United States have known that he was not just shaking the hand of another eager student from a small school in the Midwest, but one in the passing of thirty years who would succeed him into the Oval Office as the 42nd President? It is quite strange to imagine how certain circumstances unfold in a country where we are afforded so many avenues to make the most of our lives. It sort of makes us wonder whether there was some kind of a tincture in the handshake of Bill Clinton and JFK that could in any way give either of them the slightest notion that the younger of the two would eventually become elevated to our government's highest office. Whatever it was, we could not see it; and this is the same mysterious workings of democracy that cannot be captured in the hues of a flag. Indeed, it is the aura of the heart that our young people are seeking today. Do we suppose that Mr. Kennedy passed-along some type of unseeable grace or blessing to young Bill Clinton that set him on an inevitable course or a mystically paranormal inheritance to seek and secure the office of the presidency that we will all see once we are dead and gone? Imagine what it would have been like for an unsuspecting photographer to have taken a close-up snapshot of the clasped hands of Bill Clinton and John F. Kennedy when they first met? It is more than probable that it would have eventually made the front cover of *Time Magazine*. Some of the main things the two of them had in common were their vision for the future, an innate penchant for seeking ameliorative revisions to a democracy that, as (the late) Senator Robert Francis Kennedy once said, often yields much too painfully to change.

     People like these have always sought more than to advance their own careers or to etch their legacy in history. They see the chance to make a positive difference in millions of lives and take advantage of it. And, this is the struggle for fostering goodness upon the world stage and the lasting ages that we must instill in our young generation of Americans. Patriotism for the sake of national pride is a hollow virtue; and only our desire to seek freedom for everyone is what makes us greater than most all other republics. We must bring the commotion of our partisanship to a halt and recall what has made us noble inside our own country. I sometimes think that the only reason God placed quicksand on the Earth is to serve as a parable for our spiritual lives. The more we flail about in political diversity against Him, the faster and deeper we sink into the secular abyss. We are still fighting an incalculable number of civil wars of the heart—not for the sake of liberty or individual freedom; but because, deep inside, most of us abhor living around other people who are different from ourselves. Our social cohesion is larger than most of us are willing to concede; and we must be capable of thinking about other men in more expressive terms than we ever have before; past the bounds of the casual and into the absolutely sublime. If a genie emerges from a bottle in front of us in a cloud of smoke and says that God has chosen to allow us one wish to come true, we should tell him that our desire is to have a billion more wishes so that we can contemplate every facet of Creation and ask our Divine Lord to adhere to our imitations of His Son in ridding the Earth of every form of apostasy, ill-will, impurity, and theological sacrilege. We must cast our failures, suffering, inhibitions, and perennial lacking aside and make way for the newer people we have chosen to become in the sheer genius of Christian Truth. We have got to stop diluting the integrity that has made us a nation of good will seekers, and never stand for the outright malevolence which is spewing from the mouths of our political hate-mongers, while never allowing a single cynical dastard to escape into the night. Why? Because too many exceptions can render any rule to be irrelevant and ultimately unenforceable. This is how our decency has slowly been eroded; and it is why there is so much cynicism in the public sector today. What honest man or woman would ever wish to seek to serve their country when they know that not even the FBI would give their background the microscopic scrutiny that they will get from the media and their opposition? If we do not demand higher civility from our fellow countrymen, then their unchecked hatred will reciprocally become a national blemish on our own faces as well. Would it be inappropriate to describe our dismal national personality as being not unlike the scrounge we find in abandoned outhouses, attics filled with cobwebs, and in musty cellars whose doorways have not been opened for dozens of years?

If our brains formulate thoughts by sight, sound, and touch; should not the heart of our country communicate with the world on the conciliatory planes of faith, hope, and Love? If we suffer from loss of vision or become suddenly paralyzed, or are rendered deaf; does this imply that our life has ended? We survive by our will to live; and this is what we should be doing underneath the garment of God's holiness; taking our children, our fellow Americans, our government, our Colors, and the very essence of our yet-unfinished democracy with us, too. We must learn to have respect for the fairness of the facts in our future politics. We know that the days seem to pass-by too quickly now, and conversely that they are oftentimes much too long; but each one is like a cog in a wheel because a single day provides a measure of progress in the passing of our years and the accomplishment of our goals. Without any particular day in time, we would lose our footing; our forewords would seem to stumble; and we would become confused by the sudden rise of the unexpected. This is how our national tragedies such as September 11, 2001 seem to make time almost stand still and blast it into pieces. America must begin to see Eternity through the purview that every day is equally as important as its predecessor, that each one is a cameo appearance of Divine Truth in spectacular succession and our momentum toward seeking Holy Perfection itself. And, yet, nothing immortal can be confined to the mere presence or passing of twenty-four hours. If we create an America for our children in which we value every second of our lives in making true freedom of peace in the heart, then Generation X will someday eclipse our own patriotism with a skyscraping valor of their own; fit for our greatest museums of art, history, science, and industry—and all the holier for God to place in a monstrance upon His Altar in Paradise for the Angels and Saints to adore. They are trying to feed upon our leadership now, but we are placing their impressions and hopefulness in peril by tossing their spiritual breadcrumbs onto our expressways of selfishness and disdain. When will this come to an end? When Americans see our national purpose as the Eternal marriage between Almighty God and civilized man.

# Section IV
## *With a Little Child to Guide Them*

---

## Chapter XI
### *Children of a Greater God*
### *Resurrecting the Meaning of Love*

The first message to have ever been transmitted via the telegraph line is attributed to inventor Samuel Morse on May 24, 1844 when he was recorded to have said, *What hath God wrought!* It apparently did not take too much to impress him back then to make such a proclamation. Imagine what he would say about our wireless telephones, pagers, and cosmic TV transmissions that are sent and received around the world every day. How quickly did his contemporaries respond to his words? According to the World Almanac, the first transcontinental telegraph line was completed on October 24, 1861, replacing the Pony Express that had previously run from Missouri to California. We are, indeed, a people of persuasive opportunism, creative intelligence, intuition, filled with imagination, and willing to put our collective minds and hearts to the ultimate tests of fate. And, since we have become so industrious in lands where too many things do not really matter, what do we suppose it would mean for us to be able to envision the true presence of God more clearly than we do? Both our conduct and our reputation take a beating when we fall into the jowls of sinfulness and error, substance abuse, promiscuity, philandering, gambling, and the general lack of spirituality. However, the entire panorama of God's blessings rain-down upon us when we live according to His Word; fostering the growth of piety, prayerfulness, forgiveness, and empathy. Time, itself, amends and changes life of its own accord, but not always or necessarily to the better. That is why we must make a concerted effort to reunite humanity, even if only in the same archaic steps that brought Samuel Morse to invoke the power of his Almighty Maker, so that the growth of Christianity can be a worldwide interconnection of inexplicable apostolic zeal. Then, if the culmination of history's moments broadens the expanse of universal peace, will not our occasional skirmishes in defense of Christendom be recalled as having been worth the fight? We sometimes live with intense feelings of exasperation because the answers to such questions are not as readily apparent as we wish them to be. Some of what we believe to be ironclad protections against the evil influences of the underworld are oftentimes only papier-mache illusions of a false sense of security. The fact is, our souls are protected only by the supernatural Spirit of Jesus whom we cannot yet see. We have been turning somersaults over guard-rails and everglades for centuries now, trying to get a closer peek at His Glorious Face. Little do we know, however, that we do not need such things as telescopes, calipers, divining rods, triggers, armor, lances, push-buttons, toggle switches, levers, handles, or remote controls to comprehend the full nature of His Being. Nothing in the world can ever bring harm to our invisible souls because they are completely untouchable by the physical universe. Our fears are misplaced and wholly misguided if we believe that any suffering, rejection, castigation, ridicule, or even bodily harm could ever steal-away what Jesus Christ already owns.

We have put a fair amount of effort into pursuing the wrong climaxes here on the Earth; and rarely has it been because we do not know better. We have no good excuses for declining to become more engaged with God because there are plentiful Scriptural passages to keep our hearts, minds, sentiments, and emotions aligned while pondering human Salvation for the Biblical threescore and ten years' average span of our natural lives. There is no way we can concoct any legitimate alibis to convince Jesus Christ that we have been otherwise too busy to search for Him; and no amount of pandering to the Archangels will ever erase our spiritual deficiencies. By all means, no case-bound reams of lofty word-smithing could ever produce sufficient grounds to conclude that we are better-off not knowing what is about to greet us in the afterlife. Whether we know it or not, there is no burden of proof resting on God's shoulders to convince us that He exists; for nature and life itself are sufficient evidence that He does. So, when we are looking for someone to speak to who will never over-interpret what we are trying to say, the Son of God is our Man. When human Love seems more corporeal and physical than spiritually awakening, He will set our sights on the higher realms of human existence by drawing a circle around everything seeming to confine us, lifting us heart and soul from within its circumference, and allowing us to see the brevity of mortality from beyond the sparse economy of what we previously thought to be our measly portion of the voluminous expanse of all Creation. In Him, we can usurp our own sense of stability by gaining a greater impression of what it feels like to continue living outside the material world once we have finally died. However, nobody ever said that acquiring such trust would be easy; and this is what our Christian faith is for. The great Doctors of the Church have warned us about the many ways other people will chide us for believing in things we cannot see; but, guess what?—the human heart can envision them anyway! Paradise has got to be someplace, or everywhere, because the number of souls who have already passed-away from life on the Earth is no-less than ten times the population stationed on it now. Our arrogant objections, stubbornness, egoism, and materialistic greed are among the reasons why we are so reluctant to take any greater steps in relinquishing control of our everyday lives to a sovereign God who seems too notorious for hiding in the shadows. Again, from the *Faith Connection* bulletin from Allen, Texas: *Only God would pursue an ongoing relationship with a people as obstinate as humanity has shown itself to be through the ages. God fashioned a human race and endowed its people with the gift of free will, making it capable of establishing great civilizations, productive communities, and nurturing families. Fulfilling the Divine plan and living righteously, however, has always been a great personal and collective challenge for the people of God. Hardheaded, dishonest, and selfish human behavior has compromised humanity's relationship with God from the time of creation. Yet, God continues to try to reconcile the breach caused by such behavior with generous portions of sanctifying faith, hope, and love. The Angel Gabriel reminded Mary, "Nothing is impossible with God" (Luke 1:37). God wills the Salvation of His beloved human race, and all Creation with it. God's mysterious possibility of a world order that promotes the peace, welfare, and freedom of all people has captured the imagination of the people of God—like King David, young Mother Mary, and the preacher Paul. It continues to capture the imagination of 21st century Americans like us as well. Despite our shortcomings, God consistently reaches-out, inviting human participation in the Divine work of Redemption. God, the all-powerful Author and initiator, requires our active and free collaboration in the Divine plan to save the world. Sometimes, like David, we fix our minds on our own idea of what we believe God wants and needs of us. We need to remember that God rejected David's plan to build a holy temple, seeking instead to build a Kingdom that will last forever through Him.* (Published during the Season of Advent, December 22, 2002).

We must know, therefore, that our faith is a portion of our Love for God. If we were allowed to see Him in all of His brilliance before we die, would this not mean that our reason for faith would be diminished and, as an effect, our Love for Him become diluted by some appreciable degree? We are required to boast of our affections for Him now as prolifically as we will the very moment our souls are left standing bare in the absence of our flesh before His Heavenly Throne on Judgement Day. Anything short of this, it seems, will bring us only to greater frustration in our search for His Truth. When we fail to see Heaven as clearly as we think we ought to be allowed, we file our disappointment under the proverbial "...and this, too, shall pass" recycle bin until later when we have time to take the matter up again. We muster the troops of our own defeatism, paranoia, and self-doubt in an effort to bolster the blind garrison of our false assumptions about the purpose of our being here, and then set-out to destroy anything that looks even slightly like a holy relic that would require the unconditional surrender of our worldliness into the arms of sustainable faith, carrying-on as though we have been commissioned by some raw atheism to expunge anything in our path upon which our Love for God might choose to feed. And, in such uniform militance, we are completely missing the point about our spiritual conversion because the clear and evident explanation for the subsistence of the human race is founded in the Sorrowful Crucifixion of the Savior of the World at precisely 1500-hours local time on Mount Calvary on Good Friday, almost 2,000 years ago. (Luke 23:33).

It is an extremely rare human heart that would try to refute these facts—although there have been a few such losers throughout the course of history—because deep within each of us lives the capacity to accept what has been revealed for centuries as being the unalterable veracity of God to surrender the Life of His Only Begotten Son to a rowdy group of belligerent agnostics whose sinful first parents were earlier evicted from the Garden of Eden in order to save our souls. Who would have ever dared to step forth on the Earth twenty centuries ago and proclaim that He is the Messiah? Jesus Christ! And, He is the same Person of Divine Truth and Revelation who lives inside our hearts today in the Church, within the Sacraments, and in our intercessory prayers. We believe these things without having seen them with our own eyes. There were no journalists or television networks to report it back then, no relay satellites floating in the void of outer-space, and not even an English-speaking prophet upon whom we could depend to translate it. And, yet, this is the Truth as it was foretold by God to Moses and Abraham, through every humble soul who ever returned His Love with a defensible faith of their own, in His Martyrs' untimely executions, the Pontificates of all His Popes who succeeded Saint Peter as the Vicars of Christ, and by the works of great Christian servants like (the late) Mother Teresa in our modern times. There is no doubt that such a transcending and Sacred Mystery of our human involvement in the purification of the world is evidenced by eradicating the suffering of poor people everywhere; but the genesis of our desire to do so cannot be seen with the naked eye. Not unlike the transparency and historical significance of the United States flag, what makes us best in everything we do is a matter of the insatiable desire of man to become as benevolent as God. And, this is what He fully seeks in us and expects us to embrace, while giving us both the venue and resources to effectively make it so. Why can we not see this power with a casual focus of our vision? Because there is too much Mystical Providence, exaltation, converging power, and imminent prophecy to behold for it to be concealed inside a single-dimensioned backdrop. Trying to understand the extemporaneous ingenuity of the human potential once it is empowered by the Holy Spirit of God by looking no further in the universe than the trees and stars would be like trying to see our nighttime dreams more clearly by wearing reading glasses to bed. For all of this, we must learn for ourselves and for the generations to come that we are the children of a greater God than we often wish Him to be. The self-imposed curfew we hold against our spirits which seems to imply that we should not think about Love and devotion except during the hours when we are sitting in Church or at someone's wedding or funeral ought to be expunged from the matrix of our consciousness. The great TV screenplay writer, Rod Serling, once said that prejudices can kill and suspicions can destroy; and such is the fate of those who are not given to the more holy of things. We must begin, therefore, to recapture the solemnity of the Church from the demagoguery of modern revisionists and new-fashion seekers. Parishioners should do their part by becoming more pious in the presence of greater Reverence; for Love can greet itself inside us if we choose to allow it to. How many times have we humbly bowed our heads during the Holy Sacrifice of the Mass and heard someone's pager go off or their cellular phone begin playing John Philip Sousa's *Stars and Stripes Forever* at the moment when the priest confers Consecration upon the gifts of bread and wine into the Eucharistic Body and Blood of Jesus Christ? This is the same type of unprecedented lack of respect for the Holy Mass about which I am speaking.

However, to articulate every such malignment of the sanctity of the Mother Church would be a diversion from the purpose of this chapter, so suffice it to say that we are never quite as reverent as we ought to be while participating in the Liturgies and receiving the Sacraments of our religious faith. There is no doubt that the portly excesses of our worldliness and our almost tepid attempts at piety must surely be rather repugnant to God. If my readers will indulge me at this juncture, I would like to address another metaphor that will assist in clarifying the temperance which still seems to be lacking amongst a few in our flock. I know that there are many facets about our faith which can never be abridged, suspended, or reversed; such as the orthodoxy of our Canons, the real and true gifts that the untold lives of the Saints have yielded through their loyalties, and the multiple-millions of private sacrifices that Christians everywhere make everyday to allow God's Creation to become a better place. But, I believe that the eminent cutting-edge for all conversion is not a flat line of razor-thin tenets. For all we know, the cultivation of the heart is serrated into staggered dimensions of varying heights and degrees. Such is the timely progress of our Mystical evolution. Why? Because popular holiness as defined by the Catechism is oftentimes more difficult to achieve, retain, and display for some people than it is for others. It is not that we are standing on a different plateau from those who appear to be the closest to God like one might envision the summits of a mountain range, but more like the leading edge of the ocean's waves crashing against a shore. We are all one body in the Sacred Heart of Christ; and I truly believe that He loves the most wretched among us as affectionately as He does the righteous. It is as though Christians from the earliest centuries established a beachhead in a stark world of lost sinners; and most of them died in the first battle against the evil which thereupon ensued. In due course, those of us who are alive today have inherited the challenge which was fashioned after the early Christians upon completing their original oaths. The problem is manifested when too many people's imagination gets the best of them about what Jesus really wants; or they somehow see the mission of His faith-Church on the Earth as being as whimsically amendable as the secular world. In other words, they have lost the meaning of valorous Love in favor of some watered-down version of modernized brotherhood and an intermittent social piety of institutionalized religiosity that revolves in and out of faddish belief. Conversely, everything we know about organized Christianity tells us that God is more consistent in the Traditions of His Church. He seeks in contemporary humanity the precise perseverance which was reflected by His Son, with the exact same Beatitudes that were peculiar to His day. I realize that it is not politically correct to be writing in this vein; but I am convinced that Jesus will return someday and rescind every aberration we have ever implemented against His Original Apostolic Church; including, but not limited to, the Protestant Reformation, gender-neutral Liturgies, our reduction to symbolism of His factual Articles of Truth, and the rubber-stamp appeasement that has been given to those who have opposed the Roman Catholic Church by various yellow-spined parochial vicars and feminist parishioners all across America. He will restore the spiritual and physical integrity that has been stripped from within the Church during the past forty years and grab those who are responsible for committing it by the throat with a grip of one hand and slam their backs against the wall of Creation with their feet dangling in mid-air. Through their grossly systemic errors, the world has heaped the stench of mortality upon the meaning of Ecclesiastical Love; and Christ will make it an important part of His mission to resurrect it from its entombment when He returns to the Earth the final time.

After that, the various heretical pastors and ecumenical lay-persons who are now declining to partake of His Sacred Blood in the Communion Cup because they do not like receiving His Eucharistic Species under the presence of Consecrated Wine will storm against the gateways of our finest vineyards and rush massive quantities of it by the truckload into the hands of our priests. People such as these are in ranks farthest from the fore of Christian fortitude because they are unwilling to engage the fight on behalf of Roman Catholicism against the negative influences of other religions in distant quarters of the world. They may be a portion of the same oceanic wave, but they are laying back, bringing-up the rear in hopes that the tide of time will reverse the fate of the Earth before it impacts the inevitable Truth. These are lost children of their greater God who seem to be among the last to comprehend the usefulness of the Resurrection of His Messianic Love. And, physical maturity is not enough to fill the vacuum left by their refusal to seek His Divine Wisdom because time is never a substitute for evangelizing our Salvation. If we think more deeply about our impending legacies, about how we can affect the rest of humanity during our mortal years and also be conversely changed by them, about the passing images that are exchanged between ourselves and the spiritual ideologies of other men, and our inner-desire to be remembered fondly after we are gone as having made a profound impression upon the greater world, we will correct our lives when we see them drifting occasionally into distasteful waters. If we really stop to think about how we will be eulogized upon our death, does it not make us pause for at least a moment to ponder how we are now prescribing that event? Wouldn't it be grand if our last act was to instill a higher sense of devotion to God upon our families, friends, and peers? And, do we not already pray for our successors to cite passages from the visionary speeches we deliver nowadays when our souls and the Holy Spirit of Jesus Christ seem to be so finely intertwined? Our legacies must be that we render the whole of Creation more compassionately consoled, more enriched by the goodness of our works, cleansed through our merciful admonishments, enlightened by our charitable advice, and brought to a better understanding of servitude with a spirit of self-denial in the wake of our own authentic sacrifices. Just because our souls may pass beyond the boundaries of the Earth, the spiritual genius of our hearts should live-on through the deeds of other men. In the final analysis, the world is a wreck in which billions of our predecessors have already perished; and so shall we likewise proceed. However, our passing need not be either catastrophically fatal or irreversibly permanent because the entire meaning of our immortal Love has been instilled, refined, and raised from among the deceased in the Sacredness of Jesus Christ. We already know what He continues to tell us anyway; that we are supposed to be more concerned about caring for our brothers and sisters in a spiritually-sustaining way rather than pirating their personal dignity for the purpose of subjugating their lives in order to satisfy our selfish motivations. Why should we try to inhibit their ability to effect their own contributions upon the moral values of society?

God communicates His thoughts to the Earth through the language of signs in these present times; but He is certainly not muted because He deploys the intentions of His Will through so many faithful human voices.

And, the business that a lot of people make out of ignoring His messengers and fighting-off the sureness of having to face Him someday is only more of the needless fallout that will come when He finally proves to the world that He has always been in charge of His Kingdom of certain fate, fortune, deliverance, and freedom.   From what most of us have seen, however, His Angels could probably go ahead and conduct a post-mortem autopsy on some people's consciences because they have long-been dead in the grave.  But, this is where we Christians come in.  We are meant to exert the energy of our faith to live in the likeness of the Son of Mary, *...for unto us a Child is born, a Son is given to us; and upon His shoulder Dominion rests.  They name Him Wonderful Counselor, God-Hero, Father-Forever, and the Prince of Peace.* (Isaiah 9:5).  Once Jesus began His public ministry between the ages of thirty and thirty-three years, he took advantage of every opportunity to impress upon anyone who wanted to know their God to know *Him* first, for in Him also lives the Father.  He asked the people of His century on behalf of every generation which followed them to emulate His Supreme Love through any way a man could possibly invoke a blessing; nourishing, teaching, praying, and respecting the overall dignity of human life.  For all the modern Saints to be—those who do not yet realize that He knows them by name—we are to become the seed of the awakening of the dead spirits of the forsaken in our midst.  We must walk outwardly into the world and seek those who were given names like Jonathan, Cedric, Jason, Lawrence, Reuben, Michael, Silas, and Ulysses; and all the sons of modern man; and tell them that the Kingdom of Heaven is at hand and their souls are the inheritance of the Almighty Father whom Jesus Christ has pleased by His Passion and Crucifixion on the Cross.  When Our Lord was Resurrected from the Sepulcher, He brought-forth new life in us who believe in Him to rescue the future of our brethren from the bottomless pit of their selfishness and deliver them to the Font of the Redeemed.  Indeed, for all of God's women who bear our little children with names like Etta, Carolyn, Cindy, Alexandra, Eleanor, Mary, Elaine, Lynette, Sabrina, Nadine, Veronica, and Victoria; a new title has been given to each and every one of them by the goodness of the works of the disciples of Heaven; which is the surname of "Saint."  If God shall Love humanity through Jesus Christ, then we should hail Him, also, by dispensing our warmth and all the sustaining graces He has implanted in our hearts by the power of the Providential Paraclete for lifting-up the world in His Holy Name.  We are the breathers of new life into the walking dead; the purveyors of goodness, peace, harmony, joy, and the Light of the Godhead who came in the night as our Emmanuel in the Manger, He who lay so provocatively as the Morning Star.

What does any of this have to do with the younger generation of American children whom we are attempting to persuade into garnering a more precise perception of God? If we were to observe the profile of the Church from a future age in time, we would obviously see that it is *their* participation in its Mission that will sustain its life. Once the rest of us are gone and all of our influences have passed-away, the world that remains will be another step closer to becoming the New Heaven and the New Earth that Jesus has promised to reveal at the end of mortal time. So, everything we do to shape the spiritual faith and conscience of our children today is tremendously important to how dutifully they will remain true to the Holy Gospel prior to that impending gift. The shoreline where the ingenuity of man greets the artful consonance of the physical world is inscribed not by the inanimate elements of the universe as we have known them before, but by the presence of a fuller deposit of righteousness that is growing in the hearts of our children. And this, in itself, must become more wholesome than that of any previous age. For all the industrious progress we have achieved since we first invented the wheel, humanity as a whole has grown nearer to its Divine Creator only by the things we cannot touch with the palms of our hands or fabricate into tangible products because such is not the synthesis to which we are being called. The subliminal manifestations of faith, hope, and Love are not always perceivable within the focus of our vision, unlike such phenomenon as the movement of our frames through the element of space, the utility of our crafts and works, and the temporal ways we impact the world through the exertion of our bodies and the effects of our labors. If we could reflect upon what it would be like to see the sound of music or feel the scent of roses, we would come closer to comprehending the intangible interface between the curiosity of man and the Divinity of God. For all of our faults and failures, we still hold within our midst the means to do these things because of the power of the invisible Spirit of Jesus Christ as He has cloaked Himself within the flesh of our hearts with every attribute of His irrefutable Truth intact. From here forward, the best of what we shall become is a revelation that has already been accorded by Him in response to our decision to let it be. For those who still cannot relate to this concept, let them stand at the leading edge of a precipice overlooking a large canyon opposite an equally towering cliff on the other side and wonder how they might ever span such a chasmic breach without the risk of falling to their death. Depending upon whether their life and limb were left hanging in the balance by their crossing-over the gorge, they might imagine what they would give if only there was a bridge before them to aid in their passage across the humongous cleft. This is the concept that comes to mind with respect to the reunion of God and His people. Jesus is the bridge whose return we have not yet seen on a lateral plane, although He is still truthfully here.  If we allow our spirits to walk through life undaunted by our fears of letting go, He will carry the weight of our inhibitions and bear us the strength to go on.  In His presence, we will always be elevated, protected, and delivered through the graces of the Cross despite the ghosts that are holding us back.  We may never be capable of soaring like nighthawks while trapped inside our bodies, but our souls are given wings for the flight to Heaven in the Resurrection of Christ, which is a windward vestment capable of defying the gravity of the Earth and the logic of mortal men.  We know, therefore, that we are children of a greater God than we originally thought Him to be through the observations of the everyday world; and the enhancement of His Kingdom will become more prevalent if we commend our offspring to join us in this faith.

# Chapter XII
## *The Providence of Human Suffering*
## *For the Sake of Lost Souls*

Before the English language took a sudden turn toward a more modern mode, people used to equate the terms *suffer* and *allow* as being synonymous. Some dictionaries even cite the expression, *Will you suffer us to leave?*, as one such example. Others have suggested that the meaning of pain, distress, loss, injury, agony, hardship, and endurance refer to the occurrence of some misfortune *by sufferance*, or by passive permission resulting from a lack of outside interference. Can it be true that the Will of God is such that He realizes the converting power of human tribulation and, therefore, condones it so we can better understand the kind of Passion that has purified and remade the Earth by Jesus Christ? The Church refers to someone's personal torment as a portion of the cleansing of humanity, i.e., that each of us shares in our own unique way in the Sorrowful Suffering of the Savior of the World as an offering of ullage to complement the Holy Sacrifice of Jesus in reparation for our sins. There can be no doubt that if we are to become like Him in every possible way, such pain of mind and heart must surely be our fate, as well. But, why? How can it be true that God takes pleasure in rectifying our disobedience to His Will by allowing innocent people to pay the price for the guilty? There is no question that He does, however, which is proven beyond a shadow in the way Our Divine Lord was tortured and slain by the people of His day. While the Sacred Mysteries about this miraculous Truth have yet to be fully divulged to us, we know for a fact that the Passionate Suffering of Christ is the expiation of the transgressions of all humankind; past, present, and future. Since He lives in us as the Holy Spirit, He also suffers with us when we lay in pain and agony or our feelings are degraded by those who hate us because we belong to Him. Many denominations maintain that Jesus died on the Cross almost 2000 years ago, that He was Raised on the Third Day, and Ascended into Heaven 40 days after Easter Sunday; which seems to be a basis for our traditional faith that every true Protestant, Catholic, and all other Christian congregations agree upon. But, the fact that we poor sinners suffer terrible scourges in reparation for the continuing sinfulness of modern man seems to be an area of stark disagreement within the mix. The Roman Catholic Church is on the side of the Truth—that whatever is heaped upon us in the form of pain and agony is our emulation of the Crucifixion of Jesus Christ; as involuntary as it may appear to be. We may never be required to submit to crucifixion to satisfy a secular court of law or endure a trial before our religious peers as being amenable if we choose to offer our suffering to God for the conversion of His people. Surely this is the goodness and Mercy that shall follow His little ones all the days of their lives so no harm will ever befall their counterparts. (Psalm 23:6). Who are we to say that the tensions of our exile cannot be accepted by our Almighty Father in any ameliorative way He might deign to choose? We need not look too far for answers once we understand the edict which was made by Jesus from the Holy Cross that *It is finished*, just after languishing in agony for Three Hours, inducing God to proclaim the world to be liberated from facing the wage of sin. If this is insufficient to prove the validity of the power of our crosses in the wake of His Sacrifice, then where could it otherwise rest?

Many people have approached me about this subject and asked an obvious question: if it is true that we give ourselves to pain without asking God why, or even in advance, then why are so many little children around the world stricken with poverty and disease when they are yet too young to know that it is their own portion of the Cross? Remembering that Sacred Mysteries continue to be mysterious, could it be possible that our children are also the Christological offspring of the Most Blessed Trinity whose lives are the filaments through which the Light of Love brings such efficacious healing and protection to the multitudes who are given years of health and happiness beyond the present hours? God gives us birth not out of spite, but through the bountiful nature of His Will. And, when He calls us to bended knee before the Monstrance of His Exposition on the Holy Altar bearing His Eucharistic Son, are we not thereby reminded that we belong to Him in heart, soul, mind, body, and despair? Are we not summoned to be broken as equally as Him who is the retraction of the pride of deceitful men and *The Way* by which we are reunited with the future and beyond? And, are we not also co-Eternal and like sufferers on the Earth in reflection of the Christ Child who was later impaled so timelessly on the Cross as the antidote for our fate of fixated death? Therefore, as the Roman Catholic Church proclaims, the Crucifixion of Christ is the domain of reparation, the origin of the whole economy of our Salvation, the harvesting of the Fruits of the Divine Love of God, and the beautifully-blinding Light of Paradise which has cut through the darkness of the ages so we can see our way back home. Our Lord will continue to be Crucified until no mortal man ever sins again. He has been Resurrected and has Ascended into Heaven for sure; but His Passionate Suffering continues on the Earth in the poverty of the poor, the emaciating flesh of the sick and diseased, the weeping tears of the sorrowful, and the last gasps of the dying. How? By virtue of the fact that these things are brought to Creation *by sufferance*, by what the Providence of our ingenious Creator is allowing, and through His assertion that there is no greater Love than in he who surrenders his life for his friends. Is this not, therefore, what we are doing in an immortal way here, atop the ground where so many wrongs are being committed against the weak and afraid, and in our time when it seems as though the suffering of Jesus Christ is having its most profound effect? Let us not be so afraid anymore that He has called us to the summit of such human misery, for in this shall we be rewarded with the Crowns of Saints who were not cowards, who withstood the fight without flinching from the buffets of the netherworld by which we are pummeled everyday, and in the faith that our call on behalf of Divine Truth cannot be real unless we are willing to endure the consequences as though we were otherwise guilty as charged. Is this not what our dear Jesus has done? Was He not taken to the pinnacle of agony as an innocent Man and ruthlessly bludgeoned as though everything He was accused of being was a matter of fact?

> *Have pity on me, O God;*
> *have pity on me,*
> *for in You I take refuge.*
> *In the shadow of Your wings*
> *I take refuge 'till harm pass by.*
> *Then, do my enemies turn back,*
> *when I call upon You;*
> *Now, I know that God is with me.*
> *In God, in whose Promise I glory,*
> *in God I trust without fear;*
> *What can flesh do against me?*

The Psalter 56-57

We are birthed and Born Again so our spirits cannot die anymore. Whatever shall come, so says Saint Paul, that would put our joy asunder and plunder the feasts on our dinner tables, nothing of any consequence within the realms of this Earth can strip us of our blessedness in the Bloodshed of the Lamb of God. Why did He have to suffer; why does He agonize still; and why are His followers of this modern age subjected to such indignity and pain? Because we wish to be like Jesus; and we know to call upon the Lord in Heaven for strength to bear the plight of our lives with acceptance and humility. Never once did Jesus turn to His Father in Heaven and ask *why* He had to suffer; He inquired only as to the reason for His seeming to have been so forsaken from above. He knew upon the completion of His mortal years that His Hour had come; and He likewise knows that we, too, shall understand from the perspective of the fullness of Eternity when He closes the doorway on the evolving of time. When Saint Paul wrote to the congregation of Colossians in the Lycus Valley in Asia Minor, he said of these things, *Now, I rejoice in my sufferings for your sake; and in my flesh, I am filling-up what is lacking in the afflictions of Christ on behalf of His Body, which is the Church, of which I am a minister in accordance with God's stewardship given to me to bring to completion for you the Word of God, the Mystery hidden from ages and from generations past. But, now it has been manifested to His holy ones, to whom God chose to make known the riches of the Glory of this Mystery among the Gentiles; it is Christ in you, the hope for the Glory. It is He whom we proclaim, admonishing everyone and teaching everyone with all Wisdom, that we may present everyone perfect in Christ. For this, I labor and struggle in accord with the exercise of His power working within me.* (Colossians 1: 24-29).

When all is finally said and done, we will realize that we have been groveling below the constellations in a world we will not always remember; but we have been sustained by a Divine Love we shall never forget. I am convinced that human grief is not a parasite that is feeding on our piety, and that the fear of anything other than the justifiable Wrath of God in deference to His Holy Wisdom is unworthy of our valuable time. Broken-down into microscopic pieces, life is a sparkle in an engagement ring that encircles the girth of Our Divine Lord's wedding finger as we are united with every fiber of our intrinsic beings to His unseen creative Love. In this, we live never to ourselves, but to the Maker of our souls; to be laden and saddled with mortality so as to carry the burden of righteousness past the broadness of the mountain ranges, back into the corridor of the Paradise we lost, and into the very presence of the Almighty Father while we are vested in raiments of prostrated humility. This is the nature that is lacking in us now; it is the Truth we have avoided by being so shallow in seeking peace and far too prolific at making war; and also adept at prejudice; and it is the mainstay of Justice-reunited with the dying Earth for which the boundless Providence of Heaven has been so electrified that it flashes before us in jagged bolts, spires, monsoons, and deluges. Our global planet is upside down right now because the moonbeams were supposed to be the footlights emanating from below the stage of our having played-out the Scriptures of unparalleled Love to a humanity we have never truly embraced. The vessel of our hopes and dreams is listing back and forth in the tears which have flooded our lands because we are too sad, it seems, to saturate them with compassion, instead. We think we do sometimes, but we suddenly change our minds before the Spirit of Christendom has the chance to slip quietly past our tongues like the slowing of the evening in our consciences—that last swallow of fine wine across our palates before we don our nightcaps and set sail upon a crest of dusky images while waiting for another dawn to come. All the while, our unborn children suffer the fate of being evacuated from their mothers' wombs as aborted fetuses; impoverished infants cry-out in hunger on the sheetless mattresses in their cribs, our adolescents angrily pound their fists into the ground from hallucinogenic pills, and the forsaken elderly who are the epitome of them all together have been crammed like insects in roach motels in dark corners of our nation's hospices and private nursing homes.  All of this is too sad for casual observers to take, so they turn it off, tune it out, and come to the wrong conclusion that God must not be as loving as they first believed, for surely He would have changed it all by now.  What we fail to remember is that Jesus Christ bled both for us and with us; and we for Him; so that the sacred union of God and man can be overtly canonized in the sweetness of our deaths.  If we carry our arms to Judgement Day, but feel too disenfranchised to discharge them against the evil in our midst, will not our enemies think that they have won without the slightest whimper of retaliation to be heard from the bunkers above which the enamored Cross resides?  Little do our foes realize that our bushel baskets are turned upright to allow the Light of Christ to shine anew, that they are filled beyond capacity with the rapture of a Newer World which is seeping into our errant one a Chalice at a time, willed by the concession of God to dispense the nectar of Salvation from the veins of His executed Son.  These are the battlefields of the Earth—the invisible scenes where our souls resurge, and from where we shall someday ultimately pass while leaving our frail and inhumane casualties behind; sparing us from enduring the sting of death and defeat, too; and stripping from the hands of His adversaries the spoils of Victory that were never really theirs to share.

There are multi-fashioned reasons why Jesus commends us all to become like little children before He shall allow our entry into Paradise than readily meet the eye.  It is obvious that by doing so, we will be far less conniving, not as materialistic, and not as apt to rationalize the principles of His sacred teachings.  Put rather simply, little children recognize His presence and Grace with greater distinction than adults do because they have not yet been assimilated into the twisting armature of the spontaneous world.  We learn everyday that our conduct can be unwittingly courageous and can evolve from the most unlikely sources, not the least of which is derived from the behavior of our youngest ones.  In a world that is riddled with symptoms of post-traumatic stress, anxiety, depression, post-partum clinical psychosis, and the estrangement that often occurs between spouses, their siblings, and their parents; one might wonder what it is going to take to try to put the fallen Humpty Dumpty of our personal relationships back together again.  Herein, the answers reside in the miracles from God that are rarely seen with mortal vision. Heaven has been communicating with us since time immemorial through the presence of the angels; and their intercession has been the greater portion of our knowing what God has wished for us during critical tides throughout the history of the Earth. How far back do our written records go? To Wit: *Moses was tending the flock of his father-in-law Jethro, the priest of Midian. Leading the flock across the desert, he came to Horeb, the mountain of God. There, an angel of the Lord appeared to him in fire flaming out of a bush...When the Lord saw him coming over to look at it more closely, God called out to him from the bush, 'Moses! Moses! Here I am!...the God of your father, the God of Abraham, the God of Isaac, the God of Jacob!..I have witnessed the affliction of My people in Egypt and have heard their cry of complaint against their slave drivers; so I know well what they are suffering. Therefore, I have come down to rescue them from the hands of the Egyptians and lead them out of that land into a good and spacious land, a land flowing with milk and honey...Come, now, I will send you to Pharaoh to lead My people, the Israelites, out of Egypt...I will be with you; and this shall be your proof that it is I who have sent you: when you bring My people out of Egypt, you will worship God on this very mountain.' 'But,' said Moses to God, 'when I go to the Israelites and say to them, 'the God of your fathers has sent me to you,' if they ask me, 'What is His Name,' what am I to tell them?' God replied, 'I am who am! This is what you should tell the Israelites: I AM sent me to you...This is My Name forever! This is My title for all generations!'* (Exodus 3:1-15).

Henceforth, we know from the start that the angels have played a seminal role in enlightening humanity about the presence of our Creator, the desire of His Will, and the Wisdom we have needed throughout history to carry it forward. The word *angel* is derived from the Greek term *angelos*, which has the literal definition of *messenger from God*. And, the Sacred Scriptures are peppered with evidence of their holy service on His behalf in the Old and New Testaments alike. Their most crucial revelation to come into the world was when God dispatched the Archangel Gabriel to Mary, the Immaculate Conception and daughter to Joachim and Anne, who was betrothed to Joseph the carpenter. It was by Her Fiat that Jesus Christ was conceived in Her Womb, thereby allowing the Word of God to be born Incarnate in Bethlehem. Angels likewise announced the births of Ishmael (Genesis 16:11), Sampson (Judges 13:3-5), John the Baptist (Luke 1:19), the Child Jesus (Luke 1:26); and also proclaimed Our Lord's Resurrection at Easter (Matthew 28:5). The angels have been our guard against impending danger throughout the ages; for it was one of them who stopped Abraham from sacrificing Isaac (Genesis 22:11), who protected Jacob from danger (Genesis 48:16), and shielded Israel from the Egyptians at the Red Sea (Exodus 14:19). An angel forewarned Joseph to take Mary and Jesus and escape to Egypt (Matthew 2:13); they consoled Our Lord on the Mount of Olives (Luke 22:43), and freed Peter from prison (Acts 12:7).

In Psalm 91:10-11, *No evil shall befall you, nor shall affliction come near your tent, for to His angels He has given command about you, that they guard you in all your ways.* Accordingly, in Matthew 18:10, *See that you do not despise one of these little ones, for I say to you that their angels in Heaven always look upon the Face of My Heavenly Father.* Likewise, from the Roman Catholic Missal, Eucharistic Prayer One, *Almighty God, we pray that your angel may take this Sacrifice to your Altar in Heaven.* And, as an intercessory petition for the dead, *May the angels lead you into Paradise.* Therefore, anyone who says that he is a Christian but does not accept the existence of angels is not in total compliance with the Gospel. There are nine recorded Orders of them: seraphim, cherubim, thrones, dominions, virtues, powers, principalities, archangels, and angels. The Catechism celebrates the existence and usefulness of the angels in Part One, Chapter One, 328-336, confirming that the presence of such spiritual (non-corporeal) beings called angels is a factual Truth of faith and that, with their whole beings, they are servants and messengers from God who, *have intelligence and a will: they are personal and immortal creatures, surpassing in perfection all visible creatures, as the splendor of their Glory bears witness.* Psalm 103:20 states, *Bless the Lord, all you angels, you mighty in strength who do His bidding, obeying His spoken word.* From Hebrews 1: 6-7, *When He leads His First Born into the world, He says, 'Let all the angels of God worship Him.' Of the angels, He says: 'He makes His angels winds and His ministers a fiery flame.'* Therefore, we live in the midst of an entire bevy of spiritual benefactors upon which only a few fortunate seers in the history of Creation have been allowed to feast their eyes, and on the rare occasion that these benevolent creatures have taken-on a visible form. According to the Church, *...from infancy to death, human life is surrounded by their watchful care and intercession. Beside each believer stands an angel as protector and shepherd leading him to life. Already here on Earth, the Christian life shares by faith in the company of angels and men united to God.* (Catechism 336). So, we should believe in all those testimonials that come from the mouths of babes and their elders, alike, when they tell us that they have been in the company of angels, while too many who hear their stories claim that they are deluded by a repugnant faith, that their imagination is getting the best of them, or they are suffering from mental instability. How broken their hearts must be when people who doubt what they are saying look at them with incredulous eyes or pat them on the top of the head in pity. But, what happens when our little children, who are much too young to know what deception is, confirm that they have witnessed the angels of God? Now, we have an entirely different set of circumstances on our hands!

A news story that was placed on the wire in December 2001 tells about a woman named Tobi Gabriel and her three-year-old son Gage who were inside an automobile that veered off a cliff and wrecked on the rocks beside the shore off Lower Cove Road near Joggins in Cumberland County, Canada on Christmas Eve. The woman was killed instantly, but the boy survived the crash and spent the night alone shivering on the beach where he waited approximately 12 hours before some passers-by found him at 9:00 a.m. on Christmas Day. He suffered frostbitten toes and a bruise on his head, but was otherwise uninjured in the mishap. Upon being interviewed by police who were dispatched to the scene, Gage said that two "angels" appeared on the water above the Bay of Fundy where his mother's corpse floated near their overturned car; and that they just kept smiling at him, keeping him company. According to Amherst RCMP Sergeant David Bogle, *...one of our officers was talking to him and he mentioned that he saw a couple of angels with wings on the water. Anything's possible; let's face it, when you look at someone surviving a crash like that.* Tobi's grandfather, Roy Gabriel, stood by his great-grandson's story, believing they saved his life. *He said he saw two women in white dresses standing in the water smiling at him all night. That's what kept him alive. If it wasn't for that, the boy would have died there in the rain.* Sergeant Bogle said he believes Gage's testimony about the angels because the toddler hadn't talked to any adults before he told it. *It sets you back on your heels in a way. He's three-years-old—how could he come up with this? There's a higher body than me or you.* (Halifax Daily News, Global Communications Corp., Canada). Need we be reminded that the little boy's family and the Archangel that greeted the Virgin Mary on the occasion of The Annunciation share the same surname? Another similar incident occurred in Perry, Georgia as told by Shelly Parker in the October 2002 issue of a trade magazine published by The National Reigning Horse Association, the *NRHA Reiner.* According to Ms. Parker, one of their best-known horse trainers and fellow cowboys, Ed Fear, suffered a cardiac arrest during an event in Perry, and a physician by the name of John Dorminy was unsuccessful in reviving him. Parker was saddened by the passing of her friend, but she was more moved by seeing the reaction of a young spectator in the grandstand named Aubrey Galbraith from Palm Beach Gardens, Florida. The little girl was sitting on another person's lap almost asleep when Ed Fear entered the rodeo ring. According to Ms. Parker, the child raised her head quite coherently and trained her attention poignantly upon him from the moment he first appeared before the crowd, after completing his rodeo ride, and until he walked out of the pen. She just could not seem to take her eyes off of him; and Ms. Parker was quite amazed by whatever it was that had surreally captured the attention of little Aubrey. That is when a large group of people gathered around him and the doctor began the procedure of trying to restore the regular beat of Mr. Fear's fibrillating heart. Shelly Parker concluded her magazine article by saying, *I'm sure to the untrained eye it would seem that he was hurting Ed rather than helping. Aubrey (was asked) to put her head down and go to sleep, but (she) would have no part of that. She asked a question that stood the hair up on my arms. 'Why are they killing that man?' Meagan Boswell, on whose lap the little girl lay, told her, 'Baby, they're trying to help him, not kill him.' Aubrey replied, 'No, they're trying to kill him. I see two angels with him. They're trying to help him.' Meagan tried to comfort Aubrey by saying, 'No, baby, God's with him. He's going to be alright.' Aubrey insisted, 'I know he's going to be alright because I see the angels with him.' Understanding the innocence of a child, I believe they get to see what we, as adults, are no longer able to see. That night, I do believe that Aubrey Galbraith saw two angels with Ed Fear.*

There are many other such stories which recount harrowing events involving our little children that have been reported in the news and spread like wildfire in the streets and on various TV talk shows. When we see all of them in their gory detail, it makes us feel glad to be alive, blessed to be members of the Church, and honored to be chosen worthy of sharing in the Passion of Jesus Christ. All of these have earned us the title of "disciples" in the Kingdom of God, and deemed credible in our faith so sufficiently that we are given an honorary role to play in Redeeming humanity. Although we are incapable of seeing it with our eyes, God metabolizes the food of our sacrifices into a nutritional ambrosia which keeps the hopes and spiritual well-being alive for millions of people around the globe. On the other hand, it is nearly inconceivable what some people will do only for themselves and try to pulverize it with makeup in an effort to convince Jesus Christ that their labors have always been for Him. However, the tangible fruits and the manifestation of the fertile cultures of Grace we are harvesting cannot be misconstrued in such awkward ways. The question always remains in the back of people's minds as to what sort of contribution such individuals as Gage's mother make whose lives are ended much too precipitously, those who die suddenly in the wrecks of airplanes, trains, and motor-cars. What about the thousands who die in America every year by physical violence, gunfire, and other such cataclysmic tragedies? What role do they play in building-up the Body of Christ and growing the life of His Church? The answer is that they are among the hundreds-of-thousands of anonymous Martyrs whose lives become entangled in the recklessness of the Earth; and God is calling them to His side to focus our attention back upon the Cross. And, while we may not know where every unfortunate accident occurs every day or when somebody's life is snuffed-out by upheaval and carelessness, the identity of every single one of them is known by Divine prefiguration to the Author of human life. There are a couple of Midwestern cliches which apply to the dangerous world in which we live today and how Satan takes advantage of our lacking any substantial defense against the peril in which he places our lives. They are "loose cannon" and "fly off the handle." Am I saying that God watches in disinterest while evil forces ambush the most delicate and vulnerable attributes of our existence between the gnarling teeth of catastrophe and neglect? This is absolutely not the case; rather it is that we humans open the door for outright lethal sorcery to walk in by refusing to embrace the fortified security of His Resurrected Son. We give venue to the fiendish demons in Creation to wreak havoc, destruction, and death upon God's people because we decline to live prayerfully or give our guardian angels the opportunity to protect us. Most people do not believe in them anyway or ask them to come within earshot of their whimpering, while still wondering how to evoke God's greater compassion. We frighten the angels away like scattering doves because they would rather not be located anywhere within the proximity of the demons inside us. It is the enemies of the peace of Jesus Christ who coax us into believing that it is spiritually beneficent to fly overhead like bees and daredevils in acrobatic circles inside jet fighters, pop wheelies and jump midair across canyons on motorcycles, and drive 200+ miles-per-hour in high-tech race cars around blacktop tracks. There is never enough danger, it would seem, in human life as it is without our creating even more; establishing conditions in which such participants are routinely subjected to being either seriously harmed or qualified for the fate of death. If any competitor in the Indianapolis 500 or at the Daytona International Speedway ever asked his guardian angel to hop into his car and hold-on for the ride, his invisible advocate from the other side of life would probably quickly retort, *No, but thanks anyway. I'm doing perfectly fine hovering right where I am!* Even though angels are fully immune to death, there is no doubt that they would never endorse the antics of a flippant human being who gambles with it like it is a penny-ante in a gin-rummy game. We would amend our conduct for the better if more of us believed in them and heeded their warning from God.

What we are learning is that injecting ourselves into harm's way is an act of defiance to the Creator who gives us life; and the survivors of the victims are the ones who really suffer. It is their grief which becomes the nourishment for the ever-changing face of our refined human conversion. When we make fateful decisions too hastily, off-the-cuff, or to benefit only our own personal expedience, other people get hurt; and they are usually the innocent ones. We may try to hide our negligence from one another once in awhile to coerce our friends into condoning our perilous schemes, but our reputation will always precede us in the eyes of Jesus Christ; for He knows full-well what we are capable of doing. There are many occasions when the Holy Spirit has attempted to circumvent our carelessness by interceding with more protection from Heaven than we really know about. This is why such things have happened as when Gerald Kelly and his wife Nelda went to a private airport in New Mexico and rented a single-engine Cessna airplane to take a short flight. When Gerald began to taxi onto the runway, his eyeglasses fogged-over for no apparent reason. He gave them to his wife and asked her to wipe them for him, which she did, and handed them back. Almost immediately, they fogged-up again. Somehow, Gerald knew that something was amiss, so he turned the plane around and headed back to the terminal. Almost immediately thereafter, the engine stopped running. After getting out of the cockpit and securing the services of a mechanic, they removed the engine cowling and discovered a faulty fuel valve that had killed the engine without notice. If he had not returned, the plane would have malfunctioned in mid-flight, and Gerald and Nelda Kelly would have died in the crash. What was causing his eyeglasses to fog? We may all get to Heaven someday and see the Son of God blowing His breath upon the lenses of Gerald's spectacles so he could not see to fly. Such close calls are oftentimes so frequent that they are too numerous to mention here; but there are televised programs on the airwaves all the time to recount the inexplicable good fortune of some people whose parachutes have failed to open, who have fallen into dry wells and off of tenth-floor balconies, been exposed alone for days without food or shelter in inclement weather, or who lost their way back to safety on wilderness trails; and many of them survived without so much as a scratch.

There was even a testimony that aired in 1992 about a couple named Robert Shay and Janet Rule who were married and conceived a little boy, Teddy. His parents had been lovers since they were young and in school, and Robert once penned the letters ILVU4FR in Janet's school yearbook, which was an acronym for "I love you forever." He had studied to become a commercial artist, and was successful in landing a job with a firm in New York City. He went there to make the arrangements, and was planning to return home to move Janet and Ted to New York with him when he was involved in a fatal traffic accident with another driver who was intoxicated behind the wheel. His death left both Janet and little Ted, who was four-years-old at the time, completely unable to fend for themselves. The $6,000 that Robert and Janet had saved in the bank had dwindled to $1,200 after Janet paid his funeral expenses. She was in total despair as to what to do next. One day, while Janet and Ted were sitting at their kitchen table, she nearly broke into tears wondering how they would survive. She called upon Robert from the depths of her despondence and, at that very moment, little Ted took his crayons in hand and began to etch characters onto his drawing paper. He offered them to his mother and told her that his Daddy had just spoken to him and asked him to show her the drawings he had inscribed. But, she did not know what they could have possibly meant. So, she went to visit one of her late husband's college friends, Jack Knowles, who said that he recognized what Ted had written as the likeness of the shorthand that he and Robert shared between them when they were in school. So, he took the drawing paper upon which Ted had written the characters and translated the following coded message: ILVU24FR. Then, Janet's heart began to race with joy because she recognized the inscription from Robert's earlier writing in her school yearbook. This time, however, he added a "2" because Robert wished to tell his little son that he loved him, also. Keep in mind that Teddy could not read or write a single letter of the alphabet. The rest of the message that he wrote was as follows: MDTNBK34STBX1142. After some mutual consultation, Jack and Janet came to the conclusion that the message had something to do with Robert's affairs in New York City. It occurred to them that the code referred to: Midtown Bank, 34th Street in Manhattan, lockbox number 1142. So, she traveled to New York, went into the bank, and asked the teller there if she could look into their lockbox with that number. After verifying Robert's signature on the box lease, she was allowed into the vault; and it is there that she opened lockbox number 1142 and discovered $925.00 cash currency in bills tied together with a rubber band. Knowing that this would barely cover the costs of her flight to New York, she reached to close the box when she noticed another envelope in the corner. She quickly opened it and found a life insurance policy that Robert had taken-out not long before he died with a face value of $100,000. And, it carried an extra benefit of double indemnity in case Robert lost his life by accidental death. Janet and Teddy now owned $200,000 with which to continue their lives. The obvious question is, was it a voice from the man in the grave who miraculously transmitted to his son the information that played such a crucial role in ensuring the well-being and fiscal solvency of his surviving family members?

It is very important that the entire globe hear testimonies such as these because they are proof of the intervention of the Kingdom of God into our material world. However, it is too bad that so many opportunists, ambulance chasers, rumor-mills, and media outlets scandalize the suffering of other people by attempting to profit from their publicity. With regard to the latter, if any one of them ever inherited a suitable conscience, he would turn to the others in his profession while thinking about the things that keep the Earth in so much turmoil and declare with a signal of firm conviction, *We've seen the enemy, and he's us!* The prying eyes and sensational rhetoric that surrounds our personal grief at times is a great tragedy in its own right. The devastated lives of our sorrowing neighbors and friends should never be used as tools for copping the profits of free speech. There is something to be said about better discretion, and we could all take a lesson from the dignified way that most people handle themselves during times of sudden misfortune, even when they have no time to adjust to the abrupt alterations of their otherwise normal lives or to prepare for the loss of someone dear. God apparently knows it, too, or He would not have our faithfully departed relatives speaking to their little children who are stationed in front of their coloring books. We try to be helpless romantics at times, but fate will not always accord us the conditions under which we can capture the aura. We know that onlookers always cheer the loudest when "the good guys" take the lead; our friends always seem closer to us after they have passed-away; and cold beer always tastes best when the bartender shouts, "last call," as he turns the rheostat to bring-up the house lights. But, there is no way we can romanticize about the matter-of-fact suffering that some people endure. There is precious little we can do to reverse the critical effects of time, and a smaller amount that would restore normalcy to the lives that have been changed for the worse by losing their relatives who may have lingered for months on their deathbeds and are, themselves, quite grateful to now be in Heaven. What good offices do we hold to explain the article that was in the news in June 2002 about a little 22-month-old girl named Miracle who survived ten days on whatever food she could find in her family's kitchen cabinets and pantry after her pregnant mother, Lawarna Stevenson, age 26, died in their apartment in Atlanta? Authorities responded to complaints from her neighbors of a foul odor and swarms of flies, broke down her door, and found the toddler standing next to her deceased mother's body that was so decomposed that the woman had to be identified by her dental records and fingerprints. A medical examiner later ruled that Ms. Stevenson died from complications of sugar diabetes and elevated blood pressure. As for little Miracle, she was taken to the hospital and treated for malnutrition and dehydration, and then released into her grandfather's custody. Let's see if we have this right—the little girl was still sixty days shy of being a full two years old! We have yet to hear all there is to learn about this story, knowing what the angels probably said to her about where to find her food, and how to cleanse herself. But, we will someday! We shall discover the mystery surrounding the child named Miracle. It is inevitable and a mathematical certainty that the entire world will know.

And, then, what will the uncertain future hold for the millions of people around the globe who have previously scoffed at the supernatural intercession of God as being a mere coincidence, happenstance, or a matter of the configuration of the stars in the skies?  If all else fails us now, let our faith never give way or surrender to the daily mantra of things we cast-off in favor of more visible attractions.  There are still too many Glory-days to come for us to succumb to the delusion of the cyclical trauma of mortal life and the tinny sounds of panhandlers' pleas and butcher knives.  There are thousands more little heroes for us to rescue and imitate, and too much going on behind the scenes for us to assume that it all has nothing to do with us.  Once the panorama of unseen Creation comes bursting through the seams of the physical world, we will be inundated by the flood of Divine Truth slapping us in the face; and our dyadic systems will all defer to the Singular God of Preeminent Domain.  Isn't it ironic that He has seen fit to reveal His presence to the mortal Earth as One God in Three, the thrice-Blessed Trinity: the Father, the Son, and the Holy Spirit; and yet the entire mesmerization of America during the 1990s was a product of a binary code?  In the computer world, a zero is used to represent the electronic state of *off*, and a "1" to represent the electronic state of *on*.  A binary digit is a "bit" and a group of eight bits is a "byte" in which there are 256 possibilities that can be represented by using all the combinations of 0s and 1s.  From this simple phenomenon, entire computer languages have been written, two of which are the American Standard Code for Information Exchange (ASCII), and the Extended Binary Coded Decimal Interchange Code (EBCDIC), the latter for use primarily on mainframe computers.  Within the Kingdom of Jesus Christ, however, there are no such things as circuit motherboards, megabytes, or digitizing.  Human suffering cannot be measured by an on-off switch or colored in two distinct hues of black and white.  It may affect humanity indiscriminately as a living species, but quite disproportionately when seen through the eyes of the poor.  And, it is to the poor that God has given Himself, Body and Soul, to endure their poverty so they can share in His Eternal Divinity.  Hereafter, those whose joy seems difficult in coming will discover its exaltation rather easily; the blunt-force of negligence will surrender to the pampering of suppliant Love, and the Light of resurrected humankind will outshine the monstrosities of hatred which have been the ritual of the world since God first took a pensive look at the inequities we have created of our own accord below His Heavenly Throne.  There is a gaping hole left to be filled in the void we have manufactured between what we have promised Him we would do upon the occasion of our Baptism and the paltry amount we are actually doing to set aside our prejudices in favor of a single-minded world in search of the advantages of the heart.  When we are Baptized in Christ, we are telling Him that we wish to bear the burdens of the rest of humanity with ours.  We are not saying, "God, please save my soul, and to Hell with everybody else."  It is a revealing moment during which our eyes are opened to the grotesque poverty into which billions of people around the globe are thrown because of the blindness of the rich. We hold an historic opportunity in our hands these days to convince God that we trust His Will, believe in His power, embrace His Love, and respect His Judgement; and that it is our own flawed decision-making processes that are the begetting of so much international grief.

When we stand in the Light of Truth someday and crank our necks around to see our own shadows, what will be there? Will our past show us to have taken-on a gruesome configuration that we never really knew we had? The mirror in front of our faces before which we stand today to greet the morning dawn does not always reveal everything that is haunting us from the inside. Indeed, if we could miraculously hear it, what would be the substance of a private conversation between our mind, body, and soul if they could actually speak to one another? There is no doubt that in those who espouse only hatred, their spirit turns to their flesh to say, "It is as cold as ice in here," to which their flesh responds, "it's because the heart of the man we comprise is as frozen as the Yukon Klondike." The function of the human heart is not only to keep the physical body alive, but the Son of God has employed it as a parable in His spiritual teachings, i.e, we believe that Love comes from the heart, and it is this same Love that sustains our lives beyond the darkness of the grave. It is our lack of affection that causes us to fall prey to the evil legions of the world and to describe our brothers as being scum-bags, sleazy freaks, and skuzz-balls instead of our poor fellow sinners. I have come to the conclusion that it is to mitigate such things as these that God allows some people to suffer; especially the innocent; to evoke pity from the whole of humanity toward the untold numbers who are afflicted. No one is a solitary piece of driftwood on the high-seas of reality anymore because He has reconstructed us into a unified frigate of Mystical Grace whose commission is to reach the shores of His Paradisial Arms. We belong to a Divine Omnipotence of such great magnitude that our passage into immortality will leave the physical nature of our present existence absolutely breathless; as it has for the countless souls who have already crossed the Bar. For all practical purposes, we die in order to Live again; and this should more than satisfy our voracious curiosity for discovering everything that is yet unknown. If we try to draw a comparison between the way we are suffering here in America today and that of the ages past, and even in other lands, it may not be accepted very well in the eyes of God because of the lavishness with which we have surrounded ourselves. But, even in all of this, we live in a free society that is fraught with dead-ends, traffic jams, nauseating hang-overs, gross transiency, marked irresolution, our brethren's pretenses, and their capitalistic chatter-boxing. How do we know? What kind of civility can be found in the United States when its 41st President campaigns for re-election in October 1992 and speaks of the two opposing candidates for the office of president and vice-president, to whom he eventually lost, by exclaiming, *My dog Millie knows more about foreign policy than these two Bozos!* So, must the rest of us suffer in order for the world to regain a sense or semblance of dignity from the human infestation residing upon it like ticks and fleas? We may have to wait until the end of time to find the answers to some of these questions. But, meanwhile, it looks like our materialistic world will continue to grovel in such rationalistic themes as inorganic asynchronous modes, virtual reality, streaming videos, proxy servers, multitasking, and defragmentation.

Let's try another dose of hard reality on for size as a case in point. A woman named Tammy Hill, her seven-year-old son Titus, and her two younger daughters Tiffany and Tier were riding home in her pickup truck from a Thanksgiving dinner in November 2002 near Greeley, Colorado when the vehicle veered-off the road and rolled over several times. The children were all wearing pajamas, and they all escaped serious injury. But, their mother was thrown from the truck and was rendered unconscious. So Titus, whose last name is Adams, walked without any shoes to get her help. His father, Glenn Adams, said that the boy trekked across a muddy field, squeezed under an electric fence, and had to break a gate on another fence to get through. He came upon some dairy workers who were standing nearby and told them about the accident; and they called the authorities to respond. The paramedics who arrived at the scene said that it was apparent that the woman would not have survived if Titus had waited for a passerby, rather than running for help. The police and medical staff said he was a hero, according to his father, claiming that he had saved his mother's life. (Associated Press). In a related incident, another six-year-old boy by the name of Brent Moral from Springfield, Illinois was just as heroic. His mother, Laura Moral, had gone-out of the house to her 1998 Toyota Sienna and fastened her two youngest children into their car seats one day in February 2002, while Brent belted himself in. The vehicle would not start, so Ms. Moral put the shift-lever in neutral and began to push it out of the garage, hoping to get a jump-start. But, her driveway was on a hillside and the SUV began to roll away from her. She was pulled underneath it and dragged to the end of the driveway near the curb where she became pinned beneath it with its weight resting on her chest. She started screaming, not really knowing what else to do. She told Brent to run into the house where his uncles and cousins were asleep inside. He replied, *OK, Mommy, I'll be right back!* But, rather than try to explain it to his relatives, the little boy rushed into the home, picked-up the telephone, and dialed 911. It was later learned that Brent's parents had recently allowed him to visit Fire Station No. 7 in Springfield with a group of Boy Scouts only a month prior to the incident to teach them about the importance of the 911 emergency system. (Sarah Antonacci, *The State Journal Register*, Springfield, Illinois). After a while, does the world not begin to see the strength and innovation which emanates from our little children? Are not many of them our true heroes, while we adults who hide behind our fears and material possessions the real cowards of Creation. There is one thing that the likes of Gage Gabriel, Aubrey Galbraith, Teddy Shay, Miracle Stevenson, Titus Adams, and Brent Moral have in common. They are the consummate incarnation of greatness that comes only from God; that innocent and innovative desire for human survival based upon the Truth they know, and in direct contradiction to the lies they never learned. When we see them in their unintentional valor, it makes us believe that the same valiancy can live in us, too.

How do we bring such goodness to the peaks of our consciousness like cream in our confections? By imitating the acts of our young offspring as we approach daily life with the Sacred Heart of God on our minds. And, if the Most Blessed Virgin Mary comes to us in the dark of night through the many miracles of which the Earth is full, tells us that the transgressions of the human race are too burdensome for Her Immaculate Heart to bear, and that we should climb to the summits of the globe and tell all the world that Jesus Christ has expunged them for us, we should move as briskly as any six-year-old can scamper up the driveway while saying at the top of our lungs, *OK, Mommy, I'll be right back!* We should never stop to ask Her why, always understand that our pathways will be made clear, continue to repeat the message in our heads, and never allow a single obstacle to keep us from our mission or any enticement to distract us into looking another way. The temporal world is not just gruesome, it is often repugnant, grisly, shocking, horrid, and horrendous. If the condition of our collective souls were to be listed on the public record, God would have the right to proclaim us to be in gravely serious spiritual health—close to losing everything we have to the perils of our vast mortality. Little children suffer because we impose inordinate agony upon them, requiring them to hoist the effects of our loathsome indignation upon their little shoulders that even our greatest war Generals have never commanded from their most highly-trained foot soldiers. Why suffering? Because God knows it to be the only way we will stop celebrating our own arrogance long enough to listen to the perfection of His Holy Love that is pouring-down from Heaven in gushes to aid in our glorification of Him. Jesus was born as a little Baby in Bethlehem because He wishes us to become like Him in every way pertaining to a child who is dependent upon his mother and his God for guidance and nourishment. And, why do we know only very little about His years between the ages of twelve and thirty? In my view, it is because we are supposed to see Him as the innocent Alpha and the humble-but-courageous Sacrificial Omega. His first and last acts as a sinless man embrace the innocuous manifestations of a King in the Flesh of a Baby and a Martyr of 33 years who was willing to die to prove it. Let the record show that He did both with the perfection of the God in whose shoes He walked with courage amidst the land mines of the Earth. In Him, we shall live as all those little champions who know not to retreat when they see the suffering of other men, but who remain composed in the strength of the Holy Spirit, yearn to seek the Truth when the world languishes in torment, and trust the angels to protect us when the cup of human suffering is suddenly passed to us.

Fortunately for them, and on behalf of the God who loves them, there are multitudes of insightful citizens who really care what they mean to Creation and the future of humanity. When they fall into illness and sickness, Jesus places healers and caretakers among them to deliver the *masse* shot of loving compassion that only His Kingdom can effect. These are the people of upright nobility who stand perpendicular to the ordinary passivity of the everyday world. Their purpose is to imitate the service of the canonized Saints; and many in their number have lived and died in our age; people such as "the Lady with the Lamp," the humble nurse Florence Nightingale (1820-1910); Louis Pasteur (1822-1895) whose discoveries in immunology and bacteriology led to the disease preventing process called the pasteurization of milk which bears his name; American microbiologist Jonas Salk (1914-1995), who founded the University of Pittsburgh's Research Laboratory and in 1954 discovered the first successful vaccine against Polio, and the countless number of other doctors and medical professionals in our modern day whose research and labors have become the restoration of good health and convalescence of millions of children around the globe. One in particular whose work is worthy of citation especially in America is Dr. Peter Doherty, PhD in Immunology, who was awarded the Nobel Prize for Medicine in 1996 for his laboratory excellence in his field. Dr. Doherty worked extensively through the St. Jude Children's Research Hospital in Memphis, Tennessee, which was started by a popular Hollywood entertainer in 1962. The history of this dignitary's founding of the Hospital is an evocative dissertation in its own right. His birth name was Muzyad Yakhoob of Arabic descent, and he later took the surname Amos Jacobs. He is remembered best, however, as the talented stage-player and children's advocate, Danny Thomas (1912-1991). Anyway, it is widely known that he began as a pauper in search of a new beginning in America. He had $7.00 in his pocket one day, walked into a Church in Detroit, knelt down to pray for help before a statue of St. Jude Thaddeus (the Patron Saint of hopeless

*The Providence of Human Suffering*     *147*

cases), and said, *Show me my way in life, and I will build you a shrine.* His prayers were answered after he moved his family to Chicago, Illinois and he went on to greater things. His career as an entertainer burgeoned through film-screen and television; and it was not long before he became a nationally known figure. And, Danny Thomas kept his promise to his old friend, St. Jude, the 1st century son of Alphaeus, who was a playmate and comrade to another little boy known as Jesus Christ in the backyards and alleyways of their youthful boroughs. Danny remembered his oath to erect a shrine. So, with the help of his friends of Arabic heritage, he raised the money to found the St. Jude Children's Hospital in Memphis. According to their global Web site, www.stjude.org, it is now recognized as one of the premier centers for the study and treatment of catastrophic illnesses in children. They practice research and curing pediatric leukemia, performing bone marrow transplantation, chemotherapy, studying the biochemistry of cancerous cells, radiation treatment, parasitic viruses, hereditary diseases, influenza, and the psychological effects accompanying these illnesses. As of the beginning of 2003, St. Jude had treated more than 19,000 children from across America and 60 foreign nations. And, every one of them was accepted by physician referral because the patient had a newly diagnosed disease that was under research at the St. Jude facility. What is another revealing fact? All St. Jude patients are admitted regardless of their ability to pay. And, because of the massive involvement of pediatric care for blood cancers and solid-tumor malignancies, the Hospital has an average daily operating cost of $700,000. They accept donations from the general public to offset these expenses; and every Christian should remember them in their charitable giving. Danny Thomas died on February 6, 1991 and was laid to rest at the Pavilion on the grounds of the Hospital in Memphis. Rose Marie Thomas, his wife, died on July 12, 2000 and is buried beside her husband in the Memorial Garden.

As Our Lord Himself once said, there is not enough room in the universe to contain all the books that could be written about His life and teachings, the biographies and histories of all the people He touched, and how we continue to move with great compassion to become His likeness in a world that is agonizing more now than during any period in its previous existence. However, I would like to elegize one more little girl in particular whose suffering was well known in the southern Illinois counties of Clinton, Bond, and Madison because of her obvious debilitated condition. She was Judy Kay Heather, who was born on March 7, 1944 to (the late) Thomas W. Heather and his wife, Alta (Parsons)Heather, who hailed from the Village of Keyesport, Illinois on the bank of the Kaskaskia River for the better part of their younger years, later moving to my hometown of Ashland in 1956. God gave little Judy to the Heather family when not a great deal was known about congenital diseases other than those deformities which were obvious to the naked eye. Her eldest sister, Carolyn Jane (Heather) McDonald, who relocated to Davenport, Iowa in the late 1960s, was very kind to offer a testimonial for this book that she penned on October 2, 2002 about Judy, which I will always treasure as being a prayer from her heart. Its text  reads as follows: *A very special little girl, who only lived to be five-years-old, was born an invalid. The doctors told Mom and Dad that she was born with "infantile paralysis." I don't think anyone knows for sure why she was born that way, or what it means. Although she could not walk, talk, or do anything that a five-year-old child could do, she tugged at the strings of my heart; for she was my little sister. From the time she was born, we all knew that she was a very special little girl. Although I was only four-years-old when she was born, I grew-up taking care of her. I talked to her everyday; and I was nine-years-old the day she passed-away. I can remember it like it was yesterday. I always took care of her when I got home from school; that was my first stop when I got there. It was as though she knew my voice; and she would smile at me when I talked to her. Sometimes, I would put her in her highchair—she would have to be tied into it so she wouldn't fall out. She had a beautiful smile; and she loved to sit in that chair. She loved it when I would take her by the hands and play 'patty cakes' with her; and she would kind-of smile at me and make a sighing noise like she was trying to laugh. She would tire easily, though, so she spent most of her time in bed. She was a beautiful child with blonde hair and blue eyes—such a tiny thing for five years. I came home from school one day and could tell something was wrong. Mom and Dad were visibly upset and tried to stop me before I went into the bedroom. But, it was too late. When I saw the empty crib, I knew that my little sister Judy had gone to Heaven. I was devastated the day she passed-away. I hid in the hallway and cried for hours; until I cried myself to sleep. It left a very empty feeling in my heart; and when I think of her now after all these years, I still have that 'empty' feeling. Sometimes it overwhelms me because I didn't get to tell her goodbye. I'm happy I was there for her because we had a very special relationship. For some reason, we always connected with each other. I will always remember her because she was a gift from God to us; and He had special plans for her. He needed another angel.*

Judy Kay Heather died in January 1949; and her etiologies that were common in such pediatric patients back then were the direct result of the inflammation of the nerve cells; mainly in the arms, legs, neck, and spinal cord; which resulted in the paralysis of the limbs, followed by muscular atrophy and deterioration into permanent disability. Upon further research, we discovered that the medical term for "infant paralysis" is poliomyelitis, or Polio. The Jonas Salk vaccine came a mere decade too late to stop the virus that took the life of little Judy Kay Heather. Because of the paralysis of the diaphragm in her abdomen that involuntarily controls the breathing in humans, the medical examiner concluded that her death was caused by acute asphyxiation. In effect, she just went to sleep one day and woke-up on the other side of life in the Arms of Jesus Christ and in the presence of the Angels and Saints, where she is still resting to this very hour. There were twelve children born to the Heather family, three of them who died very young, including another daughter named Patty who was struck and killed by an automobile in 1959 near the schoolhouse in Ashland, not long after their family had relocated there. We can look in almost any direction and see someone who has either been afflicted by the ravages of disease or has lost one of their loved-ones under severe duress. People like Florence Nightingale and Danny Thomas knew it, all our physicians and scientists know it, and so do the hundreds-of-thousands of people who are working the clock around to somehow manifest a cure for every kind of ailment that still brings the curse of infirmity upon the peoples of the world. There is too much work for us to do to sit on our hands and wait for an occasional hero to emerge. We are the elect who have been chosen by God to employ the power of the intellect for the only two good roles it will ever play: to the eradication of human suffering and the enlightenment of the collective human spirit about our Salvation in the Blood of Jesus on the Cross. We do not become Christians with a disclaimer that says that if we are given an opportunity to act but feel unmoved to do so because of the trepidation of the fight, we are excused from trying. There is no such thing as waiting for another day when we think conditions will be more amenable for us to act without having to pour-out our heart and soul in succeeding.

There is another organization that is taking world poverty head-on with this same kind of courage: Catholic Relief Services. Their mission is to help the poor and vulnerable overseas; and 90% of all their support goes directly to those who are in need. Their main office is located in Baltimore, Maryland; and their global Web site is www.catholicrelief.org. The arrival of 2003 brought the anniversary of their 60th year in operation, having begun their charitable works of feeding, housing, and caring for impoverished people in the international community in 1943. It was started in an effort to assist the victims of the Second World War in Europe; and they now have an outreach program that spans the undeveloped regions of 80 countries. In places where the spread of AIDS is rampant, they deliver food and other provisions to those who have fallen victim to its horrible effects, and to the families who survive. In Africa alone, more people will die of AIDS by 2010 than perished in all the world wars of the 20th century! Starving refugees are fleeing to safety in places like Kosova, Bosnia, Afghanistan, Pakistan, and other Third World countries whose names most Americans have never even heard of. Afghan families have been uprooted by recent years of drought, twenty years of war, and the aftermath of the military strikes by the United States in response to the terrorist attacks of September 11, 2001. We tend to forget here in America that the price for our western freedom oftentimes comes at the suffering of innocent civilians who are caught in the crossfire between our U.S. armaments and our intended targets in their lands. When the Catholic Relief Services takes their caravans of charitable gifts into such places as Kenya, Nairobi, Nicaragua, Egypt, Cambodia, Ethiopia, and the Democratic Republic of Congo, they see firsthand the squalid conditions in which we in the richest nation on Earth have allowed their poor children to live. This brings great shame upon America; and we shall pay the price before the Throne of God for our stinginess someday! In North Viet Nam, the floods of 2002 were the worst in 25 years. Did we read about them on the front page of our local express? Two typhoons hit the Mekong Delta during that same year and uprooted 200,000 people from their homes; and hundreds of unsuspecting people were flushed-down its open gullies to their deaths. Where was this grave news next to the DOW Jones Industrial Average? Countless homes, farms, streets, churches, and villages were destroyed in the Indian states of Orissa, West Bengal, Assam, and Uttar Pradesh. A massive super-cyclone hit Orissa in 1999 killing 30,000 people and virtually destroying the lives of millions more. And, through all of these catastrophes, Catholic Relief Services was there to lend a hand. They need America's help now, more than ever. Let there be no mistake, it does not take tree-twisting winds and waterfall monsoons to bring a civilization to its knees. There are over 40 million people who are living with HIV/AIDS worldwide as the third millennium opens; and these cases are only the ones we know about.

It seems as though our hopes always go "kaput" when we hear facts and statistics such as these because we feel helpless as to what we can really do for them while we are all trying to keep up with the Jones's here at home. We should likewise be unsurprised to learn that not every nation mourned with us when those terrorists did their dirty-work on the soil of our beloved homeland in September 2001. Why? Because America is seen as the world's gluttonous fat-cat whose greed is causing the peoples on other continents of the Earth to suffer so greatly. How soon we forget that we are not only one nation under God, but a single humanity as well. Surely our holy mosques, temples, synagogues, basilicas, cathedrals, and chapels are positioned out of kilter on an otherwise horizontal playing field if we choose to ignore the pleading wails of our brothers and sisters who spend their entire lives trying to fend for themselves in the bowels of our social gutters. Organized religion is only a hollow virtue if it is never used to manifest the good works of the past generations from whom we have inherited our faith. While I will be speaking about a *pendulum* again in Chapter XVI of this manuscript; and for reasons that are far beyond sublime; we must begin thinking about the reversal of fortune and fate by which the rich and poor are now improperly maligned in matters of magnitude and significance. If the relevance of the Holy Gospel is going to be duly incorporated into the architecture of this new century, we are going to be persuaded by our own compliance to do something to effect the equilibrium that has heretofore been lacking. Again, I am not advocating a single world government with socialistic ideals because there are not enough well-intentioned leaders in our midst to keep themselves honest. We should be searching for values that are much more telling than how we shall be governed in the future as segregated republics; but how we might pull together as a species with a common cause, regardless of the color of our skin, national origin, gender, ethnic background, or financial status. Each of us is a subpart of the whole of "something" that only few visionary icons in the annals of history have been capable of defining. Even then, many of their voices have become silenced by thugs and assassins' bullets and drowned-out by the rattling of sabers echoing across the white-capped seas. Or, they may have finally seen enough indignance in other men that they have foregone their hopes of ever changing the Earth, so they have crawled into a hole of anonymity in sorrowful resignation. There is a religious sect that still practices their beliefs quite prolifically around the world that was founded in England by a peaceful man named George Fox in AD 1650 called the Religious Society of Friends, otherwise known as Quakers. They are commonly opposed to any oath-taking, and are staunchly against engaging in any kind of warfare. Their members have reached prominent places of power and influence in society and governmental affairs; and one example is the 37th President of the United States, Richard Milhous Nixon. As a matter of record, he took the oath of office and engaged in the tactics of war for our nation's defense. I remember watching his funeral broadcasted on live television from Yorba Linda, California upon his death in mid-April 1994, and how the venerable Reverend Billy Graham, who was his personal friend, kept referring to the late President as a Saint who had rejoined his earlier departed wife, Pat, with God in Heaven. On a side note; even though I was very young when he held office, I have always respected President Nixon very much for the dignified way he addressed the people of the United States and the billions of foreigners in other lands he visited during his trips abroad. I believe to this day that one of the reasons why the People's Republic of China has not blown the Western Hemisphere completely off the map is because of the kind diplomacy of leaders like Richard M. Nixon. He was also said to have been pretty adept at playing the piano—a trait that I have always admired in anyone who is so inclined and ambidextrous!

But, how could a practicing Quaker continue to embrace his deep religious convictions and become the Commander-in-Chief of the greatest military in the history of civilization? Inside the answer to this question is the key to the coexistence of secularism and ecclesiastical religiosity. Like President Nixon, who stopped the Viet Nam war on January 27, 1973, we must ultimately decide whether the waging of the hottest battles of human conflict is worth the price of the melt-down that might ensue if the war, itself, is ever to be won. We held the nuclear arsenals in our possession to flatten North Viet Nam in the same way we did Japan in WWII, but we did not wish to initiate the nuclear holocaust that would result. We learned a valuable lesson in Southeast Asia because we were willing to concede to conventional fighting for fear of destroying the entire planet if we chose a more lethal campaign of nuclear annihilation. This discussion, therefore, is a perfect microcosm of how we approach the strife and turmoil of a poor humanity in this post-modern era. How? It seems as though we can never eradicate poverty from every last nook and cranny of the Earth, so we draw a line in the sand and conclude that it would be better to sustain ourselves with what provisions we have at our disposal than to "drop the big one" on Satan by utterly dismantling our capitalist democracy, selling our civilian and military assets to the world's billionaires, and procuring food for every last soul who now relies on those benevolent relief organizations that I spoke about in the previous paragraphs. The problem is that our definition of "the war" is not as clear as we think it is. We see our enemies as anyone who tries to take away our material possessions, limit our human rights, and infringe upon our self-capacity to choose our public officials by the majority-rule of our nation's electorate—which are quite worthy and tenable issues to defend. On the other hand, if ever there existed a nation which espouses Christianity as an open spiritual institution that lives in almost diametric opposition to the Commandments and the Messianic Beatitudes that Jesus pronounced in the Sermon on the Mount, it is the United States of America. If we ever suddenly became humble enough to relinquish our heirlooms of self-ingratiation, individual pride, public expedience, personal partisanship, and isolationist independence, who is to say that the Son of God might not respond in-kind by summarily delivering every happiness we ever hoped for to our nation's doorstep anyway? After all, stranger things than this have occurred. Just ask the Biblical figures Saul, Job, and Jonah. The thesis of this discussion, therefore, centers around our reluctance to become poor in the physical sense so as to grow rich in spiritual Love. This is what made the likes of Richard Nixon arrive at the conclusion that there is really no mandate for interpersonal conflict.

I also recall seeing Edward Nixon seated in the row of mourners during his brother's 1994 funeral service in Yorba Linda. He was slouching with a rather broken posture and a sad look on his face while the assembled dignitaries and the President's former colleagues offered eulogies for whom former Secretary of State, Dr. Henry Kissinger, called...*our gallant friend.* One speaker after the next took to the microphone to honor the life of Mr. Nixon; such notable public servants as Senator Robert Dole from Kansas, then-California Governor Pete Wilson, and other high ranking officials. I particularly remember Senator Dole breaking into tears at the end of his speech during which he would say something notable that Richard Nixon had done while repeating the phrase,...*how American!* Let's be clear about one more thing in passing. If there is anyone alive on the Earth who does not respect honored heroes like Robert Dole and U.S. Senator John McCain (R-AZ), they have got some extremely serious psychological problems. Ed Nixon shed a few tears that day, too; along with the rest of us, because he was shorn of words that could accurately describe the compassion in his heart for a man and an American legend whom he loved and admired. My question is this: why must we wait until the greatness in us dies into the dust before we hear any eloquent speeches about it? Remembering true remarkableness only for the purpose of sealing history inside a wooden coffin beneath the surface of the ground seems too much like petting a dog *after* he has bitten you. The point is, let us travel the globe with the gifts of nourishment, sustenance, and dignity in our hands to the alleviation of human suffering before our brethren are forced into their own graves by our defiant negligence. If we do this, then the hierarchy of Heaven will yield the podium so that we can deliver our valedictory address before the entire gamut of galaxies and universes; just in time for Christ to hand us over to His Father as being justified in our faith. When Pope Paul VI (1897-1978) proclaimed, *If you want peace, then search for Justice,* perhaps his audience included individuals like President Nixon, who died at 81, so that a Quaker could run for the office of U.S. president and not violate the tenets of his religious faith. And, it is the same reason why we should struggle for equal rights between the nations of the Earth in our day; not waiting a moment longer to begin the process of releasing our counterparts around the globe from the chains of poverty and disease. Then, and only then, will there be Justice; and thereafter, surer peace. I certainly do not propose to imply that solving such international problems will ever be an easy task. But, making the appropriate choices through the elimination of the agony of mortal men is something that is well within the concepts and capacity of the designs of Creation. Satan does not have the horsepower, the venue, or the fortitude to lay waste to the Mystical Body of Christ if we band together and remain united against the evil legions who are the enemies of our personal dignity and Eternal Salvation.  If it seems as though they are defeating us anyway, it is because the prince of darkness has us assuming that we do not own the power to preside over his demise through the Light of the Cross.  Why have we failed to succeed?  Because we are still far too divided and not soundly convinced that we have already won.  Indeed, it appears that any attempt to station the provost of good will on the surface of the globe next to our human egocentrism is like carrying a flea beside a herd of African elephants across America on the roof of a Volkswagen Beetle.

This image is in direct contradiction to the acclamation that was made by Senator Dole at the funeral of Richard Nixon.  *He used to lay in bed as a young boy and listen to the train whistle in the night,* said Mr. Dole when reflecting upon the life of the fallen President.  And, that sound gave him the hope that there was an entire world of opportunity just waiting to be seized.  If we learn nothing more about the passing of great men, let us recall in their wakes that they, like the billions around the globe today, were once little children.  And, their heritage takes us back there time and again.  It is in this recollection that we shall reach-out with arms wide-open and innocence anew.  I penned the end of this chapter about the providence of human suffering realizing that there would be a fair number of knowing nods from readers everywhere who could grasp some sense of the decency and responsibility to which I have referred.  If we do not make good on our promises to become the extramundane essence of Wisdom and courage in our age, will we not be sorely lacking in the virtuous graces that have taken so many of our mentors to the heights of larger-than-life distinction?  If we decline to affirm our golden pledges to those whose hopes we see during our youthful days, like Danny Thomas did fifty years ago, or set-out with honesty to redeem them through the best means by which God has granted us the power, we will have a lot more to worry about come the end of time than which Saint we will see first when we get back to Paradise.  Changing the face of the Earth is going to take a lot more work than just clipping-off an occasional stray hair of inequity in East Timor or dabbing a smudge of rouge over the squalid corridors of Israel where the ugliness of crime and death are rampantly out of control.  Beyond any other parting; if we fail to deploy every sound weapon of righteousness against the prevailing forces of malevolence that are tearing our people's lives apart at the seams, then we are no better at being Christians than the secular masses have been in evangelizing Our Lord's Paschal Resurrection.  Are we so hypocritical that we place our spare coins in the Sunday collection plate with the expectation that we can bribe our way into immortal freedom? If we stand beside the Cross but never come into contact with it, we are only casual observers of Divine

Love who will someday soon be ushered out of the arena of God's Kingdom and cast into the darkness once again to beg, barter, and steal for an opportunity to garner a second chance.

In Jesus Christ, we are given the Grace that has become the healing of Creation, and to the interior beatification of the spirit which hears His call for us to begin the journey back, through Him, to the blessed fields of Love still blooming from His Crucifixion.   It seems, therefore, that we are both enlightened and burdened by Christianity because the liberties it espouses give us the freedom to bear our brothers' slights and shortcomings. This should be very good news ! It is true that there are too many millions who do not take their faith seriously; but even so, history has been spotted like a kingly leopard with giants among us who embraced and served humanity because it was the only way their consciences could survive.   Nobody ever said that the adornment of enrichment upon broken-humanity would be an exercise in leisure.   We need not look much farther than the life of Mother Teresa of Calcutta (1910-1997) as a prefigured example.   She attended a Eucharistic Congress in Pescara, Italy on September 20, 1977, the precise date of my sixteenth birthday, where she prayed deeply for those who were not only poor, but the tens-of-thousands who have been silently chosen by God to serve them.   No person on Earth knows more about self-sacrifice to ease the agony of the impoverished than she did. However, she was as human as anyone could be; and her heart had to fight against that slow, creeping depression that sometimes sets-in when Christians see that the rest of the world is not listening. It is to her memory that I dedicate this chapter; for Mother Teresa, like Pope John Paul II, has been the incarnate charity of the Son of God, Himself, during our latter age. She was awarded the Nobel Peace Prize in 1979 for the way she focused attention upon the horrible scourge of poverty that has claimed so many victims since the first man ever placed his greedy clutches on a copper penny and said, "...this is mine, and you can't have it." It was not the money that Mother Teresa wanted, but their promise of Love from the depths of their hearts which always produces its Fruits in magnanimously charitable ways—the giving of time, resources, and supplications which are so profound that it almost makes the Heavens shield its eyes from the sudden flash of light. And, most importantly, Mother Teresa asked us to pray, especially for unborn little children, so their mothers would comprehend the Eminent Creativity of Almighty God that He implants inside their wombs when our little progeny are first conceived. She penned a diary when she was younger, before she founded the Missionaries of Charity in 1946, that included her desires to fight the same anguish that some Christians suffer today, wherein she pined to know Jesus better. The despair we feel, she said, is only a smidgeon of Our Lord's pain on the Earth. She wrote as early as 1937 in her diary that her life was never strewn with roses, but that she simply offered herself to Him. Mother Teresa of Calcutta will be canonized by the Catholic Church to Sainthood very soon; and it is fitting that we remember why. She may not have been able to leap over tall buildings in a single bound or make the Earth shudder through the meekness of her voice. But, on behalf of the suffering poor to whom her life was devoted, she understood its providence in the nature of all things.

# The Providence of Human Suffering

*I consider that the sufferings of this present time are as nothing compared with the Glory to be revealed for us. For Creation awaits with eager expectation the revelation of the children of God; for Creation was made subject to futility, not of its own accord, but because of the one who subjected it, in hope that Creation itself would be set free from slavery to corruption and share in the glorious freedom of the children of God. We know that all Creation is groaning in labor pains, even until now; and not only that, but we ourselves who have the firstfruits of the Spirit; we also groan within ourselves as we wait for adoption, the redemption of our bodies. For in hope we were saved. Now, hope that sees for itself is not hope. For who hopes for what one sees? But, if we hope for what we do not see, we wait with endurance. In the same way, the Spirit too comes to the aid of our weakness; for we do not know how to pray as we ought, but the Spirit itself intercedes with inexpressible groanings. And, the one who searches hearts knows what is the intention of the Spirit because it intercedes for the holy ones according to God's Will....What, then shall we say to this? If God is for us, who can be against us? He, who did not spare His own Son, but handed Him over for us all, how will He not also give us everything else along with Him? Who will bring a charge against God's chosen ones? It is God who acquits us. Who will condemn? It is Christ Jesus who died, rather, was raised, who also is at the right hand of God, who indeed intercedes for us. What will separate us from the Love of Christ? Will anguish, or distress, or persecution, or famine, or nakedness, or peril, or the sword? As it is written: 'For your sake we are being slain all the day; we are looked upon as sheep to be slaughtered.' No, in all these things, we conquer overwhelmingly through Him who loved us. For, I am convinced that neither death, nor life, nor angels, nor principalities, nor present things, nor future things, nor powers, nor height, nor depth, nor any other creature will be able to separate us from the Love of God in Christ Jesus, Our Lord.*

St. Paul to the Romans (8:18-39)

# Chapter XIII
## *The Scourge of Infanticide*
## *The Abortion of Unborn Innocents*

A girl by the name of Lisa Dillon from Springfield, Illinois wrote a letter to the editor of a newspaper that appeared July 19, 1994 complaining about an apparent inconsistency that was troubling her. She noted that she had seen an article in the same publication a short time earlier where a man was charged with murdering his girlfriend who was four and a half months pregnant; and that he was being indicted for two murders—the woman and her unborn baby. Ms. Dillon posed a question whose answer seemed rather poignant. *If the girlfriend had gone to an abortion clinic and had the baby's life terminated, that would be OK under the law. But, how would the woman's 'choice' differ in any way from the actions of the murderer?* Almost three years later, on Friday, March 14, 1997, two children were playing in a field near the City of San Bernardino, California at 5:30 in the afternoon when they discovered five cardboard boxes containing thirty human fetuses. According to Sheriff's deputy Sergeant Paul Cappitelli, it was evident that they had come from a nearby abortion clinic. After their telling of the find to one of the children's parents, authorities were called to the scene where they found the boxes that were sealed with duct tape, containing six fetuses each. The burial crypts measured three-by-five feet; and they lacked any identifiable markings. There were 30 dead fetuses in all; each one stuffed in a sterilized plastic container. While none of us fears stating the obvious, where are the blatant criminals who ripped these unborn children from their mothers' wombs, crammed their limp remains into petroleum-based bags, and concealed them in an open field like someone might bury a pack of wild dogs that had been put to sleep by an animal control warden? Where are the mothers of these dead offspring who are the accomplices to these homicides? The debate over the abortion of unborn children is one of the most gruesome discussions to ever take place here in America. There are so many sides to the issue which the proponents of abortion attempt to raise that they hope the intrinsic value of the lives of the little children who are killed get riddled in the mix. They pose such distractions as personal freedom, the ability of a family to determine their own size, and even the proposition that God has given humankind the dominion to decide the ultimate fate of our gestating species. Perhaps a recollection of history might be in order for those who do not know all the facts. Back in 1970, a woman by the name of Norma McCorvey, a waitress who lived in Texas, claimed she had been raped and needed an abortion. At the same time, Henry Wade, District Attorney for the jurisdiction of Dallas County who was responsible for upholding the law prohibiting abortion except to save a woman's life, filed charges against her to protect the life of her unborn child. Earlier, in 1964, he had helped lead the prosecution of Jack Ruby, the nightclub owner who shot to death the man charged with assassinating President John F. Kennedy, Lee Harvey Oswald. The jury took less than two hours to sentence Ruby to death. And, while DA Wade was one of the most successful prosecutors in America at the time, it was the decision by the U.S. Supreme Court against him in the infamous *Roe v. Wade* lawsuit of January 22, 1973 that overshadowed his previous successes. He died in March 2001 at the age of 86; but it is the 40 million aborted children whose lives he tried to save for which humanity will most remember him.

According to Associated Press Reporter Richard Ostling in an October 1998 article, Ms. McCorvey, who was "Jane Roe" in the Supreme Court documents, came forward in the 1980s to reveal her true identity in interviews and a made-for-TV movie. She confessed, said Ostling, that her story about having been raped in 1970 was a complete fabrication and that she was, instead, an unwed mother who later put the child up for adoption. In 1995, she was said to have converted to Christianity, joined the pro-life movement Operation Rescue for a brief time, and was confirmed a Roman Catholic in August 1998. However, the damage to the soul of humankind had already been done by then. She sued Dallas DA Henry Wade using her pseudonym of Jane Roe, and the case traveled up the ladder to the U.S. Supreme Court, where its first oral arguments were heard on December 13, 1971. The most revealing interchange in the case was during its second hearing on October 11, 1972 in the presence of the following Supreme Court Justices: Warren E. Burger (Chief Justice), William O. Douglas, William J. Brennan, Potter Stewart, Byron R. White, Thurgood Marshall, Harry A. Blackmun, Lewis F. Powell, and William H. Rehnquist. From the sixty-five minutes of 10:04 a.m. until 11:09 a.m. during that formal reargument, the destiny of the lives of millions of unborn little children who would be conceived in their mothers' wombs hung in the balance; and the unseen evil forces that were so apparent in the early 1970s prevailed, as the Court voted 7-2 to allow the infanticide of our unborn progeny to proceed. The Justices ruled that the fetus is not a person with constitutional rights, and that the right to privacy pursuant to the Fourteenth Amendment of the United States Constitution regarding the guarantee of due process and personal liberty protected a woman's right to have an abortion. If they had ruled the other way, the 30 dead babies that were found by those two children who were playing in a field near San Bernardino, California might have grown-up to be some of the brightest, most productive citizens that this nation has ever known. Arguing on behalf of *Roe, et al* before the Supreme Court was Mrs. Sarah R. Weddington, an attorney from Austin. Robert C. Flowers, Esq.,

Assistant Attorney General of Texas, pled for the Defendant, Henry Wade, on behalf of the People. While it would not be practical to cite the entire transcript of their testimonies here, it seems painfully obvious that most of the Justices had presupposed their opinions before hearing both sides of the case. If anyone is interested in reviewing it, it is *Roe v. Wade,*. 410 U.S. 113, No. 70-18 (1973). My impression after reading the transcript is that the temperament of the Court that day was not one that reflected the grave consequences of the Justices' actions. Only Mr. Flowers, testifying for the sanctity of unborn human life, seemed to take his role seriously. One of his first motions was to remind the Court that the case was moot because the Plaintiff, Jane Roe, was no longer pregnant since the introduction of her first complaint nearly three years prior. Mysteriously, the Justices insisted upon hearing the case anyway. Mrs. Weddington, who was attempting to persuade them to overturn the law in Texas that made abortion illegal, tried to convince the Court that an unborn fetus is not a living human being, and that, *There are women who, for various reasons, do not wish to continue their pregnancy, whether because of personal health considerations, whether because of their family situation, whether because of financial situations; education, working situations, some of the many things we discussed at the last hearing.* Justice White asked the more pertinent question as to whether Mrs. Weddington believed that, under the Constitution, the unborn fetus is a person for the purpose of being protected within the due process clause of the 14th Amendment, to which she said, *All of the cases, the prior history of this statute, the common law history would indicate that it is not...We are asking in this case that the Court declare the (Texas) statute unconstitutional, the State having proved no compelling interest at all.*

For his part, Assistant Attorney General Flowers stood before the Court and affirmed that it was the position of the State of Texas that an unborn fetus is a human being upon conception, and therefore, a person protected by the Constitution of the United States. Justice Stewart asked him if he knew of any cases where it was held that an unborn fetus is a person within the meaning of the Fourteenth Amendment, to which Mr. Flowers directed the Court's attention to the intent of the framers of the Constitution. Justice Stewart refuted by claiming that the original framers are not the people who promulgated the 14th Amendment because it came much later. Mr. Flowers counter-argued that under the Fifth Amendment, no one shall be deprived of the right to life, liberty, and property without the due process of law. It was at this juncture that a horrible assumption was made by Justice Stewart. He said, *Yes, but then the Fourteenth Amendment defines a 'person' as somebody who's born, doesn't it?* Before allowing Mr. Flowers to respond, Justice Stewart said, *Well, it does.* Undaunted, the latter turned to Justice Stewart and said, *Your honor, it's our position that the definition of a person is so basic; it's so fundamental that the framers of the Constitution had not even set out to define (it.) We can only go to what the teachings (were) at the time the Constitution was framed.* Suffice it to say that neither the attorneys nor the Justices of the United States Supreme Court came to a general consensus as to when the life of a human being begins—either at conception or upon the point of live birth. Mr. Flowers cited several lower court cases where the dignity of the embryo had been protected from harm and wrongful death; but his pleading, for the most part, fell upon deaf ears. Moments prior to the rebuttal put forth by Jane Roe's attorney, Mr. Flowers petitioned for the Justices to rule on his behalf based upon the knowledge that, *This Court has been diligent in protecting the rights of the minority. And, gentlemen, we say that this is a minority, a silent minority, the truly silent minority. Who is speaking for these children? Where is the counsel for these unborn children whose life is (sic) being taken? Where is the safeguard of the right to trial by jury? Are we to place this power in the hands of a mother and a doctor? All of the constitutional rights, if this person has the person concept; what would keep a legislature under this ground from deciding who else might or might not be a human being, or might not be a person?*

It is my view that the following excerpt from the rebuttal testimony of Mrs. Sarah Weddington on October 11, 1972 sealed the sentence of death upon untold millions of unborn children, *We are here to advocate that the decision as to whether or not a particular woman will continue to carry or will terminate a pregnancy is a decision that should be made by that individual, that in fact she has a constitutional right to make that decision for herself, and that the State (of Texas) has shown no interest in interfering with that decision....The woman should be given that freedom, just as the doctor has the freedom to decide what procedures he will carry out, and what he will refuse to his patients.* And, in an interchange with Messrs. White and Blackmun, Mrs. Weddington assured the Court that a physician had the constitutional right to reject any woman's plea for an abortion based upon his judgement under the Hippocratic Oath because it was yet to be determined by the Court whether an unborn child is an actual living human being. When questioned by Justice Blackmun about what might happen if a pregnant woman visits a physician and he tells her that he does not perform abortion procedures, she replied, *She goes elsewhere, if she so chooses. If she stays with that, you know, that's an impossible question. Certainly, I don't think the State could say the first doctor a woman goes to shall make that determination and she cannot go elsewhere.* Thereupon, the matter was concluded at precisely nine minutes past eleven o'clock in the morning Eastern Time on October 11, 1972 pursuant to the following deadly epitaph which is inscribed in history by the bloodshed and execution of our unborn little children:

Chief Justice Burger:     *Your time is up now, Mrs. Weddington.*

Mrs. Weddington:     *Thank you.*

Chief Justice Burger:     *Thank you, Mrs. Weddington.*
*Thank you, Mr. Flowers.*

The case was then submitted for judgement; and their decision was rendered by the majority rule of the U.S. Supreme Court under the date of January 22, 1973 that our unborn children have no rights of protection under the Fourteenth Amendment of the U.S. Constitution; and none of the States has the authority to infringe upon a woman's right to procure an abortion. Thereafter, any mother has been allowed to terminate her pregnancy at her discretion as a matter of public law. And, this is the culture of death that the more civilized and God-fearing nations around the globe have condemned on a massive scale; not only on religious grounds, but for the reason that the USA has become the great murderer of helpless little innocents, which is quite an ironic prospect when we tout our desire to uphold the human and civil rights of our own people and condemn other foreign countries who do not. The disingenuous levity that marked the tone of Justice Thurgood Marshall and others during the testimonies at the Supreme Court was not slightly worthy of the serious nature of the debate that was ongoing. Indeed, the decision by the Court to legalize abortion has left a gaping crater in its credibility before the world as a body of freedom, justice, and decency. As for the jurist who wrote the final decision on their behalf, Justice Harry Blackmun took-on that task. He was appointed as a staunch conservative by President Nixon in 1970 and served until his retirement in 1994, a span of twenty-four years. His writing of the decision of the Court in 1973 resulted in countless threats against his life. It was widely reported that he received 70,000 pieces of mail calling him a murderer and comparing him to Adolf Hitler and the Nazi Germany plague of genocide during World War II. He later said that he tried to read every one of them because he wanted to know what people thought of him; but it never brought him to change his mind about having ruled in favor of Jane Roe or making abortion on demand illegal again. His heart was later converted regarding the institution of capital punishment, to which I have referred in Chapter XVI of this book. He passed-away on March 4, 1999 at the age of 90; and his sorrowful legacy has been one of gross immorality, sacrilege, and political expediency since that fateful day in the cold-hearted frigidity of an American January in 1973.

According to the National Right to Life Committee, "abortion" defines any premature expulsion of a human fetus from the womb of its mother, whether by miscarriage or artificially induced. They claim that the *Doe v. Bolton* decision by the U.S. Supreme Court, also in 1973, legalized infanticide in all fifty states during all nine months of pregnancy for any reason, medical or otherwise.   Prenatal abortion terminates a pregnancy by destroying and removing the gestating child. The heartbeat of the baby can be detected about thirty days subsequent to its mother's last menstrual period; but abortions rarely take place until after that, usually during the seventh week of pregnancy. At that time, the unborn infant has developed his or her arms and legs and discernable brain waves. By the end of the tenth week, when most abortions are performed, the child has fingernails, genitalia, and a recognizably human face. This, however, whether detected by sonogram or traditional obstetric methods, does not deter abortionists from taking the life of the child. How do they do it? There are several techniques utilized in America today. Suction Aspiration and Dilation-Curettage are surgical procedures that are used primarily during the First Trimester of pregnancy. Dilation-Evacuation is a surgical operation which is completed during the Second Trimester. There are chemical methods of killing unborn children, such as Salt Poisoning, Urea, and Prostaglandin, each of which is used during the Second and Third Trimesters. Other surgical procedures in the Second and Third Trimesters include Partial-Birth Abortion and Hysterotomy. During the Suction Aspiration procedure, a powerful vacuum tube with a sharp cutting edge is inserted into the womb through the dilated cervix. The suction dismembers the body of the baby and tears the placenta from the wall of the uterus, vacuuming blood, amniotic fluid, placental tissue, and fetal parts into a collection container. Using the Dilation-Curettage method, the cervix is stretched so that a loop-shaped steel knife can be inserted into the womb. The body of the baby is cut into pieces and removed and the placenta is scraped off the uterine wall. To abort unborn children as old as six months, the Dilation-Evacuation procedure is employed where forceps with razor-like metal jaws are used to grab onto the body of the baby and twisted like an auger to slice the child into tiny pieces, which are suctioned from the mother's body. Because the baby's head has developed into bony tissue by this time, the skull is crushed to facilitate the complete removal of the body. Physicians are oftentimes concerned that the sharp edges of the collapsed baby's head will lacerate the cervix of the mother receiving the abortion procedure.

Instillation Methods of abortion, also known as chemical poisoning, involve the injection of drugs or liquids through the abdomen of the mother into the amniotic sac, causing the baby to die previous to being extracted from the uterus.  During the Salt Poisoning procedure, a hypodermic needle is inserted into the mother so that 50-250 milliliters (the equivalent of about a cup) of amniotic fluid is drawn and replaced with a concentrated brine solution. It is used after the first four months of pregnancy.  The unborn baby inhales, swallows the salt, and is fatally poisoned.  But, before that, the chemical solution causes painful burning and the deterioration of the baby's skin because it takes about an hour for the child to die.  The mother goes into labor around 36 hours later and delivers a dead, scalded, and shriveled baby.  Roughly 97% of these mothers deliver their deceased children within 72 hours.  As for the other two surgical methods which are utilized in late-term pregnancies, Partial-Birth Abortion and the Hysterotomy, the former is composed of five steps and is used to abort infants of women who are eight months pregnant, and sometimes even nine.  Through the medium of ultrasound, the abortionist reaches into the uterus with forceps, grabs the unborn baby's legs, and pulls the child from the womb.  The surgeon delivers the baby's entire body, except for the head, which is intentionally left inside the birth canal.  The child is alive and breathing during this process.  The abortionist then jams scissors into the posterior of the baby's skull, spreading their tips apart so as to enlarge the wound.  After the removal of the scissors, a suction catheter is inserted into the skull to extract the baby's brain.  The collapsed head is then removed from the uterus and the child is delivered dead.  Lastly, the Hysterotomy is a surgical procedure that is similar to the Caesarean Section and is employed when chemical methods such as Salt Poisoning fail.  The surgeon makes an incision in the mother's abdomen and uterus; then the child, the placenta, and the amniotic sac are removed.  Babies are sometimes born alive during this procedure, but are allowed to die of their own accord.  No attempt is made to resuscitate the newborn baby in these cases; and the postnatal protocol that is ordinarily followed is suspended.  This would include such matters as checking vital signs, certifying birth records, and complying with established procedures for the OB care of the child.

The information that is contained in the previous two paragraphs seems almost too barbaric to be real.  They describe the actions of a savage, philistine, brutal, hostile, obscene, cruel, and bloodthirsty sect of American citizens whose actions are the direct result of the influence of the Antichrist. Any person whose hands are used to perform such abominable acts is a disciple of Satan.  This is not an opinion that is held by someone who is a religious fanatic or bent on forcing the Truth of the Love of God down other people's throats.  It is a fact which has been stated as clear as the light of day in religions of all kinds throughout history and around the world.  We in America are the epitome of the culture of death against which Pope John Paul II has spoken so profoundly because he knows that the very soul of the United States of America is headed for the bowels of Hell. He is not our judge or maker; and neither does it take a man who has written about such Divine Splendor as him to realize that the fate of the people who espouse, pursue, allow, facilitate, and perform abortions is one that is unworthy of anyone who will someday go to Heaven. Even though we believe that God is a forgiving Creator; and there is no doubt that He is; we are responsible for the little ones who are placed in our care. It is the duty of every mother and father to engage the proper course both in history and in fact that will reveal us as the living validity of His preservation of our Holy Innocents, *before* they are sent to their deaths! If any one of us expects to receive the exculpating pardon that comes with our Christian faith at the end of time, we had better get off our lazy buttocks and tell those who are responsible for the grisly horror of abortion that they are in the service of evil legions. It has been said, and widely so, that we do not yet know who among us will be saved and who will be condemned. However, our vision is clear that the people who are murdering our unborn children are in grave danger before the Judgement of Jesus Christ. Deep down inside, each one of them must know that they are effecting a horrible scourge on the face of the Earth. If they do not, they cannot be the disciples of Christ. When we affirm to Him that we do well always and everywhere to give Him thanks and praise, we will fall woefully short if the time arrives for His Return and the Supreme Court's January 22, 1973 decision allowing women to abort their unborn children is still the law of this land. While I do not always agree with the pious platitudes and fundamental extremism of Reverend Jerry Falwell and television evangelist and politico Pat Robertson, I cannot argue against their claim that some of the terrorist acts toward the United States are being allowed by Jesus Christ to teach us that Heaven is offended by our refusal to preserve the dignity of all human life.

Whether or not we ultimately choose to accept it; and regardless of the political lunacy that has engulfed people like Justice Harry Blackmun, our decisions are never autonomous from the surveillance of God because they are a portion of the criteria by which He judges us. While there is a different set of circumstances surrounding the psychological dysfunction that would bring a mother to walk into an abortion clinic, someone who is so intellectual that they have qualified for appointment to the U.S. Supreme Court, was seated, and then refused to protect the lives of the unborn must surely have had their own conscience surgically extracted by some sinister force. This entire bane has been like a decades-long nightmare from which the good citizens in America who have a Christian conscience would like to awaken. The destruction of little children in the womb must surely be the most grievous act that could ever be perpetrated in the entire world of human sinners from the moment Adam and Eve were first cast down from Paradise until our time at the beginning of this 21st century. We are laying waste to the future of our promises, conceding defeat to the despair which has slain the Wisdom of the heart, and striding headlong into the evil traps that Jesus Christ warned us to avoid. We seem to be looking upon human existence as a means to enhance the number of matters we control; from where we live, what our gainful employment will be, who or whether we will marry, what we eat, and how we choose to perceive either the dominion or irrelevance of our unseen God. What we fail to recognize is that there are more parameters in the broadness of life over which we have absolutely no control than those we do. It is quite obvious to me that about 99% of the operative functions of the earthen globe continue to be unbeknownst to us; notwithstanding what we have already discovered inside the composure of living cells and the infinite traits that are involved in our mutual exchanges everyday. What we assume to be an inanimate Creation that lives beyond our vision is the true life with which we come into contact only after we accept the Messiah of the God who put it in place. Our concession must become more than studying the movements and catalysts of the universe, but complying with the procession of His Truth and Will. Creation will never be whole until we, His thirsting humanity, fully comprehend that we have no authority to cease the making of His people as He places them in their mothers' wombs. How could the Justices of the U.S. Supreme Court conclude that an unborn child is not a viable person when they, themselves, sprung into being from this same origin at the wellspring of their mothers' love? What occurred on January 22, 1973 was a horrendous error made by a collection of nitwit mortals whose own opportunity to be born had been cherished like fine jewels by their respective parents, but a mystical treasure they declined to bequeath to 40 million unborn babies they have allowed to be executed since. Justice Harry Blackmun was born November 12, 1908 in Nashville, Illinois; and he celebrated his birthday with jubilation for nine decades thereafter. But, he and six associate judges of the Supreme Court decided with outright malice that untold millions of their successors should not have that right. So, if we hear someone screaming about flames leaping against their soul in the middle of the night, let us pray to God that it is not a vision of what Jesus Christ has done to any of the Justices from the United States' Highest Court who have already died.

And, while it seems as though their catastrophic blunder took such a brief time to commit from the first oral arguments in December 1971 until the decision was rendered some thirteen months later, it has knocked our American nation completely off its moral center and has us sprawled flat on our collective bellies in guilt and shame. As a result, it is going to take a wholesale amount of praying on our knees to induce the Angels and Saints into discarding their disdain for us long enough to help our country back onto its feet again. To date, we are lacking any sufficiently demonstrative effort toward reversing our cruel assault against the dignity of America's unborn infants. They all have names waiting to be given to them; gloves and booties prepared for the warmth of their velvet skin, and a world filled with tidings of affection from loving people everywhere who see them as the endearing promise of hope for the generations to come. The witty American barrister Clarence Seward Darrow (1857-1938) once said that he'd never killed a man, but he had read many an obituary with pleasure. Perhaps this is how millions of people ponder the fate of those who are responsible for the vile infanticide that has taken such a tragic toll on America and the entire world; from the mothers who no longer care, the doctors who commit the murders, the legislatures that allow it, and the media outlets who turn their faces the other way as though they have no role to play in revealing the Truth about equal protection under the law. They know deep down inside what the rest of us realize: that the social conditions under which we live today meet none of the criteria that properly comply with the definitions of "dilemma" or "impasse" because the correlation of protecting unborn life with Divine Truth makes it a unilateral decision. As our adolescents would say, the fact that abortion must come to an abrupt halt is a "no brainer." One of the more eloquent ways of stating that children in the womb are of invaluable significance to God and the entirety of His Creation was printed by His Excellency, Bishop George J. Lucas, from the Catholic Diocese of Springfield, Illinois on the 30th anniversary of *Roe vs. Wade* in an editorial of his diocesan paper, *Catholic Times* on January 19, 2003, wherein he mentioned the annual March for Life in Washington DC that has been an annual event for three decades, *...we have not forgotten the primacy of God's Law about the sanctity of human life. This yearly demonstration makes the point peacefully...that any law or legal decision that so blatantly contradicts Divine Law cannot be allowed to stand...There are many who are dedicated to making our society and our institutions more 'inclusive.' At this moment, it would be good to look around and ask, 'Who is missing?' After 30 years and millions of abortions, we are missing people who could have been our neighbors and friends. The talents of people who would be in the prime of life; serving in health care, education, social work, business, and in religious life are not enriching our American experience. Most of all, we have been deprived of so many unique reflections of God's creative Love, whose very lives give glory to the One who fashioned them. There is no doubt that our nation has been diminished by 'Roe vs. Wade' and all of the deadly choices it has sanctioned. Our young people believe in the sanctity of human life and...may very well be able to accomplish a change on behalf of human life in this country that my generation has failed to accomplish. In any case, they make us all proud and humble.*

His Excellency, Bishop Lucas, knows what everyone should begin to understand: that the fight for life must never end. Humankind should not desist in protecting its dignity from its own heinous crimes. We owe it to the Creator who deigns to implant mortal souls in our mothers' wombs, and we must definitely accept our mandate from Him in seeing that His Holy Will is done. Too many selfish Americans have stood for the wrong principles in the past fifty years; and we are only now beginning to see the destruction that their mistakes have wrought. Justice Blackmun knew he was the proud "cock of the walk" when he pronounced the sentence of death upon those millions of aborted children about whom Bishop Lucas spoke in January 2003. If only he and his fellow Justices would have solicited the opinion of the Church before they acted, or consulted their own consciences, perhaps our offspring would have been spared. Instead, however, Satan had a field day through the snaking abomination of the U.S. Judicial system, knowing well in advance that he could seduce the Supreme Court into believing that a developing fetus is not a living human being. God will deal with them in a way that is commensurate with their error; so we need not worry that our prayers will ever be in vain. To every man is given a sense of both morality and contempt. And, how we wield them underscores the defining moments in the history of the world that are read and adjudicated by the Messiah from Nazareth who walked, talked, and laid-down His life by Crucifixion on Mt. Calvary so that our righteousness might be preserved. The abortion of our unborn children is our way of casting Him aside; telling Him that we do not need His institutionalized form of piety in order to be scrupulous in matters of the world. This human trait of domineering conceit will come back to haunt us someday; and we ought not to be too surprised when it does. We should remember that it was the pride of the first of our species that got us all expelled from Heaven in the beginning, having something to do with not taking a bite of the fruit from a tree. Unfortunately, however, we have now bitten-off more than we can chew. Our very existence on the Earth is gagging over the horrendous mistake it has been trying to swallow since January 22, 1973 when a cast of aristocrats in the U.S. Capitol decided to legalize abortion and begin the slaughter of 40 million unborn infants and counting. Some day soon, we will hear the voice of Jesus Christ speaking to every person on the globe, sounding not unlike the words of Chief Justice Warren Burger to end the oral arguments in Case No. 70-18, *...your time is up, Mrs. Weddington.* It is at that moment when those who are responsible for killing our children will look down and see *her* identification tag, stained by the blood of our unborn innocents, pinned to their own lapels.

# Section V
## *The Mother and Child Reunion*

---

## Chapter XIV
### *The Immaculate Conception*
### *The Most Blessed Virgin Mary*

I am just a poor sinner who has written plainly about the throes of our subordinate existence here on the Earth and the pitiable strife by which we sadly endure the present hours. However, my cause could have never become a portion of the sumptuous Truth without directing the renditions of my soul like a beeline into the depths of the Immaculate Heart of the Most Blessed Virgin Mary. I have spoken heretofore for 170 pages about liabilities and wares, the sunrise and darkness; of telltales and tragedies; summonses, prose, and poisons; oratory, interplay, and obsequies; starlets and commoners; vespers, warlocks, cavaliers, corpses, shadows, airships, and gauntlets; mayhem, warfare, armor, friendship, depravity, devotion, and forgiveness; and of cribs, empathy, gladness, dreams, and dynasties. With what broad stroke or encompassing wit can I remind you that none of these matters anymore to those who can see human life as a monumental flash of genius given to us through the Wisdom of the Mother of God? All of our diaries and dissertations are only pious conjectures within the element of time, which in itself is but a subset of true Glory, because it is extremely difficult to capture the consummate union between the Holy Spirit and the Handmaid of the Lord with a pen laid onto a page. There is no place in Creation which is marked by either time or space that is sufficient for the proper veneration of the inviolate perfection of the Virgin Mary; for Her Grace is the pinnacle of all spiraling summits of holiness and Love, both seen and unseen; and She is the foundress and vessel by whom humankind is purified and elevated. She is our Matriarchal Sentry in the shadows of human desperation, the Supremacy of the Motherhood of man; Divine, formidable, awesome, revered, pristine, undefiled, sublime, chaste, noble, inspiring, majestic, splendorous, stately, dignified, regal, exalted, brilliant, superb, Glorious, eloquent, rapturous, and always invincible. How could anyone conclude a manuscript within the realms of Eminent Omnipotence without referencing the Queen of human sanctification? How do we know this to be true? We need not look any farther than the Gospel of St. Luke*, wherein it is stated that God dispatched the Archangel Gabriel to a humble Virgin who was betrothed to Joseph of the house of David in the town of

Galilee called Nazareth. *Hail, full of grace! The Lord is with thee! Blessed art thou among women!...Do not be afraid, Mary, for thou hast found favor with God. Behold, thou shalt conceive in thy Womb and shalt bring forth a Son; and thou shalt call his name Jesus. He shall be great and shall be called the 'Son of the Most High,' and the Lord God will give Him the Throne of David, His father; and He shall be King over the house of Jacob forever; and of His Kingdom, there shall be no end. The Holy Spirit shall come upon thee; and the power of the Most High shall overshadow thee. And therefore, the Holy One to be born shall be called 'the Son of God.'* Even in these kismetic moments, Mary conceded to the deigning voice of the Holy Spirit by which She was being urged. Rather than decline His wish or tell the Archangel to return to the Throne of God and deliver Her regrets, the Immaculate Virgin said *Yes* before the enemies of human sanctification had an opportunity to begin their clamoring opposition in the midst of such an auspicious occasion as the swift aptness of Her reply. *Behold, the handmaid of the Lord; be it done to me according to thy word,* she said, whereupon the Canticle of Her allegiance to the God of Abraham was inscribed into the Sacred Scriptures and immortal time, by which all future generations would be led, consoled, and blessed.

There is no doubt that Mary was as taken-aback as any of us might be, should we be privy to such a miraculous visitation appearing from out of the blue. However, She was not the least hesitant; and not once did She question the motivation of the Archangel. From that moment forward, Her acceptance won the affections of the Most Sacred Heart of the Son whom She was about to bear; and now the crescents and orbs, the stars and moon, and the very meaning of life were transformed as the Divine and the mortal have been reunited in Her Mystical Grace. Forever after, the garish sun would bring forth drink instead of thirst. The moorland meadows of the Earth would be replenished again with the flowering of the heather and edelweiss; the constellations would begin to move into formation and dress in their best attire because they knew that the entirety of humankind would look upward to see from whence this great manifestation of worthiness and promise had come. The Mother of Jesus Christ set our Redemption into motion by granting Her concession to the Will of God not only because She is an obedient Daughter of the New Jerusalem, but is its Eternal Mother as well. To this day, we recite the Sacred Mysteries of the Holy Rosary with these things in mind. We echo this same Angelic Salutation that brought Gabriel to reveal the Truth about the sinless nature of Mary from the instant She was but the brilliance of the contemplations of God. He pined for His people to be reconciled with Him

*\* Confraternity for Christian Doctrine Edition - Copyright 1957*

once again; and what better way than for Him to appear in the Flesh in the Person of His Only Begotten Son so that men, women, and children from every walk of life could see for themselves what a perfect mortal Man could do? Ergo, the Son of God was born from the Womb of the Blessed Virgin Mary in a Manger in Bethlehem that we who believe in Him shall have life everlasting. (John 3:16). All of this is by virtue of the same Grace of which the Mother of Our Lord is full! Can we see such a benevolent power with the bland facility of our eyes? Yes! By the very nature of this Grace! *From His fullness, we have all received grace in place of grace because, while the Law was given through Moses, grace and Truth came through Jesus Christ. No one has ever seen God. The only Son, God, who is at the Father's side, has revealed Him.* (John 1:16-18). Hence, the Mosaic Law has been supplanted by the New Covenant.

Too many sinners have walked awkwardly and without this same allegiance because they proclaim that such Grace has never been overtly divulged. According to the Church, it entails the wholly favored, free, and undeserved help that Heaven gives us to respond to God so as to become His children, partakers of His Divinity, and beneficiaries of Eternal Life. The Catechism proclaims that Grace is our own participation in the very Life of God, in the Person of Jesus Christ, in whom we are introduced into an intimate relationship with the Holy Trinity by our Baptism, through which we participate in the Grace of Christ (1997). Let there be no mistake: this is our new vocation as justified children of our Divine Creator; meaning that we are separated from sin through the power of His Son. And, without His Grace, we could never be so justified. Where do we find it? In the Child of Mary Immaculate, in whose Blood we have been Redeemed. This, in itself, is nothing short of a supernaturally exculpating event. *Yet, we do speak a Wisdom to those who are mature; but not a Wisdom of this age, nor of the rulers of this age who are passing away. Rather, we speak God's Wisdom, mysterious, hidden, which God predetermined before the ages for our Glory, and which none of the rulers of this age knew; for if they had known it, they would not have crucified the Lord of Glory.* (1 Cor. 2:6-8). This is the authority by which the Virgin Mary speaks to humankind today, which is a fruit of the supplication She lifted through the Annunciation of the Archangel Gabriel on behalf of our mortified souls. It is the duty of a mother to give the fullness of life. And, the gift of our Salvation, who is Jesus, the Fruit of Mary's Womb, is our Life after we have closed our mortal eyes in death. No greater blessing could have been given to the fallen souls of man than this. According to the Council of Trent (1547: DS 1533-1534) which is cited in the Catechism (2005), the Grace of Heaven supercedes our sentence in exile and is known only by our faith. We cannot rely solely upon our feelings and good works to know that we are justified and saved.

However, according to Matthew 7:20, *...you will know them by their fruits;* meaning that the blessing of God upon our lives guarantees that His Grace is at work deep within us, growing our trust, and casting our souls into an inextinguishable Light of prayer, service, and humility.  When asked under duress by her ecclesiastical judges whether she knew if she was in a state of God's Grace, Saint Joan of Arc replied, *If I am not, may it please God to put me in it.  If I am, may it please God to keep me there.*  The implication is that Grace is not seen with the naked eye, but its effects are discernable because its presence enhances the Kingdom of God through the more pious works of our hands.  Therefore, when we claim that the Mother of God is full of Grace, we are attesting that Her entire Being consists of His same Divinity and that the Virginal Nativity of Jesus Christ was modeled after Hers.  Mary, Wife of Joseph, is the only Immaculate Woman to have been conceived anywhere in Creation; and She is the only immortally-born of Her gender that God ever gave the breath of life.

Hereafter, since the Son of Man was given to the Earth from the mansions of Heaven through the Handmaid of the Lord, it is through Her Grace that we are introduced to the Savior of the World.  Although the study of Mariology has become somewhat of a novelty in our modern times, the certainty of Her stature before God as our role model for Love can never be refuted.  He has placed the entire repatriation of the Mystical Body of His Crucified Son upon the Pillar of Divine obedience, who is Mary, so that we can cast-away our pride and arrogance in favor of a more suppliant attitude of contrition and peace.  He will never force the Salvation of our souls upon us because He gave us a human will by which we live of our own accord.  However, if that same will is not in alignment with His, then we shall never inherit the Kingdom that He promised.  Jesus does not employ scare-tactics to procure our faithful allegiance because He knows that Satan terrifies us enough.  Once we have seen a sufficient amount of tragedy and horror, and wonder why we cannot escape them, He stands firmly within the grasp of our hearts and offers Himself as the civilly righteous alternative.  How can anyone desist, therefore, in pursing Him and the definitive gift of His Truth by holding fast to fashions of the flesh?  All the arbors and atriums under which we shall ever be entrained while studying matters of the universe and the limits of the world cannot take us to the Grace by which we are broadly designed to seek His Love again.  We are not expected to throw ourselves off the top of towering cliffs to see whether Our Lord will spare us from harm before we hit bottom and rack our brains on the crust of the earthen floor.  This is not the kind of Salvation the Bible preaches.  I am not sure that the type of Grace we require will yield to such ambivalence on our part.  The inward soul and the unseen spirit are the valuable facets to which God is speaking through the Holy Paraclete. And, once we have accepted Him, the surety of His protection applies to the paranormal aspects of our intrinsic being, too. Hereafter, there is a transparent safety-net to keep our souls from falling into the fiery dungeons of Hell; and this is all that should matter anymore. Saint Paul was correct in asserting that everything else is only vanity for the travails that have no bearing on the outcome of God's Kingdom. Above all else, while our faith must be both fervent and true, we should never seem bellicose or ostentatious about the crucial nature of the conversion of man because there is too much at stake right now. We have learned in times past that genuine Grace thrives by simple piety, and that it is cultured by our spiritual meekness. It is probably accurate to assume that we have no power to amend the Grace of God, but only to wield it, and to procure our absolution before Heaven and Earth.

It is this homiletic Wisdom that teaches us to recognize the Grace of God in one another and in the powerful presence of the Immaculate Virgin who gave Him birth in Bethlehem. Mankind has been blessed with the mystical capacity to underscore the spiritual nature of human existence and to be consumed by it, too. The literary term for this is *gnosis*, which is an ancient Greek word that defines the parameters of human knowledge on a level that allows us to recognize Divine Truth with transcending Love. By contemplative prayer and peace, our understanding of His Providence and purpose becomes much more clear; and this is what we learn through our faith-works and religiousness as the offspring of Mary. She is neither God nor a part of the Holy Trinity. But, no creature has ever known Him better; and nary a soul besides this Auxiliary Benefactor has been the harborage of the Crucifixion and Resurrection of Jesus Christ as She who has spread His Eternal Being over the annals of the Earth since He was first chartered to engender the faculties of the Divine. Her Mantle is our backdrop, tapestry, and portico under which all Creation huddles in wait for the breaking of the Celestial Dawn. We need not fool ourselves into believing that we can earn this Grace any more than we can wager, pilfer, or buy our justification in Jesus Christ. It is only by His Love for us that we are saved; and anything beyond this is our supplication to the advancement of His Will. Simple men are not required to become Doctors of the Church before their time, even though such felicity should be hastened, in order for God's Grace to envelope the world. The hermits and marabou of Northern Africa have no more grasp on the supernatural conveyance of His Love than a child sitting on a school bus in Central Boston. He knows us all well and with clarity of the heart; and His fairness has no equal among the social orders of civilized people everywhere. This, likewise, is the adherent defense that the simpler of souls garners from the Most Blessed Virgin Mary.

Why? Because, as it is stated in the Marian Canticle in the First Chapter of St. Luke (46-55), *My soul proclaims the greatness of the Lord,...Behold, from now on will all ages call Me blessed...He has shown might with His Arm, dispersed the arrogant of mind and heart. He has thrown down the rulers from their thrones, but lifted-up the lowly. The hungry He has filled with good things; the rich He has sent away empty.* Thus, we each have equal representation before the Cross of Jesus Christ in the person of Mary, Queen of Saints; for She knows the intentions of our will, the effect of our laboring, and whether we have given ourselves to Her Son or to the vileness of the netherworld.

Moreover, it seems obvious to me that the Holy Mother serves a much greater capacity than Her role as intercessor on our behalf before the Divine Mercy of Her Son; as critically important as that is; but that She is also our model for all Christian Virtue; and for prudence, prayer, fortitude, justice, temperance, purity, and truthfulness; and for faith, hope, charity, and Love. These are among the cardinal, moral, and theological virtues that keep us in common with the Divine; along with the Grace of the Seven Sacraments. Indeed, the notable precepts of judicious conduct, almsgiving, charisma, consecration, mutual pardoning, freedom, goodness, modesty, penance, reparation, sacrifice, duty, and worship all revolve around and flow from the Grace that defines the constancy of Immortal Love which blooms so prolifically from Our Lady's Immaculate Heart. Her purposes are not to provide the Earth any new revelations about the Kingdom of God, but to complement that which is already dispensed through the Church. The Roman Catechism (67) clearly states that Her miraculous apparitions and other such manifestations are in addition to the original deposit of faith; and that they serve specifically to help us live more fully by Christ's definitive Revelation during a certain period of history. (Cf. Timothy 6:14, Titus 2:13). And, in a larger sense, what do we make of this thing called "prudence?" We know that in Christianity it must imply more than the application of our simple regard for practical matters because the entire economy of human Salvation seems too mysteriously abstract. Perhaps, therefore, it is best defined as our guard against temptation and sin; our care, caution, good judgement, and Wisdom to see what lies ahead through the venues of foresight we are afforded in our spiritual union in Christ. We have no definitive way of planning for all the external conditions by which we are affected nearly everyday or a means of foreseeing the contingencies we should install into place to avoid pitfalling into extremely unfortunate circumstances. These are among the values we learn from the Mother of God, through the intercession of the Holy Spirit, because She knows that we are unprepared to greet the perfection of Her Son on the last day of life. Her concern is a direct reflection of Her Love for us, and by reason that we will indict ourselves as being unworthy of Redemption if we do not arrive at the Final Judgement dressed in our Baptismal gowns free from the stain of sin.  This is why She perpetually reminds us to enter the Sacrament of Reconciliation on a regular basis, and so as to be worthy of receiving Her Eucharistic Son.  But, behind it all, Her call to humanity is more than to a simpler discipline.  The Queen of Heaven has plenty more to say about the condition of the world and the fate of our souls.  Why?  Because She loves us with the same Redemptive compassion that took Christ to His death on the Holy Cross.  When She speaks in the overwhelming ways that God is allowing, Her sentiments turn to matters of the heart—the resilience of Love and the sustenance of peace.  In the final analysis, when our human condition is fully reflected against the Pauline purview, we see that we have also been persecuting the Catholic Church when we fail to exercise every discretion that it teaches or have not prevented ourselves or someone else from dabbling in the artifices that will always be unsightly before the vision of Our Lord.  I have no whit of doubt that the single thread by which we are stitched to the hem of the garment of His forgiveness is fixed upon whether we loved His people from the character of our being and through the fond and most genuine trust to which we have predisposed ourselves to embrace His Sacrifice during our mortal years on Earth.

This is the essence of human Salvation—Love, and Love again—to the point that there is nothing left in the world but Love; not to demand it, but to give it in all possible ways to the creatures of God and the Kingdom by which we are blessed.  If I could write literary masterpieces like William Shakespeare, I would have already made my point about this miracle on the first page of Chapter I of this book.  Perhaps, I could have penned a verse of striking poetry or a sonnet with a twist; or I would have added an encore to the Acts of Henry IV, King Lear, or Twelfth Night that would have called for the dissolution of every fibrous particle on the face of the planet that has nothing to do with conveying holiness at home and abroad or surrendering to the bounty of our prefigured Salvation.  *It is only Love, and nothing less, to whom we are dispatched; that welcomed contagion through which our inexpressible desires for change are cultured, so that we can see more clearly beyond the lore of fabled men whose destiny was borne at the price of God's Blood splattered in drops like zeppelins crashing to the ground.  Now, we stand at the brink of hailing the cynosures from which we have procured our long-lasting life, and have sorted-out the real Messiah from the pack and rim of deities that our feathered scalpers took by mistake as being the reverend sun and moon by which they were led; full, comprised, undaunted, appealed, and reserved—all within the vast dynamic of Christ-exhumed and Crowned again.  Our missive motions and secular accidents tick-tock across our breasts like salamander swordfish while we swim in human mockery to trebles and treks in the presence of old-fashioned, Cross-bearing Saints whose martyrdom has been our exculpation for today.* Somewhere deep inside these things which spring from my interior rests the image of our Love for Jesus and one another that those who spate upon the importance of Mary in human Redemption will never come to know. No history can erase Her from the preponderance of God to place Her in our midst for the purpose of reeling us in like minnows through the beauty of Her Face to feast upon the Paradise of the European shores. No modern fad or winking "wanna-be" can imitate Her Grace or steal from Her our apportioned lot of the incalculable Divine. We discover in Her that Love is greater than the sum of every expressed affection of our ancestors and ourselves, or that which we may see fit to dispense upon our progeny to keep our legacies alive long after we, too, are gone. What we make of our Love for God must be the filler of every canyon we have ever seen, and those whose concave throats have yet to belch the voice of Truth into the wiles of outer space. This seems almost too surreal and positively metaphysical enough to constrain the logic inside our textbooks and never allow their covers to be reopened until the Son of Man finishes His Reign over the laborers who bound them together with glue and press. Mary calls for this visionary romance to be perfected in us all, so that we can manifest a newness of life that has nothing to do with cart blanche cruises on ocean liners that will only make us vomit anyway from the rolling waves telling us to get off their beatific crests at the closest seaport, and never set foot or trespass upon their foaming whitecaps again.

The spiritual Truth to which the Mother of God is leading us has nothing to do with triceps or clavicles; or mainsails, keels, and captains; and only very little reference to anything we might remember tomorrow about how we earned a buck today. If this is the limit to how we live, then we will wake-up with a terrible headache in the morning and only make it worse by bumping our skulls on the sky that is not sufficiently elevated to hold all the junk we have created in our trains of thought that are railing against the probability that we will recognize the Face of Jesus Christ once He Returns in Glory on a cloud. With what great hope does Mary help us permeate the bonds of the three dimensions in which God has encapsulated us for as long as we shall live? Do we see our existence as a form of imprisonment from which we will eventually be set free so as to regale the Saints with the story of our lives as commemorated by fashions of Truth? We should hope this to be the case! What will they assume if we tell them about shells and cockleburs when there are presently so many reprobates and infidels on our city walks and country lanes whose souls rest in our hands? Will the Hosts of Heaven not be fully justified to rebuke us before the Son of Man for not forewarning them that damnation and Hell are real and present dangers? When the Mother of God tells us to *evangelize* the Holy Gospel of Her Crucified Son, She is not asking us to speak only to ourselves! God may turn unto us and say that He gave us the power through the white-feathered Paraclete He perched upon our shoulders to convert them into Saints! And, if not for the intercession of His Immaculate Mother, we may have looked into the mirror and seen ourselves as grungy pirates with parrots sitting on our epaulettes instead. It is the benefit of the vision of Paradise which She has already seen that Christ is revealing to us now. This same Virgin has taken humanity by the hand and through the heart to accept the Will of God by living inside Him, as unachievable as it may sound. Sometimes when in prayer, we can peer downward into a world that our bodies have never even departed because the Handmaid of the Lord has prepared us to fly like invisible eagles above the grave and burdensome wreck in which we have caused human decency to die. And, the sooner we learn that the most premier significance about the Mother God is the powerful prayers She wields before the Throne of the Almighty Father on mankind's behalf, the more quickly we will recover from the fatality of our wounds. God is alive; and Mary is real. To those who refuse to believe in the Providence of either one, *Get over it! Get a life! You lose!* Contrary to the sentiments of some agnostic zealots, it is neither fanatical nor coltish to believe in a God who is still interested in interacting with His Creation on a daily basis by which we decipher the expiration of the clock. And, it is not considered delusional to hail the Queen of Paradise to come to the aid of our agonizing souls whenever our suffering reaches its peak. Good Christians who summon Her loveliness and generate a distinct loyalty to Her Grace are always more confident in their faith, better able to endure the hardships by which we are exposed from the pagans in the world, and no longer fear the prospect of dying in good favor with the God of the Gospel Truth.

The Lord has sent Our Lady onto the Earth to infiltrate it with His sublime purity and righteousness so, by Her simple faith, we can become chaste of heart again. Her intention is to augment our journey back to holiness and to assist in refining our personal daily examen through which we focus upon our areas of laxity and eliminate any distractions that keep us from knowing Jesus better. She rejuvenates our consciences and leads us away from our infatuation with the high crimes and misdemeanors of the temporal globe—the mortal and venial sins and transgressions which keep us separated from the fullness of Heaven. She complements the Holy Spirit in interrogating our souls from the moment we first recognize that God has vested Her Immaculate Heart with the authority to manifest His miracles in the Name of Jesus Christ.

She is the Patron Saint of the United States; and She has Her work cut-out for Her in prompting us to understand the true meaning of Divine Sacrifice. Most of us see an America in which we ought to be allowed to drive Cadillacs and Lincoln Town Cars with tinted windows and wet-bars, while She sees us as needing to become as benign as those anonymous street dwellers and paupers who can be found carrying their belongings in plastics bags around their belt lines and pushing grocery carts overflowing with empty cardboard boxes alongside the railroad tracks. She is searching for cadres of benevolent heroes who are willing to reach-out to the lost and vulnerable in the vastness of Creation to join in the long line of Saints before whom She is poised to reproach the Earth. When the popular singer Carole King released her song *Been to Canaan* in December 1972, she was hailing the aura of peace and happiness for which we are all searching in the depths of our spirits; *a land of, green fields and rolling hills, room enough to do what we will. Sweet dreams of yestertime are running through my mind of a place I left behind. It's been so long, I can't remember when. But, I've been to Canaan, and I want to go back again. Though I'm content with myself, sometimes I long to be somewhere else. I try to do what I can, for with our day-to-day demands, we all need a Promised Land. It's been so long, I'm living 'til then; because I've been to Canaan, and I won't rest until I go back again.* We all know that the Biblical land of Canaan is the ancient region lying between the River Jordan, the Dead Sea, and the Mediterranean Sea in the Middle East, the homeland promised by God to Abraham in Genesis 12:5-9; also referred to as Palestine. What the Blessed Virgin Mary knows it to be is the unseen Kingdom of Divine Salvation to which Jesus Christ will deliver the departed souls of those who have been faithful to Him. This spiritual bounty; a place of placid rest and undying tranquility is also in the longing of the human heart for the God we have yet to see. We know who He is through the Wisdom of our faith, and by every means we offer to enhance our vision of His indomitable Love. Indeed, it is to this internal pining that Carole King devoted her singing. So many people might ask how she could have held such expectation for a place of Light and Truth that she had never even seen. How could she have already been to Canaan and wanted to go back again? The answer is simply that, as of the Winter of 1972, she had envisioned human life through the eyes of a contrite human spirit; and that this must surely be a part of the Kingdom of Heaven residing among us on the Earth. She rediscovered the true value of mortal anticipation despite the nihilism by which the rest of the world was effacing the dignity of the Holy Spirit in the name of raw secularism, terrorism, and anarchy. How clearly it seems that we are three decades into the future, and so many of us are still struggling for the paradisial foresight that led Carole King to place the longing in her humble heart into musical lyrics and artistically harmonic tones.  Do not fret little Carole!  The Mother of God has come to instill the vision you have seen into the soul of every human being!  She knows that Jesus Christ, Her Beloved Son, is the Way, the Truth, and the Life.  And, She never shies-away from aggressively teaching us that we are too far from Love; and She never minces Her words in telling us so.  The supernatural manifestations that are cited in the final two chapters of this book will discuss it more clearly, which by no means is foreign to the doctrines of orthodox Christianity.  The miracles that were performed by Jesus in the Sacred Scriptures were granted at the behest of His own Mother; and the Catholic Catechism provides a quite remarkable recounting of Her crucial role in human Salvation, 502-507, 963-972, and 2617-2619.  *The Virgin Mary is acknowledged and honored as being truly the Mother of God and of the Redeemer...She is clearly the Mother of the members of Christ...since She has, by Her charity, joined in bringing about the birth of believers in the Church, who are members of its head.  Mary, Mother of Christ, (is the) Mother of the Church* (963).  It is imperative for lost sinners to petition the invocation of the prayers of Our Lady on their behalf.  When we pray for one another in humble supplication, we should ask Her to go to the aid of those whom we know to be suffering from either physical infirmity or spiritual darkness, or are being persecuted by the enemies of the Church for the authenticity of their faith.  Her prayers evoke the pity of God upon all of us, as is recorded in the New Covenant.  She was physically present in the First Community of faith in Jerusalem in the Upper Room after Jesus' Ascension into Heaven to pray in advance of the coming Pentecost along with Peter, John, James, Andrew, Philip, Thomas, Bartholomew, Matthew, James son of Alphaeus, Simon the Zealot, and Judas son of James. (Acts 1:13-14).  Why was She there?  After all, She had already given birth to the Son of Man, raised Him into adulthood, beseeched His blessings upon believers and the lost, alike; witnessed His Sorrowful Passion and Crucifixion, bathed His Corpse with Her tears atop Her lap, rejoiced with Creation when He was Resurrected, and bade Him farewell at the Ascension forty days later.  Why, then, was it so important for Her to remain among the Apostles and Disciples in the Upper Room?  Because She knew that Her role in human Salvation did not cease when the Church was given the Light of Truth in tongues of fire.  She would become the consolation of many followers of Holy Christendom even after it was Her predestined time to be Assumed into Paradise to receive Her Crown as Queen of Heaven and Earth.  Although She is just beyond our immediate sight, She is still helping humanity remain as steadfast in faith as the first Apostles who lost their lives witnessing to the Kingship of Her Son.  She pores over our efforts to become sanctified with the detail of a seamstress; never judging, but always uniting.

Contrary to popular opinion, it is not true that Love means never having to say that you are sorry, especially with regard to our relationship with our Eternal Father. When we come to terms with our own sense of good and bad and are impelled to do the right thing, nothing can shake this foundation of obedience from beneath us. In the supreme and invisible realms of Creation, the enemies of Jesus Christ cannot really see what keeps us so elevated above their lack of piety and reverence. We seem to take a pummeling anyway by having our reputation run through the muck, our ethical and moral standards assailed, and our personal integrity impugned. There is no doubt that we sometimes perceive the adversaries of the Cross with wonder and confusion. Why would anyone on the face of the Earth be so adamantly against ridding the world of sorrow and corruption? Many are the times when Christians have wished to retaliate against their persecutors, but Our Divine Lord places the prospect before us of "trust." Do we really believe that, through God, Jesus is in absolute control of His Kingdom here on Earth when we see such destruction, malice, materialism, and atrocity that headlines the newspaper and television airwaves everyday? Our answer is an unequivocal "yes" because, like that transparent plateau beneath our souls which keeps them hoisted above the fray, our faith in the Truth we cannot always see remains intact. Too many of us are insensitive to the fact that God continues to remain hidden from our immediate sight, although we can readily see Him in the beauty of nature, in our newborn children, and through the charitable works of other men. We are all fashioned and communed by His Grace to endure the primal sacrifice of watching Satan terrify the material world; and we sometimes feel helpless as to what to do to stop it. This is the value of the prayer that Jesus has taught us to lift, not only through the *Our Father*, but in the thousands of incidental hopes that seem to pop into our thoughts as we circulate among our peers throughout the day. Living beneath the protective Mantle of the Most Blessed Virgin Mary means understanding that when we see injustices and inequities in our workplaces, on the sidewalk, or in our merchants' stores, we speak on behalf of the Truth so that innocent people are not subjugated by those who hold control, as fragile as their sense of authority might really be. There is a certain malfeasance which comes along with living the dailiness of human life when we decline to incorporate every decision we make into the basic consciousness of spiritual Love. This is what Christians have known for 2,000 years; and it is what makes the Kingdom of God and the Earth seem to be at such odds sometimes. The Holy Spirit does His bidding through us once we destroy our penchant to grab for the security of the "material" and allow Him to steer us into the ever-present clearing of peaceful Light. Our consent, therefore, is the most crucial element of Christ's success. Again, we learn this obedience through the power of the Holy Paraclete and by the example which has been poised in the person of the Mother of God, whose piety and servitude are nothing-less than a miraculous concession. If we are fair and forthcoming in our reliance upon the ability of Our Lady to guide us clear of the traps that Satan places in our paths, we will not only learn how to overcome them in the future, but be able to place them into proper perspective if we ever accidently stray into one again. Clarity of the heart means seeing Paradise through a set of eyes which are not necessarily anatomical in nature, but sublimely focused through and in our spiritual union in the Sacred Heart of Christ.

The world shall do what it wills! If our enemies manifest causes of action that take us before the courts of secular judges and common citizens in jury boxes, how does this make our suffering any different from the trial of Jesus before Pontius Pilate? After all, His Truth and Love present within us are the precise reflection of their fruitful abundance inside His Flesh as the Son of Mary and Joseph. A man whose religion is unfit to be put to the test before civil jurisdictions that do not even realize they are oppressing a child of God is not very sure in his faith. God knows this to be true, Jesus Christ learned it from first-hand experience, and the Blessed Virgin Mary has been trying to teach us ever since that to become the likeness of Her Sacrificed Son is to be willing to be castigated for our belief that His Will is all that matters. When Jesus told Creation that, *It is finished,* from the Cross on Good Friday, He knew beyond any doubt that we would crouch in the corners of our dens in the 21st century and wonder how this could be true. Where is the evidence that Satan and his evil legions are dead? Why is he being allowed to ravage the Earth, scar our families, and waste our valuable time with such wretchedness and gross annihilation? The answer is this: because we are allowing him to do it! We own the power through the Crucifixion of Jesus Christ to send the enemies of human decency and Salvation packing into the bowels of Hell where Our Lord cast them from the Cross by our stature and station as His Mystical Body on Earth. We are His Living Being in this modern age who are sprawled across the ground like cowards and nightcrawlers, unwilling to either recognize or participate in the inexorable retreat of evil back into the netherworld. Now, our nations, societies, and neighborhoods are paying a terrible price. In Jesus Christ, we have a King whose largesse is us, a leader that humanity is refusing to follow, a benefactor whose vast windfall we are too blind to engage, and a Martyr whose Blood has raised the entire globe in victory like a prize-fighter's fists in the air. What we already know and everything we will ever discover about learning comes from a Wisdom which is not of this world, that originates beyond the starry hosts under which we pitch our tents at night and connect like twinkling dots to conceptualize the invisible animals and images by which astrologists resign to their fate.  If we could see our way clear to understand that evil is not inevitable in Creation, I truly believe that more people would become involved in rooting-it out of their personal lives, our governments, our churches, and our public institutions.  This is the Divine power by which we have become the slayers of God's foes and through which we place the Devil on notice that he is not the task-master he thinks he is.  The children of Heaven are simultaneously the offspring of Immaculate Mary; and She is the worst enemy of Satan.  By running to Her protection like metal filings to a magnet, we are in the best position that any form of life could discover itself as the last vestige of a flagrantly naive humankind is finally laid to rest.

It often seems as though we are too busy worrying about our own "creature comfort" in the contemporary world to be sufficiently concerned about what God will procure beyond our deaths.  We are in His hands; we were formed by them, shaped beyond the imaginings of anything we could possibly conceive on our own, and destined to be either held forever or cast-away at the discretion of His Resurrected Son.  While there is no doubt that He is wroth to see the great catastrophes which have become the product of our own making, those who believe in Him realize that His compassion far outweighs His Holy Wrath.  If this were not true, He would surely have never dispatched someone so gentle as the Queen of Paradise to put-forth His case.  The Virgin Mary is evidence aplenty that His touch is tender, regenerative, wellborn, lenient, and merciful.  In other words, for those who are seeking one last chance to set their souls aright before the Creator who has deigned to give them life, there is still time for them to convert.  It may be only a matter of seconds, or perhaps a week, depending upon when the Son of Man might glean from His Father that the hour is ripe for His Return in Glory.  But, it is important for the human family to know that we must, at least, begin moving in the direction of that spiritual perfection to which Jesus calls us in the Sacred Scriptures if we expect to be so blessed that the prayerful sacrifices of the Angels and Saints might become the ullage whereupon our suffering cleaves.  So many Christians keep crying-out for more miracles; and rightfully so.  We have seen images of the Face of the Blessed Virgin Mary that have grown into rose petals, shone radiantly on huge glass buildings after rainstorms, and countless other phenomenon that are obviously too supernatural to ignore.  There are signs, wonders, and miracles all over the world that many people seem to take for granted.  One such event occurred in Salem, Oregon to Pastor Wesley Marcle.  In December 2001, he discovered a golden crucifix that was believed to be a setting in a man's ring inside a serving of cabbage that had been cooked by his wife for dinner.  It apparently fell into the plant while it was growing at a farm in rural California, after which it was purchased by Roth's

Friendly Market and advertised for sale. According to AP, how the article fell into the cabbage patch is anyone's guess. While such things are an opportune time to confirm that Jesus Christ is trying to reveal Himself through every venue possible without appearing in person to everyone on the Earth, why not employ our good faith to understand gifts such as these as messages of Divine intervention with a definitive purpose? What do we have to lose by accepting them on a more receptive scale than their face-value might allow? Incidents like this one are not a matter of mere coincidence or chance; they are a manifestation of the prefigured landscape linking Heaven and Earth. If we downplay their significance, we diminish the Christian evolvement of our souls. As discussed in the next chapter, God has strewn the Earth with countless supernatural signs and events that are so tangibly and discernibly miraculous that only the most callous atheists could scoff at their meaning. And, the question is not whether they are authentic, but why would God be interested in communicating with His Creation in such spectacular ways? There is no doubt that it is by reason that He is soliciting our response; one of genuine human faith, conviction, participation, reverence, allegiance, and a submission of reciprocal homage.

It seems like there are too many people in America who are still trying to straddle the gap between liberality and conservatism, justice and vengeance, knowledge and Wisdom, the Spirit and the flesh, and teetotaling versus addiction. As for our relationship with God, there is no such thing as growing more deeply in holiness and refusing to surrender the fetishes of the world. If Love is a flame, He wants us to become a leaping inferno and not a smoldering wick. If life can be likened to a stream of water, we are supposed to become a veritable geyser and not a stagnant puddle in the keel of a gutter. When seafaring across the waves of righteousness, we are meant to sail the proverbial perfect line about which Jesus speaks, because in Him we buoy ourselves above the temptation to remain tethered to the forested globe while arriving safely to our resurgence in the bounty of God, revealing His Glory into the lives of the lost. Our vision will be much too small, unyielding, cold, and barren if we look only into the snakepits of the universe and ignore the forces of Creation that belong to Heaven which are calling from above. Therefore, the Lord has sent Jesus Christ onto the Earth to establish His Kingdom here; that He might catalyze the symphysis which will result in the perfect union which is described in the Holy Bible as the coming New Jerusalem—the deliverance of a purified humanity into the presence of its sovereign God. What can bring this new synchronicity into being? By what measures are we drawn to become much larger than simple mortal men and women who are wasting-away to nothing under the false assumption that it is somehow alright by Jesus that we wield no active role in evangelizing His Love? Why are we so confounded? Where did the world lose its way? How could it have ever happened? The Earth's valleys, folds, mountains, streams, and precipices cannot reveal everything that we are supposed to know about why we are here; for this is what Christianity is for. It is the source of our discovery of the Divine Revelation which has been given to our ancestors from many centuries past. It is the reason for comprehending that the Mosaic Law is the Messianic premonition which the New Covenant has fulfilled. It is not anti-Semitic to tell someone that the advancement of the Holy Gospel of Jesus Christ is the reason why Moses was born because the same Almighty God who spoke to him is the very Creator who conceived His Only Begotten Son inside the Womb of the Most Blessed Virgin Mary. There is too much ado about the distinctions between Judaism and Christianity around the world today. Mary was a Jewish handmaid, born to Jewish parents, and married a Jewish carpenter. She gave birth to Jesus Christ and conceded to His Crucifixion, setting the entire of humankind free from the throes of sin and death: Jew, Gentile, Christian, Mormon, Seventh Day Adventist, Pentecostal, Baptist, Unitarian, Roman Catholic, Lutheran, Zionist, Hindu, Missionary, Charismatic, Nazarene, Congregational, United Methodist, Greek Orthodox, Assembly of God, Presbyterian, and all the rest.

The union of all these religions and the broad expanse of the races by which they are composed is centered in One God in Three Persons; the Most Blessed Trinity. Some of them do not fully adhere to His Word by believing it, but this does not render it any less true. We are one people under Heaven and a singular body of absolved sinners in the Blood of the Cross of Jesus Christ. As I have plainly stated, one of His greatest gifts to Creation is His Immaculate Mother Mary, in whose favor we rest when we pray from the heart. The suppliance that pleases God to an immeasurable degree is the Holy Rosary. It has been a staple of the Catholic religion for hundreds of years, and was dispensed from Heaven by Our Lady, Herself, to Saint Dominic. By the Providence of the Holy Spirit, he was given this beautiful petition as a reflection of the Angelic Salutation of Gabriel at the Annunciation, *Hail, full of Grace! The Lord is with Thee! Blessed are you among women; and blessed is the Fruit of your Womb!* This is our call, too; that we summon Her aid in the likeness of the angels and Archangels. The Sacred Mysteries have long been divided into three sets of Five Meditations on the lives of Jesus and Mary; and Pope John Paul II added another Five Mysteries of Light in 2002 to the Joyful, Sorrowful, and Glorious ones that Catholics everywhere have been reciting since the age of Saint Dominic. While I have listed all twenty of them on page 189 herein, the new Mysteries of Light merit at least a cursory introduction. The Holy Father stated that it is suitable to include these Mysteries of Christ's public ministry between His Baptism and His Passion in order to bring-out fully the Christological depth of the Rosary, itself. *The Baptism in the Jordan* is the First Mystery of Light and is fashioned from Matthew 3:13 and 2 Corinthians 5:21, where Jesus descends into the waters as the innocent one and became sin for our sake, wherein the Holy Spirit vested Him to carry-out the mission for which He was born. *The Cana Wedding* is the Second Mystery (John 2:1-12) when Christ changed water into wine to further invoke the faith of His disciples, reflecting the intervention of the Virgin Mary, upon whom we call for help to this very day. *The Proclamation of the Kingdom* is the Third Mystery of Light, and it parallels the teaching of Jesus calling humanity to conversion in anticipation of the coming Revelation of the Kingdom of God (Mark 1:15, and John 20:22-23). *The Transfiguration* is the Fourth and is referred to as the Mystery of Light par excellence because the Glory of the Godhead shines forth from Jesus on Mt. Tabor in the presence of Peter, James, and John (Luke 9:28-36). God hereby commands His Apostles to listen to Him and prepare to join Him in the agony of His Passion so as to come into the fullness of joy of the Resurrection and life that is transfigured by the Holy Spirit. The final Mystery of Light is the *First Eucharist* during which Our Lord institutes the Most Blessed Sacrament by offering His Sacred Body and Blood as our spiritual food and drink under the signs of Bread and Wine, testifying to His invincible Love (Matthew 26:26-30, Mark 14:22-26, Luke 22:14-20), as He endures the ultimate Sacrifice of Crucifixion on the Cross in reparation for the sins of the whole world. The Holy Father has substantiated these additional Mysteries by citing their origin in the Sacred Scriptures as they relate to the Divinity of Christ; and this alone is sufficient reason for their inclusion in our Marian prayers as manifested through our original deposit of faith. What better way to enhance our union with God than through His miracle-working Son and to remember the significance of His gifts to humanity through the pining intercession of His Immaculate Mother? From this moment forward, can we not become the likeness of the many Saints from the annals of Christian history who have destroyed evil legions in their paths and converted multitudes for Jesus to the Light of His Cross through our veneration and devotion to the Blessed Virgin Mary? This is a certitude we must embrace in earnest because, according to Her recent apparitions, the world is near its end.

# The Sacred Mysteries of the Most Holy Rosary

### *The Joyful Mysteries*

| | |
|---|---|
| *First* | The Annunciation of the Archangel Gabriel to Mary |
| *Second* | The Visitation of Mary to Her Cousin Elizabeth |
| *Third* | The Birth of Jesus in Bethlehem |
| *Fourth* | The Presentation of Jesus at the Temple |
| *Fifth* | The Finding of the Child Jesus in the Temple |

### *The Mysteries of Light*

| | |
|---|---|
| *First* | Jesus is Baptized in the River Jordan |
| *Second* | The Miracle at the Cana Wedding Feast |
| *Third* | The Proclamation of the Kingdom of God |
| *Fourth* | The Transfiguration of Jesus on Mt. Tabor |
| *Fifth* | Jesus Institutes the Holy Eucharist |

### *The Sorrowful Mysteries*

| | |
|---|---|
| *First* | The Agony of Jesus in the Garden of Gethsemane |
| *Second* | The Scourging of Jesus at the Pillar |
| *Third* | The Mock Crowning of Jesus with Thorns |
| *Fourth* | Jesus Carries the Cross to Mount Calvary |
| *Fifth* | Jesus is Crucified on the Cross |

### *The Glorious Mysteries*

| | |
|---|---|
| *First* | The Resurrection of Jesus from the Sepulcher |
| *Second* | The Ascension of Jesus into Heaven |
| *Third* | The Descent of the Holy Spirit at Pentecost |
| *Fourth* | The Assumption of the Virgin Mary into Heaven |
| *Fifth* | The Crowning of Mary as Queen of Heaven and Earth |

# JMJ

## I Shall Sing the Lord's Mercy

*The Lord's Supper is laid,*
*Jesus sits down at table with His Apostles,*
*His Being all transformed into Love,*
*For such was the Holy Trinity's Counsel.*
*'With great desire, I desire to eat with you,*
*Before I suffer death.*
*About to leave you, Love holds Me in your midst.'*
*He sheds His Blood, gives His life,*
*for He loves immensely.*
*Love hides beneath the appearance of Bread,*
*Departing, He remains with us.*
*Such self-abasement was not needed,*
*Yet, burning Love hid Him under these Species.*
*Over the bread and wine He says these words:*
*'This is My Blood, this is My Body.'*
*Although mysterious, these are words of Love.*
*Then, He passes the Cup among His disciples.*
*Jesus grew deeply troubled within*
*and said, 'One of you will betray His Master.'*
*They fell silent, with a silence as of the Tomb,*
*And, John inclined His head upon His breast.*
*The Supper is ended.*
*Let us go to Gethsemane.*
*Love is satisfied,*
*And there the traitor is waiting.*
*O Divine Will, You are my nourishment,*
*You are my delight. Hasten, O Lord,*
*the Feast of Mercy that souls may*
*recognize the fountain of Your goodness!*

From *The Divine Mercy Diary* 1002, 1003
Sister M. Faustina Kowalska
Krakow, Poland March 1, 1937

# Chapter XV
## *Mary, the Queen of Paradise*
## *Matriarch of Humanity Redeemed*

One of my brothers-in-law is a construction contractor who pours cement driveways, foundations, and parking lots; and he once told me that there are only two types of finished concrete: the kind that is cracked, and the kind that is eventually going to crack. This is the sad fate of too many things; and our experience teaches us about certain inevitable aspects of human affairs, whether they are actual or thoughtful in nature, wherein we seem to never change course unless we fear something adversely affecting the wholesale turn-of-events for our profits and loss, or we act upon them merely to satisfy our stubborn habits. I do not believe that we conduct our lives with as much spontaneity as most of us would like because we have so many responsibilities to fulfill. When we were young, we dashed around on our bicycles and scooters with somewhat of a harum-scarum attitude about anything that even so much as looked like a direct command from our parents and elders. But, the countless miraculous apparitions of the Hosts of Heaven which have been witnessed around the globe throughout history deserve a more sincere response because they are not something we can quickly judge, ignore, or shape with our hands. They have never been confined to any particular age; and there is nothing we can do to destroy what we see before us when we opens our eyes, especially if it is the extra-terrestrial presence of someone whose soul resides in Paradise. The type of apparition to which I am referring is not a slapstick image that strikes us as awkward because of its stark contrast to our natural environment, like seeing a herd of cattle grazing in the middle of a PGA golf course fairway. And, God's miracles are never spectral in nature because it is not His intention to wreak further havoc upon the world than that which Satan has already caused. Paranormal events from the realms of Heaven sometimes look as odd, but they are manifestations of Truth that God deigns to the Earth for the purpose of enhancing the Divine Love of mortal men. Jesus Christ knows that the fulcrum of the human domain does not rest in balancing secular affairs outside the institution of His Church, but at the precise point where the soul of man is connected in a supernatural way with the life hereafter. In other words, we strike a chord of unity with Him through the economy of our holy spiritualism and leave the secular world behind. As for Creation at large, this can be achieved in toto only after all our agnostics, atheists, infidels, and reprobates have been converted to the Cross. Indeed, this is the intrinsic mission of the Church and is the reason why God has seen fit to provide mounds of irrefutable evidence of His powerful Being through such miraculous signs. As I established earlier, mankind seeks to find the moderate ground in many circumstances, even in the unintentional ways we speak, look, and behave. If we traveled south to Texas or Oklahoma on any given day, we might pull into a gas station and see a group of older gentlemen leaning-back in wooden chairs with their heads against the storefront. Walking past them to go inside for a cold drink, one of them might utter "howdy" to us in a slow drawl as we go by, then crane his neck and spate the juices of his Wintergreen maccaboy with a tinny echo into a nearby coffee can. And, if we went to the northeast states of Maine, New York, or Massachusetts, we might find somebody in a shopping mall who begins telling us about the price of commodities in Canada; but we suddenly become distracted by the way everyone seems so Bostonian in their accent, taking care to micro-pronounce every syllable of their words and intone phrases like "the cart went up the path" so that it sounds like "the cot went up the poth." Such distinctions serve to identify us personally, but they are no barometer for defining the composure of our hearts or the measures to which we Love our Lord and Savior.

This, therefore, is the reason why the Holy Spirit is engulfing the Earth today; evoking our acceptance of Christianity with full conciseness, sureness, and beyond a hint of ambiguity. There is a stark difference in living as a blind mortal creature and embracing the gift of human life while planning its role beyond the aspects of Eternity. It's the same axiom that former U.S. President George Bush (No. 41) called "the vision thing." He never really had it, and it caused his defeat for reelection in 1992. Just as sure as the Son of God turned water into wine and fed 5000 people with a couple of loaves and fishes, He and His Mother are appearing all over the world through this phenomenal gift called " apparitions" so as to grow the faith of sinners and implore us to embrace His Holy Gospel with greater sincerity than any generation before. A worldwide organization, Marian Communications Limited, produced and released a VHS video in 1991 entitled *Marian Apparitions of the 20th Century* which is a collection of color footage from around the globe where the Virgin Mary has appeared to unsuspecting souls. It clearly explains why God has sent His Mother to the Earth to warn us that humanity is on the brink of annihilation unless we respond to Her call for personal penance, prayer, conversion to Christianity, fasting, and peace. The production is narrated by Ricardo Montalban, and the urgency in his voice reflects the kindness of Our Lady in imploring us to abandon our recklessness and embrace the Son of God whose Crucifixion has set the world free from sin and death. Some of the locations cited in the film have already been discerned, authenticated, and formally approved by the Roman Catholic Church, while others are under scrutiny at the present time. Multiple sightings of Jesus and Mary have been reported in places like Fatima (Portugal), Banneux and Beauraing (Belgium),

Zeitun (Egypt), Garabandal (Spain), Akita (Japan), Betania (Venezuela), Medjugorje (Croatia), Kibeho and Rwanda (Africa), Naju (Korea), Lourdes (France), Guadalupe (Mexico) and the former Soviet Republic of Ukraine. The main urgency of these Messianic and Marian apparitions is that the world is being called to unity with God through the lifting of prayer; especially the Joyful, Luminous, Sorrowful, and Glorious Mysteries of the Rosary. Many people have asked why the Holy Rosary is such a timely petition for global peace, for the piety of souls, a tool for the propagation of Christianity, and a catalyst for charismatic contemplation upon the life of Jesus. To some, it seems too repetitious and needlessly long. But, to those who know Jesus Christ well, it is more than what many Protestants and other non-Catholics perceive it as being. Pope Paul VI said, *...by its nature, the recitation of the Rosary calls for a quiet rhythm and a lingering pace, helping (us) meditate on the Sacred Mysteries of the Lord's life as seen through the eyes of Her who was closest to Him. In this way, the unfathomable richness of these Mysteries are unfolded...As a result of modern reflection, the relationships between the Liturgy and the Rosary have been more clearly understood...The Rosary is (as it were) a branch sprung from the ancient trunk of the Christian Liturgy, the Psalter of the Blessed Virgin, whereby the humble were associated in the Church's hymn of praise and universal intercession.* (From *Marialis Cultus*). Therefore, let us please God by hailing the advocacy of His Immaculate Mother in the same way that Jesus calls upon Her now to be the consoling Matriarch and Lady of Wisdom for humanity thrice-blessed.

Thousands of anonymous people have been called upon to do just that during the previous centuries, some of whom have become household names to those who follow Our Lady closely, and others that were among the crowds who have seen God's supernatural signs and miracles of nature. The Holy Mother appeared six times in Fatima, Portugal between May 13 and October 13, 1917 to three shepherd children and told them that She had been sent by God to tell His humanity that the world which was being torn asunder by wars and bloody violence could find Love and renewed peace in prayer, reparation, and consecration to Her Immaculate Heart. The three seers were Francisco Martos, Jacinta Martos, and Lucia Dos Santos. According to those who have discerned these apparitions on behalf of the Church, the Virgin Mary wished to send an urgent message through these children that God was displeased with the lack of holiness around the world in the earlier 20th century. She told them that war is a punishment for sin and that it was God's intention to further chastise the Earth because of humankind's lack of righteousness and Love. She prophesied that Russia would spread its plague of atheism and military aggression if millions did not pray to stop it. According to Our Lady, *...If My requests are not granted, Russia will spread its errors throughout the world,* *raising-up wars and persecution against the Church. The good will be martyred, the Holy Father will suffer much, and various nations will be annihilated.* She requested for the Pope to consecrate Russia to Her Immaculate Heart and for Christians to be devoted to Her. She later also requested through Lucia (1925) *...Say to all those who, for five months, on the first Saturday, confess, receive Holy Communion, recite the Rosary, and keep Me company for 15 minutes while meditating on the fifteen Mysteries of the Rosary in a spirit of reparation, I promise to assist them at the hour of death with all the graces necessary for the Salvation of their souls.* The crux of the Fatima Message is contained in a three-part *Secret* which She confided to the little children in July 1917. The first was a vision of Hell that God showed them so everyone on Earth would believe that it is a real place of horrible suffering where the souls of condemned sinners go. The second part of the *Secret* was Our Lady's prophecy of the coming of World War II; and it specifically contained Her solemn request for the conversion of Russia which, in itself, precedes the inevitable Triumph of Her Immaculate Heart. Let there be no mistake by anyone who is involved in the Fatima movement today. Pope John Paul II is solely responsible for the fall of the Soviet Union and the propagation of Roman Catholicism across the expanse of its separate republics. The final part of the *Secret* which was revealed by the Vatican on May 13, 2000 deals particularly with this same Pope. It was inscribed by Lucia Dos Santos, the last living Fatima seer, and was transferred to the Holy See in 1957. Its text included an image of a Bishop in white vestments who seemed afflicted by pain and sorrow as he was ascending a mountain and passing through a city which lay in ruins. He was praying for numerous corpses he had seen along the way. He reached the summit and fell to his knees in front of a large Cross where he was killed by a group of soldiers who fired bullets at him, along with countless other Bishops, priests, nuns, and devoted lay people. Lucia described the presence of two Angels below the arms of the Cross holding a crystal aspersorium in their hands into which they gathered the blood of all the Martyrs and sprinkled the souls who were making their way toward God. It has been revealed that the "Bishop in White" whom Lucia saw was Pope John Paul II during the attempted assassination on his life on May 13, 1981. Indeed, the world responded sufficiently to Our Lady of Fatima and the Holy Father was spared through Her intercession. The date of the attempt on his life fell on the day and month of Our Lady's first apparition to the three seers in Fatima, Portugal.

A huge manifestation occurred on October 13, 1917 in Fatima when 70,000 people saw the "miracle of the sun." Our Lady told the children well in advance that it would occur by saying, *...On the last month, I will perform a miracle so that all may believe.* The thousands of pilgrims had gathered in the precise location that the seers told them it would happen. According to the testimonies of those who were present, it was a very rainy day and the ground beneath them was so saturated that they could hardly walk in the mud without losing their shoes. Suddenly, the overcast skies became clear and the pilgrims could see the sun shining very brightly overhead. It began to spin like a fiery wheel in the sky and throw sparks into the atmosphere; and the people below were able to see it without shielding their eyes. Then, to the uproar of thousands of voices, it appeared to descend from above on a course that would have it nearly collide with the Earth. Many pilgrims spoke of seeing the solar spires with vivid clarity reflecting from the amber skin tones of each other's faces. With a great whirl, it turned into a red-hot hue and descended upon them with an overwhelming flash. Soon after these terrifying moments, it retreated to its original position in the sky and the atmosphere returned to normal. But, God had left the soil upon which the 70,000 people stood parched and dry; and their footprints that had been previously trod into the mud were cast like concrete into the earthen floor. Their previously rain-drenched clothes were dried in a matter of only a few seconds. This supernatural event has become known as one of the greatest Marian miracles to have ever been witnessed in the 20th century. And, not only as a result of this paranormal phenomenon, but of the greater miracle that the prayers of the faithful are appeasing the Wrath of God, the world no longer fears Russia the way it did prior to the intercession of Our Lady of Fatima. The Catholic Church has officially approved the Fatima Message as "worthy of belief." Several Popes have visited the site of the apparitions; and Pope John Paul II publicly acknowledged that it was through the Grace of the Blessed Virgin Mary that his life was spared during the attempt on his life in 1981. Should we assume that the revelation of the third part of the Fatima *Secret* implies that time is growing very short before the return of Jesus Christ in Glory? Sister Lucia became an elderly woman before it was finally made public. There is no question that His Holiness, Pope John Paul II, is the Bishop to whom Our Lady referred in the last portion of the *Secret* She revealed to the seers in 1917. Since this is the case, humanity can rest assured that the Fatima Message is fulfilling its purpose, and that it will always be relevant as we continue to pray for global peace, to consecrate our lives to Our Lady and to Her Son, and to do penance in reparation for the sins of the world. Indeed, the imminent Triumph of Her Immaculate Heart has already commenced!

Another private revelation which has been officially recognized by the Roman Catholic Church are the miraculous apparitions of the Mother of Jesus Christ to a 14-year-old French girl named Bernadette Soubirous. On February 11, 1858, she was walking with her sister and a friend to gather firewood for her parents' home when they came upon a stream.  They tread across the icy waters, although Bernadette had wished to remain on the shore because she suffered severe bouts of asthma.  She later reported that she heard strong gusts of wind and thunder, but the skies were clear and none of the branches on the trees were waving.  She then looked toward the Grotto of Massabielle located nearby and saw a golden cloud whereupon a beautiful Woman was standing, wearing a white gown and holding a Rosary in Her hands.  This would be the first of eighteen different times that Our Lady would appear to Bernadette, during which the Holy Mother revealed to her that She wanted her to kneel to pray and receive further instructions.  From the very moment Bernadette first saw the Virgin Mary until her final apparition on July 16, 1858, she was as docile and obedient as any human could be.  She endured the scoffing, castigation, and ridicule of her family, friends, clergy, and peers.  But, she stood firmly by her proclamation that the Mother of God had appeared to her in the grimy grotto where the pigs fed on the waste that was deposited there.  But, as time passed, the crowds grew larger to discover more about this "Lady" that Bernadette kept saying she was seeing.  Our Lady asked her to perform certain acts of obedience before the skeptical onlookers.  During the apparition of February 24, the Holy Mother stated Her main request of the miracle of Lourdes, *Repent! Penance! Penance! Pray to God for the conversion of sinners,!* after which Bernadette kissed the ground as an act of contrition.  On the following day, the Virgin Mary instructed her to drink and cleanse her face at the fountain in the Grotto.  But, looking around, there was no fountain to be seen.  Our Lady told her to dig at the foot of the Grotto, wash her face in the mud, and eat the leaves of wild grass that were sprouting there.  Once the throngs of people saw Bernadette doing this, they were convinced that she was not being truthful about her visions, and that she was in need of psychiatric care.  They left the Grotto laughing at her and mocking at her obedience to Our Lady, comparing her to the pigs that came there to root.  However, almost immediately thereafter, a gushing spring of water began to flow where Bernadette had dug with her humble little fingers.  And, to this day, the miraculous streams of this spring are a healing balm for hundreds of pilgrims who go to Lourdes to pray.  During the thirteenth apparition, Our Lady asked Bernadette to request the clergy to construct a prayer chapel on the spot where the apparitions were taking place.  Upon approaching them, they required her to go back to the Grotto and ask "the Lady's" name; and it was not until the sixteenth apparition on March 25th that She confirmed to Bernadette that She was *The Immaculate Conception.* They then recalled that, in 1854, Pope Pius IX had proclaimed the Dogma that the Mother of God was conceived free from original sin.  Bernadette did not understand the meaning of these words, but she went back to report the information they had sought. From that time forward, they knew it was the Mother of God who had appeared at the Grotto of Massabielle. The Chapel was built to reflect their faith that this little French girl was telling the truth all along. *The Basilica of Our Lady of Lourdes* was placed atop the Grotto where the Virgin Mary had appeared to Bernadette Soubirous so that the union of God in Heaven and the selfless obedience of humankind on the Earth could be visibly and permanently enshrined.

One of the most evocative sites still commemorating the miraculous apparitions of the Holy Mother in the Western Hemisphere is located in Mexico City, Mexico. It was on December 9, 1531 when a 57-year-old Aztec Indian named Juan Diego was on his way to morning Mass when the Virgin Mary appeared to him near the base of Tepeyac Hill. He heard the mellow singing of the birds as though it was the break of Spring, and proceeded to the summit of the hill where he saw Our Lady. He described Her as being extreme in grandeur, Her garments shining like the sun, and the cliff where She rested Her feet was glittering as though She was wearing diamonds around Her ankles. The Holy Mother stopped him by saying the following words, *...Know and understand well that I am the ever Virgin Holy Mary, Mother of the True God for whom we live, of the Creator of all things, Lord of Heaven and the Earth. I wish that a temple be erected here quickly so I may therein exhibit and give all My Love, compassion, help, and protection because I am your Merciful Mother, to you, and to all the inhabitants on this land and all the rest who Love Me, invoke and confide in Me; listen there to their lamentations, and remedy all their miseries, afflictions, and sorrows.* She bade him to go to his Franciscan Bishop Zumarraga in Mexico City to announce what She had just told him. Upon being greeted by the Prelate, the latter declined to believe Juan Diego's testimony. So, he returned to the site where he had seen the Blessed Virgin, whereupon She asked him to go back and make the request of the Bishop a second time. On the next day, December 10, 1531 the Bishop told him that he required a sign from the Lady whom he had seen as proof of the authenticity of Her origin. After Juan scurries back to the hill again, the Holy Mother tells him that She will provide the sign tomorrow. However, when morning came, Juan missed his appointment with Her because his uncle had fallen gravely ill and was in great need of medical attention. He set out to summon a doctor, but not finding one, he assures his dying relative that he would go to Tlatelolco the next morning to find a priest to administer the Sacraments to prepare him for his death. He awoke on Tuesday, December 12th at a very early hour and decided it better to ensure that the Sacraments were given to his uncle than for him to see the Blessed Virgin at the time, so he walked around the other side of Tepeyac Hill to avoid her. However, the Lady came down the hillside to greet him, telling him that She would restore the health of his uncle, Juan Bernardino, to whom She also appeared. After having told him of this, She asked him to climb to the top of the hill and pluck the Castilian roses that were blooming there. Juan reminded Her that they were not in season during December, but he went anyway and discovered a massive garden of them growing as if it were Springtime. He gathered them in his arms and returned to the location of the apparition where the Holy Mother carefully arranged them beneath his cactus-cloth mantle, also known as a tilma, with Her hands. She instructed him to go back to see the Bishop and he would have his sign. So, he did as She asked and presented himself yet another time to Bishop Zumarraga. He opened his cloak to give the roses to the skeptical Prelate and there, impressed upon his garment, was the miraculous image of the Blessed Virgin Mary that has now become the world-renowned Tilma of Our Lady of Guadalupe. The whole of Mexico then believed Juan Diego and the temple was built according to Our Lady's wishes. Other miracles of Guadalupe have become widely known since then. Mexico was ravaged by a typhus plague in 1736 that claimed the lives of 700,000 people in a period of only eight months. When the Catholic clergy there declared Our Lady of Guadalupe to be the Patroness Saint of Mexico in May 1737, the deadly pestilence immediately stopped spreading. There were also more than nine million conversions of Aztec Indians to Christianity as a result of Our Lady's miraculous apparitions in Mexico as early as AD 1540. As for the sacred Tilma, it continues to be displayed in the Basilica of Our Lady of Guadalupe in Mexico City where millions of pilgrims travel each year to pray. Since it was made from a poor grade of agave fibers during the time when Juan Diego wore it, its fabric would have naturally deteriorated in about twenty years time. However, it miraculously shows no sign of decay over 470 years after it was first presented to Bishop Zumarraga in 1531, defying all scientific explanations. Juan Diego was finally canonized as Mexico's first Indian Saint by Pope John Paul II before hundreds-of-thousands of faithful pilgrims on July 31, 2002 at Our Lady's Basilica during a ceremony that was rich in Mexican-Indian culture and Roman Catholic pageantry.

To all of our children, our "babes in the woods," the miraculous events of Fatima, Lourdes, and Guadalupe are evidence from God that the future of the world truly belongs to them. We can say with a high degree of certainty and appropriateness that Our Creator does not sleep inside a Palace of celestial dreams pretending that we are not suffering on the Earth below. Through the countless supernatural manifestations He is according to humanity, we have come to know Him as the orchestrator and proprietor of human life both in this world and the next. We should be grateful for the many venues of His intervening Love, spiritual designs, pious perfection, supernatural revelations, and instinctive Wisdom. There is no doubt that His Divine Plan to touch the heart of humankind through the Grace and civility of His Immaculate Mother is yet another means to heal us who live on the Earth who have become embittered through time and impatient with the deafening silence of the distant beyond. We can trust through our best intuition that the Hosts of Heaven do not make these things up on the fly, but that there is a prefigured paragon in place by which we are fortunately caught-up in the rejuvenation of our consciences so that we will always deal in the Truth. After all, there can be no Wisdom where the clarity of Divine Love is not forthrightly known. I believe that the purpose of every private revelation is based upon the premise that anyone who comes into authentic contact with the workings of the Holy Spirit is helping their God write those billions of books about human Love that Jesus Christ did not have time to inscribe. Even in all He did for humanity in a brief span of 33 years, the composite parameters of His mortal life could not contain every facet of the enlightenment of the heart which has come into the world since then. My prayers and hopes are that we will become altogether absorbed by the Christian Grace which reminds us that life is nothing short of our search for the righteousness and gentleness that Our Lord so brilliantly espoused. If we are to become courageous Americans; and if it is true that we desire to forge the conquest of that "final frontier," then we must realize that it has little relevance to touching and judging, and everything to do with the spiritually sublime. The grave and noble consequences at the center of our hearts are where our decisive battles must begin. The Virgin Mary is trying to teach us that it is time for humanity to make amends in growing our trust in Jesus Christ as well as a greater faith in His Father so the world can be unified by the inseparable Love they share.

We must take the leap into believing that if Christ is simultaneously God, and that God is asking us to be not unlike His Sacrificed Son, then we should wholeheartedly embrace a willingness to suffer gladly and become worthy of attaining the attributes that make them both flawlessly whole. Our Lord was tempted in the desert by Satan for 40 days, but He never gave-in to his evil lies or to the expediency that would have made His own discomfort measurably less. The issue He was raising back then, and the point He is making to us now, is that we are finely hewn from this same vigilance inside the Third Person of the Blessed Trinity—the Holy Spirit, in which the entire globe is fully immersed. Deep inside, we are a people of wonder and awe, a community of valor and uncontested ingenuity, and a chosen species of unparalleled intellect and definitive strength. If we should fail our God in anything reverent He is asking us to do, we should force the loss upon ourselves. So, let us fast and pray in the way Our Holy Mother has asked. If we nourish anything about us, let it be the invocation of God's Divine revelations in our hearts. We can conquer, intimidate, and terrify the very fear that is trying to haunt us now through the submission and piety that Our Lady has been revealing to the world. As for me, I have based my entire being on the conclave between Heaven and Earth which is now ongoing because I know that there are still many battles yet to come. I have no doubt that Christ is in absolute control of His Kingdom here, and that my vision is only a diminutive fraction of His sight. However, I have willed to offer my sacrifices on His behalf because I Love Him for giving me purpose and sustaining my faith. My honor, respect, intelligence, trust, and devotion belong to the Son of Mary because He has gone to extreme torment to rescue us from this living hell in which impurity and corruption are slowly tearing us apart. He is the practitioner of Redemptive Grace for a people who are proudly trying their worst to avoid being absolved. How difficult this must be for Him who has paid the price for our Salvation! We shall know what it means to be "new people" if we lend ourselves to a humility that will make us more like Him. This is the hope of the Blessed Virgin Mary in whom we have no better advocate before the Holy Cross. Let us resolve to make this the goal of our little children and of the whole world; because if the Return of Jesus Christ in Glory is ever to be delayed by so much as a second, let it not be from our dilatory stubbornness or our failure to welcome Him back again.

# Chapter XVI
## *Mary,* Morning Star Over America
### *The Miraculous Intercessor*

The nearly-exhausted ages of human existence have been strewn with monumental endeavors from the premier moment that the first inquisitive soul followed the lead of his prodding conscience and was inspired to dream of things residing in the greater realms; far beyond the boundaries of our mortal senses. Our storybook of earthborn beingness is seasoned with courageous names like Hanno and Himilco, Eriksson, Columbus, Da Gama and Magellan, Lewis, Clark, Armstrong, Aldrin, and Collins; and of course, the heroic Glenn. Each set-out into the uncharted expanse, searching for the pristine experiences of worlds greater than the musing of much lesser men, and hoping to secure the throne-room treasures of what would be discovered in the yet unknown recesses of their bold-hearted voyages. While some chose the wildering midlands, others braved the pulsating seas; and in the technology of our times, their visionary devotions have been drawn upward into the vaulting skies in rocketing capsules and lofty shuttles alike. All of this has been the byproduct of human hearts who responded to the primordial call to seek-out that which had yet to be found; to discover the realms that had never been seen, to find new beginnings and break-upon destined ends, while always starting the next day with one foot farther up the path than the day before. Why? Because our hope is the reason for which anyone has ever savored the impulse to learn. We, who are the progeny of their innumerable successes, anchor their legacies in the harbors of our civic libraries and towering halls which swell with the passionate tales of these heroic souls on the wind-swept bows of their finest days. So, let us all gather 'round this embodiment of history and spread their maps before us again. Call forth the cartographers and the decipherers, the charters and the linguists! Unfurl their parchments and open the dead captains' logs! Let us together recalculate the readings and echo the historical soundings of the fathomed depths upon which they sailed! Produce the legacy that it may be formally recognized of the one who impaled his gilt-edged banner upon the shores of Paradise and thereafter returned with its cache of Divinity. Let him step forward who succeeded in unearthing Heaven; that place of infinite bliss where the knowledge to create the wayfaring universes is gratuitously dispensed like gummy-bears to a child. Where has been found the youthful fountain that produces giggling children from restless searchers and wind-driven shipmen? Bring to the fore the ancient treasure from the paradisial Kingdom for all mankind to see; the fortune that does not require life and limb to be parlayed and plundered in the balance of the chanceful dance between triumph and tragedy; the beatitude which itself yearns for its soul-parched seekers! Cry out galaxies above the reckoning at this hailed convocation of mortal history! ......What? Is there no one who will come forward today? Has the evidence not been gleaned from our millenary engagements with the stark unknown? Are there no maps to mark this course? Surely, in all the multitudes of generations, some of our most courageous explorers must have located that which is unequivocally the only thing ever worth finding.

Why has this challenge been laid before us? To clear the board of any shallow contenders! Divine Providence so often mimics the contortions of us mortals. I do not know if it is to mock us in our station relegated so far below the heavens or to encourage us by reflecting our imitations and magnifying our smallest efforts in order to lift our dignity to its perch upon the paternal knee of the Almighty. At any rate, each of us can remember those comical moments when a military commander has asked his line of troops for a volunteer and the entire rank and file of soldiers takes a unified step backward, leaving one poor infantryman sheepishly standing as the "courageous" manservant only because he somehow missed the queue which resulted in his unfortunate predicament. Humourous? Most definitively; but have we recollected whether his method of selection really mattered at the completion of his heroic duty? Notwithstanding such improbabilities, it is time for my forward-step to be bravely extended with purposeful allegiance to the beck and call of the Queen to proclaim that Heaven has been unearthed by the movement of one Stone away from a single Tomb! Paradise has thus been openly found! The treasure chest of the Promised Land has been unlocked and is being laid-bare before the eyes of man with the booty of the "blessed" flowing and falling through the fingers of the children of God who are reciting the Holy Rosary. And, the immortal youth of Eternity is but one more decade of prayer away! There are untold numbers of humble people who find themselves at this holy juncture, wrestling with the morally-perplexing dilemma of assaying the sheer audacity and brassy temperament of a human being who has never sailed the uncharted seas, looked-out from the peaks of the world's highest mountains, or braved the barren terrains of other worlds; but who would raise-up with heavenly authority and dominion to thunder forth such abounding declarations of both revelation and beatitude in this final triumphant age. One would rightfully ask what is the source of such seeming braggadocio? What experience has nurtured and perpetuated such Divine resolutions? Whose visions have produced these eloquent thoughts?

There is truly only one answer. Our Heavenly Destination is radiantly embodied in the complete, perfect, and wondrous sign given by the God of our fathers to all humankind. *And, the Virgin shall be with child...*, an Immaculate Virgin who miraculously became the Supreme Pontifical Mother, the New Eve, and has remained ever undefiled since the immortal moment of Her Beatific Conception. I hereby declare and proclaim by the power of the Holy Spirit of Jesus Christ before man and beast alike that the Most Blessed Virgin Mary is maternally responsible for all that I have placed worthily on any page, launched into the winds from my lips, and lifted in silence from the sanctuary of my heart of hearts. She is the solemn inspiration for my every voyage, the guiding compass by which I sail true, and the victorious banner for which I lay claim to everything in my path. It was in the early morning hours of February 22, 1991 that this regal Personage of the Highest Paradise, the Queen of the Heaven that every mortal seeks, the Woman clothed with the revelatory Sun, lifted the veil between the immortal Heights and the realms of our laborious wanderings to proclaim that the *Morning Star* has risen. Yes, in our darkest hour, the single greatest Intercessor to Jesus Christ appeared for the deliverance of a Light so profound that the world itself will ultimately be launched toward Divinity from within the Ark of Her Immaculate Heart. It is time for every romantically-inspired dreamer to quit the Earth and the impossibilities by which it is sinfully constrained and partake of the gentle guidance of the Mother of Jesus Christ, the Matriarch of us all, who can be engaged the world-over in Her multiplying apparitions and crescendoing manifestations, but no more poignantly and powerfully than in the breathtaking revelation of Her Motherhood to my humble brother and me. She began Her miraculous relationship just before dawn on that cold morning in February over a decade ago. In the midwestern Roman Catholic Diocese of Springfield in Illinois, the Truth of the Ages began to unfurl its majestic standard through the most powerful cooperator to ever grace our lost planet. Through the power of God Almighty, the Most Blessed Virgin of Nazareth transcended into our daily lives from Her Mystical station in the heavenly firmament to hail all revelation, prophecy, and instruction so as to stun a slumbering humanity into a state of ecstasy that is rivaled by nothing but the humble appearance of the Christ-Child in the manger 2000 years ago. From the first moments of Her supernatural direction, a Diary was meticulously conceived containing Her every uttered pearl and ingeniously-loving parable to augment literary history with the faith-filled teachings that human civilization has been trying to perfect and transmit to every succeeding generation for seemingly centuries without end. In the fall of 1999, the synopsis of the first seven years of this personal record was published under the title *Morning Star Over America,* a work containing the chronicle of every blessed step and sacred interaction of the heavenly Hosts with two children of the mortal world who, through no merit of our own, responded with all the abandonment and trusting faith we could muster. Roman Catholics call this spiritual compliance our "Fiat," our "Yes," in imitation of Mary's response to the Archangel Gabriel some two millennia ago. Such claims as the one being laid before you now are no different from the confident tales that were passionately placed before unwitting kings and queens in centuries past, of lands discovered and treasures awaiting. But, to our great fortune, the vast expanse that must be traversed is not a treacherous ocean of crashing waves or an inhospitable void of desolate space, but the panoramic infinitude of hopes flourishing from our childlike hearts. In this discovery alone are the newer worlds which reflect our most impressive accomplishments and bear therein our grandest rewards.

I have always sought for graceful ways to place these experiences into pseudo-synonymous contexts so that the more worldly of human intellectuals could somehow grasp a tangential understanding of God's mystical interaction with His earthbound children, and in hopes that a more consistent and unified response might be invoked to such a simple relationship with the Hosts of the heavens who reside in the greater part of the yet unseen portion of Creation. If anyone on the globe ever received transmitted communication from another stellar sphere in a neighboring solar system, the entire population of the Earth, through the fanatical fervor of every reporting medium in existence, would interrogate the participants in such a dialogue to dissect their every syllable for the satisfaction of their vain curiosity and intellectual triumphalism. Can you imagine how our television anchors and pundits would vie for the honor of being the first to categorically explain the transformational significance of these events to selfishly pigeon-hole them into a historically-defined context with their own surnames attached to the byline? Envision the never-ending procession of "experts" who would be paraded before the TV cameras to tell us that the dimensions of our understanding had just been shattered by the heretofore unimaginable, and that we would never be the same as a collective species again. I have always liked the movie, *The Day the Earth Stood Still*, a cinema creation from 1951 starring Michael Rennie and Patricia Neal. It was a fictional story of an alien spaceship landing on the plaza in Washington D.C. in broad daylight before the purview of the entire world. A space traveler walked out of the huge saucer bearing a material gift for the President of the United States which he extended to the military officers who were present, saying that he had come to them in peace. A trigger-happy infantryman who was stationed nearby was so terrified that the curious gift might be an offensive weapon that he summarily shot and wounded the celestial visitor. As the plot unfolded, this emissary from outer space bore a grave message for the Earth. He told the people that if they did not stop warring and learn to live together in peace, the planet would be reduced to a burned-out cinder by the community of races that inhabited the neighboring worlds of the cosmic beyond because the egregious incivility of earthmen was not going to be allowed to spread to the other planets. And, as a sign to confirm his ominous words, he performed a seismic feat to tweak the conscience of everyone here by interrupting all electro-mechanical movement across the landscape of every culture. For one hour, at least, the Earth stood still as an apocalyptic warning to all humanity.

It is not too difficult to detect the corollary insights that can be gleaned from such fictional accounts of interaction with extraterrestrial entities outside the gestating confines of our limited environment and how such events would be enlightening and humbling for the more presumptuous and inflated posture we take about ourselves as a human race. Therefore, in all honesty, it is time for humankind to come to a full-blown awakening and accept that our imperfect understanding of God *is* being shattered in much the same means by the heretofore unimaginable intercession of the Holy Virgin Mother of Paradise. She is transcending into our temporal environment in a wholly enlightening and convalescing way, and for far greater reasons than any alien not wanting our recklessness and disregard to come to his spacial doorstep. For the record, our sinfulness will never be allowed anywhere near the Gates of Heaven, even if we wanted it to. This much She has already told us. If anyone is henceforth a true seeker of Divine Truth and desires to discover the foundations of every universe, Our Lady is dispensing such perfect Wisdom and knowledge from the Maker Himself to all of us in the most profound and powerful ways conceivable to the hearts of Her children. But, what is humanity's mutinous battle-cry? *We want to see the world come to a complete standstill before we will ever believe!* The analogy illustrating our conduct can be no more clear than this. Our atrophied consciences are deep-asleep in the nightmare of atheism and materialism as we slothfully expend our precious hours in bold-faced rebellion despite the miracles of Heaven unfolding before our jaded eyes. It is ironic, and furthermore rather prophetic, that Jesus' appearance on the Earth as a mortal Man went relatively unnoticed and certainly unappreciated in this same way by thousands upon thousands who saw Him face-to-face, passing Him off as just another religious aberration who was fifing a pipe-dream they had no time to entertain. Eternal greatness, Himself, lamented, *If only you had known the time of your visitation.* Now, if your conscience has been pricked with the slightest hint of curiosity or your heart pried-open the smallest crack by these few personal sentiments, we can together begin to share the still living and never ending saga of the greatest story that is yet being told. You see, God does indeed work miracles in our modern day; and our lives are an evangelic witness to one of His most profound. Heaven has been revealed and its treasures are being brought to us through the prodigies of the Most Blessed Virgin Mary, the Miraculous Intercessor of the

Final Age. So, ignore the naysayers now and spurn the caviling objections of the "miracle police" so that we may unimpededly delineate the Mystical purposes of the Mother of the Messiah by Her own words and emblazon Her message across our marquee-hearts while contemplating one of Her most concise and powerful deliveries that She personally and miraculously dispensed to me on the second Sunday of October in the year 2000. In all good conscience, now is the time to alert the media, to stop the presses, and let the convocation of immortal history commence; for One who knows the Eternal Truth has stepped forward to speak Her mind.

Sunday, October 8, 2000 - "That the world may be blessed,    *j(282)* purified, converted, mortified, and redeemed, I am the Mediatrix of all Divine Graces from the heavenly Throne of God. These moments in human history are greater than the ability of any historian to record them. Kept in a unique pocket of this mortal time, I have come to announce with renewal the purpose of prayer from the heart and the enlightenment of the conscience of man. There is no wealth which can purchase the Wisdom that I bring and no dissension that can drive Me away. My dear children,    *x* through the power of My Beloved Christ-Child, I hereby lay claim to the humanity who belongs to Me. I assert My authority to reign as Queen of the Saints and Intercessor to Jesus on behalf of all the faithful. It is the Holy Rosary which you must hoist to your shoulders of righteousness to serve as your shield against all evil and the spearhead of your petitions to the Father. Now, all of those who claim to be Christians must awaken and live-out the profession of their faith. Indeed, My children who profess to be Catholic must elevate the Original Apostolic Church before every soul on    *xx* the Earth, like it or not. The graces dispensed through the Catholic Church are a blessing for all humankind. That is why the world must be educated both in the Holy Gospel and the Divine Traditions of the Church, the Priesthood, and the very prayerful service of all the Clergy, the religious, and the laity. No one is exempt from service to God and His people if they expect to proceed toward the highest seat of absolution. The Angels and Saints are not just a complementary group of holy spirits who watch the world go by. They are powerful participants in the transformation of the Earth into the Kingdom of Divine Royalty through the one Paraclete of Jesus. I seek anyone who will listen to believe in bold faith that the lessons in *Morning Star Over America* are true. And, you are seeing the fruit of this now. Today is the continuing culmination of a princely Papacy which is growing the awareness of mankind in the role of their Mother! I gave you Jesus 2000 years ago, and soon I will give Him to you again in Glory which He has foretold the universe. Please pay Me no worship and pay Me no homage! It is the King in My arms who rightfully deserves this praise! Mankind would do well to remember every word I have said! There is no time for doubting, despair, rejection, and procrastination. You, O' humanity, are the heirs of the Passion which has been so despised by the indifferent ages before you! You are the beneficiaries of the patience of God and the Mercy which still feeds the lost! I beseech you to not turn your back on Redemption now! The climax has finally drawn near! The plot has unfolded and you remain to see the world inverted for the cast of all generations! Nowhere else can your heart be brought nearer to God, and at no other place can you see first-hand the closure of the ages. The thousand years in the sight of the Almighty Father is but a single dawn away! This is the millennium which will heave the haughty over the cliff of perdition and raise the humble to new heights of joy! It is not a rebuke of humanity to try to be in the number who will fly freely amongst the winds of Paradise. Indeed, bring them all with you! Shout-out your jubilation because you have known the Truth all along! Remember the wretched who really never listened to anyone. I promise that they will hear you loudly and clearly now! I give you the consolation of My Immaculate Heart in which to savor your hopes and capture your dreams. God would never allow them if they were not meant to come true! This is the hope in which you must live and the reason that you should anticipate anew the answer to your petitions. Just as sure as the candles flicker on the Altar, I bear an angel on My right and one on My left whose scent will forever tell of the knowledge I bring."

xxx

xl

l

lxc

Creation has just been changed in this very moment by a Woman whose integrity and Wisdom cannot be challenged. Our lives are now a little brighter, far more unified, infinitely more in touch with God's reality, and quantum steps farther toward deliverance than we have ever been before. Your life can never return to the way it was prior to your eyes having fallen upon these words of the Queen of Heaven, nor can the consistency of your being be recomposed into the quiescent state in which it resided just a few short moments ago because the interior essence of your soul will never peacefully deny the Truth of Almighty God. Together, we rest on a pinnacle of bold new beginnings, a hope that is rumbling across the meadows of the ages like tremors in the aftermath of a giant worldwide quake. Can you envision the multitudes of free thinking citizens whose biased-colored egoism will not allow them to respond to their Heavenly Queen with anything more than, "I don't have to believe that!?" Is it any wonder why the disposition of little children allows them to progress in spiritual grace by faithful leaps and bounds over more calloused adults? Could it be, perhaps, that our innocence has been decimated by the lying, cheating, and outright deception which has descended upon so many occasions to pillory our good trust and faith in our fellow man? It is very difficult for materially-minded humans to seriously consider, let alone embrace, the concept of the Imminent Return of a Sovereign King who owns them outright and everything they have envisioned from the moment they were conceived, He who has arranged and sustains every last element of the physical world before their eyes, and who will soon reappear from the vaults of Heaven with a Divine Authority and Eternal agendum that is of an Absolute Finality beyond the capacity of our fondest imagining. Doesn't the existence of the very message that you just read reaffirm with clarion eloquence that the thoughts and understandings we hold about our closely-guarded lives are not yet in union with the Truth that is reverberating from the farther side of our mortal passing? The destiny of all Creation is poised for the beatific climax of the reconciliation between God and man; a promise in faith that the reunion of the seen and unseen has been justified for humankind inside the Paschal Mysteries of Christ, freeing us to unabashedly revel in the fulfillment of the first installments of human Redemption with a reciprocal assuredness that we have responded in-kind to the precepts engraved into earthen annals by the humble condescension of Jesus Christ in the Flesh to be Crucified for the liberation of the damned from every vestige of evil that would impede our return to His side. The Slain and Resurrected Messiah is the revelation of Eternal Love upon the Earth, and is rivaled by no other in history. His is the only Power that can Redeem the world because His perfect Reflection of the Unseen Father of Creation is the uniting element which flickers in the glowing soul of every man.

He has shown His hungry people what Love in the human heart really looks like, leaving us with no excuse for not invoking His Grace or remaining on a path other than the Salvation He has wrought through His Bloodshed, sweat, devotion and tears.  There is no other deliverance for us, not a moment of peace or a hope that can be fulfilled which does not originate in the spiring Beatitude of His Sacred Heart and the preeminent generosity of His Divine Will.  The Immaculate Virgin Mary wants to teach us who Her Son really is, and the power that He liberally animates in our deferential beings.  The heights of human perfection are embodied in the Heart of one Mother who bore a Perfect Son, a Prince and a King from His birth, possessing the Omnipotent power and authority of every army the world would ever see.  And, She watched Him being tortured and killed because He wished Heaven to be apparent before the eyes of every person in every epoch of time.  All of this She gave to mankind through an immediate and sacrificial *Yes* to an Archangel who was dispatched as the Herald of the purification of Creation, bearing a Salutation to a humble Maiden who would be sent in our day as the greatest Advocate for humankind's Eternal Deliverance at the summit of this culminating age.  Triumphalism, indeed!  The definition of final Victory will never be the same, and it shall arrive presently in a glorious flourishing of wonderment, reward, and recreation.  The Virgin of the Virgin's Womb who was born in a manger amongst the beasts of the field is "every Divine Grace," personified to full perfection.  Henceforth, should not the Mother who bore such a Child-Miracle be wholly justified in proclaiming, *I am the Mediatrix of all Divine Graces from the heavenly Throne of God!?*  No honest person can deny this; for anyone who does so is not in union with the Truth they will one day see face-to-face, no matter how many passages of Sacred Scripture they can remember by heart.   For centuries, this overwhelming ignition of Love has burned in the hopes of Saints and sinners, preachers and paupers, and in the innocence of millions-strong who have refused to surrender to the mundane and mediocre; those who have preserved the dignity bequeathed to them from a mountaintop in the defining moments of our Eternal destiny in the shadows of Old Jerusalem.

It must be so ingrained in our spirits that it goes without saying that we must be inclusive in our visions of the perfect world which our saving God wishes to manifest upon the Earth.  The very definition of Love pronounced by Christ makes this articulately apparent.  Yet, it seems that our Blessed Mother is rather guarded on behalf of the Roman Catholic Church in Her miraculous discussions with Her children.  Does this imply that those who are not Catholic and have yet to be converted to the Seven Sacraments are somehow second-class Christians, or that they are destined for the fires of Hell?  Sentiments such as these are unworthy of the space that they conscript in the thoughts of those who are devoted to fostering peaceful lives.  Our Lady must not be misunderstood in such terms, but rather as being the Matriarch of the children of Light whose purposes always flow into a singular basin for orienting our beings toward the beneficial intentions of the Almighty Father, and to effect our everlasting joy and fulfillment.  This all-beatific clarity is given its grandest definition in the peaceful unity of mankind in the closest front-and-center seat under the Holy Cross of Jesus Christ.  Our Heavenly Mother knows that the institutional foundation of the Roman Catholic Church is firmly rooted in the bedrock of the legacies of the Saints and Martyrs who have given their lives throughout two millennia by a prefigured movement to bring forth the Sacred Deposit of knowledge of the Messiah whom they loved to their deaths, which they also witnessed as being encompassed by the faithful bounty of this same Catholic Church.  There is no other Faith on the globe that has the evangelical unity, universal scope, historical longevity, heroic heritage, scholarly integrity, charitable Truth, theological certainty, concise Dominion, or Divine authority.  It is both the Alpha and the Omega.  The Roman Catholic Church was the first to be raised to its feet in the opening days of the evangelization of humanity.  It is the only body of spiritual Wisdom to maintain its supremacy in the sight of God throughout twenty centuries; and it will be standing as a vertical Torch before the nations on the last day of the Earth, boldly illuminating the pathways beneath our feet to keep us away from the cliffs of perdition.  Sadly, the followers of Christendom are not united as one heart and mind in this great bastion of devotion and desire for a concerted advancement against the materialistic ramparts of our spiritually-wayward societies.  The Holy Mother knows that we were like shiny spheres in triangle-formation who lay on a felt landscape when we were audaciously scattered upon the cue of other weak mortals, banking us into diverse pockets of blind ignorance, loneliness, contention, and opposition.  From those first inauspicious moments of raw human arrogance, we have been subjected to the generational plight of being impacted and displaced into even more distant reaches on the broadways of Creation.  What has this done to our trinitarian unity?  Are we poised so that peace can prodigiously thrive from an authentic meeting of our hearts and minds?  Are we waiting for someone with a keener eye for correct angles or the deftness of a mystical surgeon to fashion us back into the conformity of our original order before we will ever consider nudging ourselves?  Or, do we simply need an Advocate who can produce an instrument whose dimensions precisely reflect our most prolific and original configuration and rack us within its circumference?  This parable clearly signifies the mission of the Most Blessed Virgin Mary because She is fully aware and equally observant of the premier intentions and designs of God when He laid the first foundations for our spiritual reconciliation. After all, the New Testament Scriptures are the historical diary of Her life, too; and the Old are the fertility of Her faith which became manifest in Her Womb and birthed into Her arms. Anyone who thinks that She is just another pious woman in history has completely missed the proverbial boat. She is our own Mother, *for Christ's sake;* the Miraculous Intercessor at the wedding feast of Cana, the grand cooperator with the Divine plan of God to redeem His people from its inception who has come to restore us to completeness, to recreate the human soul, to enliven us with the power to change the countenance of the globe by digging the footings whereupon the Kingdom of Heaven shall soon come to prevail forever upon the Earth. Indeed, His Heavenly Messenger at the close of these turbulent mortal ages is here! She has begun the grand finale, the culminating solidarity of man, and the reclamation of *every* child of God! She has come especially for those who are lagging behind or have yet to begin searching for their reserved plateau upon our table of human existence.

I have been confronted by a few naysayers regarding the tone of voice which is used by Our Lady in Her conversations with me because they contain a commanding contrast to the mild tenor of Her words in previous generations. The answer is embodied in the premises of their discerning question. Has the world accepted and obeyed Her meeker, soft-spoken, and gentler approach over the recent ages? No! Therefore, our conduct has required the augmentation of Her semantics to include more serious overtones and the assertiveness of Her Divine Queenship above all Creation. We should recall that humankind has the illegitimate capacity to exterminate our life as we know it on this planet in a matter of minutes; an ability we did not possess until just a few short decades ago. Does this not further signify that God has been forced to provide more profound Wisdom to our souls, lest we never see the light of another new dawn? Moreover, should we consider that the rising revelation of the Mother of Jesus Christ who preceded His first Coming portends the timeliness of His Second? Did not Our Lady say, *I gave you Jesus 2000 years ago, and soon I will give Him to you again in Glory which He has foretold the universe.?* No man knows the day nor the hour, not even His Blessed Mother; but Our Lord admonishes us in the Scriptures to be as wise about the season of His Return as we are in our knowledge of an approaching winter through the hues of the leaves on the trees. Isn't the tenor of the Queen of Paradise likewise changing? Let us continue henceforth by delving even more deeply into the Mystery of human existence by opening our hearts altogether to these words from Our Lady that She gave to me in early 1997.

Saturday, March 8, 1997 - "Good evening, My children of   *g(067)*
Light and Love. Thank you for joining Me at the window of
your hearts through which you focus upon the paradisial
summit awaiting your challenge of its heights. Together, we
have taken you near the heights of human holiness. It is
your obligation to finish the journey as I watch and pray. My
little ones, your final journey to the top is equivalent to the
journey of Jesus upon the Mountain Calvary where I also
watched and prayed. God will never allow you to be either
alone or abandoned. It is I who keep your footsteps sure.      *x*
I will always tell you where to place your next step... The
world must remember that it was I upon the Earth who
brought your Savior the first time. It is also I who now
prepare the world for My presentation of Him again. That
is My Love. That is why I am speaking to you now. The
time is near. The end of the Earth as you know it may well
come tomorrow or in that next century just months away.
Oh, pray that Jesus comes in great Mercy! The last century
has been horrid and treacherous for all that is good and
decent.    The past hundred years have brought the          *xx*
diminishment of human holiness never-before seen in
Creation.   Industry and technology have replaced good
works. Entertainment has replaced meditation. Materialism
has replaced prayer. Scientology has replaced faith. Despair
has destroyed hope. Selfishness has replaced charity. The
slaughter of millions of innocent victims of wars and the
scourge of abortion has left a very cringed brow over the
eyes of God. Impurity and poverty are the dead weight of a
doomed age. And, of all the mockery one could imagine, a
sinner has given birth outside the Sacraments to a child     *xxx*
named for the holy land of Lourdes. I must tell you that
God is not well pleased with human destiny of the 20th
century. His Church has been divided and ignored. And,
one of the most holy and reverend successors of Saint Peter
is being treated as a lame and ignorant servant of only
indifference. I assure you that this Pope has yet to raise his
voice to all in the way that he will! The most responsible
Vicar of Christ on Earth is now in the Chair of Saint Peter!
He is all that is keeping God from crushing the Earth! One

day, all will see what I am telling you is true. But, he will be
at home in Heaven by then.                                          *xl*

    My children, the ravages of the last hundred years
have deteriorated the collective conscience of humankind to
its lowest point in mortal history. What a fitting time for the
Master of the house to return home. When Jesus is least
expected, He will come. But, thankfully, those who are My
children will not be caught by surprise. You will be ready,
indeed. That is because you are obedient. And, to those
who are not, I assure you that My Grace will convert them.
They cannot get away from their Mother. They cannot outrun Me. They cannot hide under the furniture. I know each         *l*
child given to Me by Jesus from the Cross by name. I know
where they are playing. Many can already hear My voice
calling them Home. Those who are not listening will indeed
feel the pinch of My fingers on their ear lobes as they come
with Me, complaining all the way to the bathtub. Oh, you
will hear the water splashing, but I will not let them go until
they are clean of all that offends God. Have hope in this
promise and pray for many. Pray, indeed, for all. I will
provide prophecy, revelations, and graces as numerous as the
stars. I know the Heart of God and He knows Mine. We          *lx*
will not lose. We will reduce the transgressions of the past
100 years to a point on the tip of a fiber of straw. They are
already no more as the Cross has timelessly destroyed them.
But, it is the acceptance of the Cross by many transgressors
that is the key to this Mystical revision of human history.
That acceptance and that Cross are the union that makes all
things possible between God and man. My son, you will see
that all I have told you is the Truth, and will come to pass in
your day."

    The embarrassing litany of human transgressions which have peppered
our mortal experience has soured our contentment with a bitterness that has
given the face of Creation a rather ignoble expression. If our lives are meant
to emanate the blessed visage of our most amiable ponderings, it is the beatific
forefront of Heaven that we must recognize and reflect to the highest degree.
The Wisdom for this restorative revelation is in the innocence of a tiny infant
smiling back at its mother for the very first time, cooing and kicking with

excitement in knowing to the depth of its soul that it rests in the arms of its maternal life-giver. Our Holy Mother anticipates our budding smiles with this same satisfaction and devotion. She nurtures with patient insight the soulful development of our enlightened maturity; and without doubt, authoritatively guides every earthly mother and father who remains within the bonds of Her Grace. This is why our Heavenly Matriarch speaks in such personal terms about God's children who are shunning the majestic benisons of the Catholic Church and mocking the supernatural gift of Her healing shrines by using the sites of Her apparitions as novelties for naming their newborn children. This is an albatross that these progeny will bear until the day they finally wear them in faithful allegiance and veneration for the intercession of the Virgin Mary who gave them their signature meaning. Our respect for God and one another is characterized by the boundaries of propriety which have been timelessly erected by the Holy Gospel of Jesus Christ. Yet, we live in a society where those who are completely ignorant of Eternal Redemption would have us believe that the demarcations of self-denial that we preserve out of allegiance to the Savior of the World and in Love for our fellow man are only prison walls, erected by the religious tyrants of dark ages past which now, in these more "enlightened" times, must be scaled and razed like the toppling of the Berlin Wall, setting us free, just as Our Lady triumphed over the horrors of Soviet Communism. What a cauldron of swine swill! The Mother of Paradise is telling them in every sense of the term that God is not at all pleased with their attempts to incite mutiny upon His good ship *Salvation*. The Messianic Captain will swiftly respond the moment His Queen's mission is completed. The swashbuckling rebels who oppose Him are being given one last merciful chance to reconsecrate their allegiance to the seaworthy Prince who will soon pilot His purified stately vessel into port amidst the thundering approval of the Hosts of Heaven; an arrival that will make the port of call of the RMS Queen Mary on her finest day look like a plastic toy wobbling in the ripples of a little child's wading pool. Therefore, the Mother of Our Savior continues by articulating supplications and metaphoric images such as Her children hiding under tables, ears that are inclined to be pinched, and rag-a-muffins who are in need of a date with a bar of soap. It is a fresh image of contemporary realization that someone truly wields this kind of authority and influence over us; and it is merely the shortest span of time before God invokes the commencement of its implementation. Hear, hear! Let the splashing begin, over the porcelain sides and down the hall! She speaks further in ominous and prophetic terms regarding the service and legacy of Pope John Paul II as he attempts to embed the Word of Life into the sinews of our souls, hoping that we will reclaim our piety in peace and constructive progress toward the mitigation of human suffering in poorer quarters of the world.  Since the Church has proclaimed that the Mother of Jesus is not just another holy woman, neither is the Supreme Pontiff just another man!  He is the Vicar of Christ on the Earth; the premier representative and patriarch who advocates all that is above the Firmament which has been bestowed upon humanity in the Life, Death and Resurrection of the Crucified God-Man.  He is the pontifical lightning-rod of all personified unity, the Pastoral Shepherd of God's universal flock who serves with a firm mandate and dominion that Jesus Christ, Himself, ratifies during his every impeccable earth-bound moment and perfection-clad Eternity.  Who in their right mind would summon the audacity to be critical of the Papacy in their pigheaded opposition to him, let alone shred his photograph before a television camera on *Saturday Night Live* with millions of viewers watching, or admonish him in various public fora because he refuses to grant us blanket permission to grovel in the boweries of our own wolverine ideals?

The question at hand is whether Our Lady's method of deliverance is supposed to instill faith in humanity through threats of certain chastisements during the same time She is calling on us to trust Her Son to have Mercy. Many are perplexed trying to decide "which" God is looking at them on any given day, the wrathful one, or the kinder, gentler one.  The befuddlement swirling around this dichotomy is not lost to those who instruct others in the Mysteries of our Christian faith.  In the past two or three decades, there has been a concerted effort on the part of Christian leaders to shift the balance of our perception of the Almighty Father away from the hard images of the Old Testament containing wrathful judgement, pillars of fire, the halving of the Red Sea, the destruction of Pharaoh's army, and plagues from an angry God which may have excessively prevailed in the context of Christianity during previous generations.  Hence, we discover ourselves at present whereby our image makers have caricaturized our sublime Creator as being nothing more than an impotent figurehead who loves us anyway and will forgive us for everything we have ever done, with or without our sacrificial change-of-heart in conforming ourselves to the likeness of Jesus.  Perhaps another parable might apply. Everyone was standing in the front of a boat that was sinking by the head when somebody screams, "There's too much weight in the bow," which sends all the passengers scurrying to the stern.  For humanity, our ship-of-state is taking on water over the transom now, leaving us with as little spiritual clarity as we had before.  It can be confirmed through any discernable means that the Truth of Jesus Christ and the historicity of His perfect Life are being grudgingly assailed by the contemptuous fog of modern analytical arrogance whether it springs from theological debate, modernistic heresy, obstinate rejection, presumptuous ignorance, historical revisionism, intellectual pomposity, or ostentatious pride.

The Truth is, the universe will be brought into definitive conformity with the beatific visions of its Creator by the power of His own superintending Will whether we cooperate with Him or not. Period! God will receive homage from each and every creature He has begotten, albeit some will choose to be the chaff that He will toss into the Eternal Furnace in triumph with a purposeful ire that would render the passionate conviction of the most seasoned warrior just a capricious whim on an ordinary day. Everyone must realize that the Blessed Trinity is wrathfully just while simultaneously mercifully benevolent in His patience for humanity to transform itself into its heavenly image, one heartbeat at a time. There will someday be an outright scorched-earth policy of destroying evil; a cauterization and circumcision of the collective human spirit at the close of the ages in harmonious concert with the most clement deliverance of those who have professed themselves to be children of God by their purified lives. But, we do not have to stretch ourselves to broad lengths to understand the motivations of the masses who are overruled by their inordinate passions at the expense of their virtuous stature in humility, self-denial, penitential sacrifice, and charitable love for their neighbors and friends. Is it anywhere within the parameters of Eternal Wisdom to placate the rebellion of rancorous souls who have no intention of embracing moral decency by telling them that their God accepts them and their lives without reprisal because He is infinitely merciful and forgiving? Talk about bold presumption before the Cross of the Slain Messiah! Therefore, our Blessed Mother has been sent to relate to us the thoughts of Our Maker at this particular juncture in modern history. We no longer have to wonder with what exuberance our merciful Father is gazing upon our efforts, or lack thereof. Each of us knows deep inside just how truly we love Jesus and everything good for which He stands. Every selfish lie about our allegiance to the Sacred precepts of holiness perishes before the verity of our interior discernment. I have heard people say that our honorable God loves us too much to issue brash warnings that would cause feelings of guilt in the minds of His children. Oh, really? They are the naive contingent who are still wading waist-deep in blind ignorance at the back of the aforementioned untrimmed boat, wondering why the admiral and first officer haven't provided more friendly confines for their fare. The chastising admonishments which have been relayed through Our Lord's humble seers in the course of history are not necessarily uncivilized threats; but neither are they just idle palaver. Most people want to know their future as long as it validates everything they currently believe about themselves, their vision, their future, and their eternal destiny; at least until they discover into what sudden cataclysm their wanton error is leading them. The intercessions of the Blessed Virgin Mary are commingled and compared with the prophetic misfortune of the fate of human destiny without Her Crucified Son, and serve as a powerful encouragement to stagnant human hearts who believe that they have nothing to gain. If we are not ready to greet the Eternal Lightning of the Return of the Prince of Peace, we may forfeit our souls to the Abyss as easily as we have succumbed to the godlessness of the present hour. Therefore, our hearts should detonate into great jubilation at the opportunity to fall into the sanctuarial embrace of our Savior who is waiting with open arms to moor us in the harbor of the Saints where every indictment against us is forever rescinded; where Divine Love flourishes so prolifically that we cannot help but reciprocate anew, where the course of history is fully amended, and where the New Dawn breaks as brightly and beautifully as on the birthday of Creation. This is the concise reason for the miraculous manifestations of the Holy Mother in the lives of sinners throughout the centuries. Her kind words are highlighting the pathway of our Redemption and arcing like an electrified rainbow through the monochrome skies of our exile from its resolute inception at a manger in the little town of Bethlehem some two thousand years ago.

Saturday, March 15, 1997 - "My pretty little children, you are *g(074)* My special ones who pray to change the world. You are obedient in your supplications, strong in faith, and loving in your desires for the destiny of your brothers and sisters. You do these things for God, and because I ask. I know God. I have lived His beautiful Face as you will soon live that same Blessed Visage, your homeland and your peace. You live in a very corrupt and clandestine world. I call your hearts out of the world. Where your heart goes, your soul *x* will follow. I can assuredly capture your heart while Jesus simultaneously accepts your soul and takes you to the Father. You do not yet know Heaven. You have not reached your holiest destiny or seen the brightest Light of an ageless Paradise. But, you stand now at the doorway between Earth and Heaven. I have led you there. I have elevated you to the podium, at the lectern from which you may speak the Truth to the world. The Holy Spirit has composed every speech that any human need hear to reach the heights of *xx* happiness. It is not material wealth. It is not even perfect health. It is simply "perfection" of all human capacities, made one and Divine through the Blood and Cross of Jesus Christ. As you journey to that perfection, your worldly desires fade, but too may your faculties wane. You may feel the cold steel of ill health or captivity, but you will always be well and always be free. And, if these words were being spoken from a mountaintop, I would address tens of thousands through the plea: Come to Grace! Come united and without conflict! Cast aside all that divides you! See no color or nation, nor race, nor creed. See not disparaging language or sadness. Be not afraid to be one humanity! Be all of God's children under His guiding hand. There is no prejudice in God. All who come to God are one Love in many parts. If you can hear My voice, you can be saved. If you fear your past, take courage in your future. If you feel sorrow for your sins, take delight that they are no more; Jesus washed them all away. I call upon all who live to walk toward the Light. Cast your shadows back to the darkness in which they will not be revealed! Yes, turn your back to the darkness. Your face seeks the sun like a flower seeks the rain. Believe Me when I tell you, the wheat and grain that lie as seed beneath the Earth celebrate in their own Divine way in anticipation of breaking through their veil of soil. They are blessed by the life-giving water and living sun to seek life. Be the seeds of righteousness! Anticipate your break through the veil of darkness into the Light! Answer the call of the living Son: Come out! Drink-in the Life-giving waters given you at your Baptism. If the world is to come to fruition in time, now is that time! If you have courage to invoke, bring it now! If you have hope in your heart, let it live now! Creation has been waiting hundreds of thousands of years for the crescendo now near its peak. The groaning of the Earth is its dying gasps! The Earth will soon be replaced by a New Earth, and Heaven will be made new because you will be there. All of these imaginings are not just lost hopes. They are real and true. The family of humankind has neared its thanksgiving meal. All will sit together in harmony and will feast upon Salvation. And, your Lord Jesus will return thanks to God with His hand in yours. Jesus will be the Grace for your Eternal meal of heavenly bliss, just as He is now at Holy Mass. And, all the Saints whose ranks you will join will revel with you the Lord of all. You will be able to speak to God to His Face, an ever-present prayer of thanksgiving. And, as His Son says, *Let us return thanks*, He will have to wait the first ten-thousand years to say *Amen* because all the new Saints will still be returning thanks with every fiber of their being.

I am very happy to bring you this news. I am grateful to God for allowing Me to come to the Earth bearing words of encouragement. I bring you the Truth, just as I brought the Truth into the manger in Bethlehem. Jesus is the fruit of My womb, a fruit that will always live there. Oh, you should have seen the Life inside the Tomb as the angels witnessed the Resurrection of Jesus there. The happy tears, the dancing, the praying, the meditation! God's Word of Truth would not die! Jesus suffered and died as a mortal, but as Truth, He would not die. And, He has yet to relinquish that Crown. Indeed, He never will. I wish to bring you ever-closer to that bountiful Resurrection; for as a mortal, your body will also die. But, like Jesus, you need not die with it. You, too, are Truth when you live in Jesus. All Truth is one, and you are one in the Love He brings. Jesus wishes to melt your cold hearts, to render them a molten lava of Love which He will pour into His own Heart to cast you into the perfect shape of Love, a beauty fit for Paradise. God has plans for you! No heart is too hard for the pulse of God's loving hand upon it. No soul can resist the Love that God gives if their heart is shaped by Jesus. And, it needs very pretty attire. I have come to adorn you in beautiful Easter garments for your presentation to God. Easter morning is your invitation to accept Jesus' Resurrection. Easter is your premonition of your own victory over death! Rise with Jesus! Rise to new Life. Come to the top of this mountain to be with Me! The view is beautiful. The gate is near. Thank you for listening to these words. Thank you for your holy prayers. I will seek from God the granting of every petition you have offered. I love you always, indeed, in My Immaculate Heart."

The golden gates that majestically rise between the pillars upholding the Mystical threshold of pan-historic Revelation have been loosed from their

*lxx*

*lxxx*

*xc*

sealed installment of justified wrath by the highest powers of Divine Mercy Incarnate. Every soul of the fortunate generation of the New Living Testimony of Almighty God stands at the doorway which separates our inherent generative capacities from the effervescent Light that elucidates the virtuous perfections of the human creation. We are an impressive collage of children who are positioned within finely enamored sight of the boundless reaches of our immortal heritage. The cherished hopes born of passionate conviction to the grandest of destinies have always been given conception behind the jeweled door in the souls bedecked with peacefulness and obedience who wantingly approached the sacred Domain of the great redeeming Spirit which pulsated in the Divine recesses of their most hallowed beings. Yet, it seems that the spectacles and spasms of our mortality-laced endeavors have visited such uncertainty upon the sanctified vision of many a heart. It is on just such spiritual obscurity that Our Lady trains Her most brilliant flares of compassionate eloquence, launching salvos of Grace toward the welkin of our broken spirits to ignite a flash of spectacular Divinity which illuminates the paradisial archway like fireworks electrifying the polished steel of St. Louis' Gateway to the West on every Independence Day. We live in some of the darkest moments of spiritual history, bar none!; evidenced by the atrocities of genocidal wars fueled by ethnic, nationalistic, and racial hatreds, the unforgivable omissions of the prosperous multitudes in the face of famine and disease, the hellish barbarism of physicians who grow rich harvesting the exterminated corpses of our unborn children from the wombs of their mothers, materialistically-bipolar societies institutionalized, advanced, and protected by the selfish rich, and the utter licentious human rot of marital infidelity and the destruction of the berth of the Mystical holy family. But, Heaven's response is to inflame the sky with the reporting accompaniment of the Queen of Paradise where inside the fiery afterglow can be seen a monolithic Cross that has already defined everything that we will ultimately become. This is the *how* and the *why* Our Lady has led us to the doorway separating Heaven and Earth, asking us to contemplate the flowering dimensions of motivational Love from the pinnacle of Eternity where She is the overseeing Matriarch. Never in the course of mankind's repetitive days have we been gifted with such miraculous brilliance on such a universal scale. Her every emboldened word is a radiant blast from beyond the bulwark of the Celestial Kingdom, streaking toward the Earth on a multiple-reentry mission of healing, teaching, and redeeming. The children of Creation are rapidly approaching that fateful moment when our heavenly Father will catapult us all over the rim of mortal time like neophyte eaglets on their very first solo flight toward the blinding sun.

We have watched the creative arteries of human intelligence fruitfully flourish beyond the imaginings of the most profound romantic and socialistic dreamers in our dominating orchestration of nearly every virile element and composition of matter in the spectrum of created things; but we have never been farther from humble submission to the loving dictates of the New Jerusalem than we are at this juncture in the development of the universe. Therefore, we reconfirm our woeful arrogance every time our sentimental reminiscence sails back to the earliest days of Christianity and our errant feelings of relief deceive our atrophied consciences into naively believing that we are theologically and hermeneutically superior to the fishermen, farmers, and merchants who took to the hills and hamlets of the Judean landscape in their professions of apostolic faith and Christian zeal. Since there can be no prejudice in God, and His eternal judgement is tempered by the standard by which righteousness is given venue and opportunity, what can we say about our obdurate refusal to capitalize these prolific times by eradicating diseases across the globe, demoting poverty to an archaic word that is finally removed from our dictionaries, and discovering the convalescing response to grotesque behavior that effects the conversion and restoration of broken souls? Never has America so comprehensively gained such a powerful opportunity in every created way for the proliferation of the Truth of Almighty God and the transformation of physical existence toward the freedom of Paradisial human perfection. Now, hear this! No excuses remain; and none will likely be accepted! The sacrificial victims of mortal sanctification are becoming quite a crowd as Saint after Saint is being canonized and elevated before the world as Sacred witnesses to the Truth by Pope John Paul II. And, all the while, we seem to be too obsessed with "destroying the teeming refuse" to be in the "making all things new" business. I repeatedly encounter people who are mystified that God would create so many humans who are deformed at birth with cleft palates, Downs Syndrome, twins attached at the chest and head, little children who fall ill and die within weeks after delivery; and so many more who have no access to nourishment or healthcare, even in the richest countries. The mystery of their suffering is not so difficult to understand if we can clearly differentiate between the fashions of this world and the visions of the next, and realize the ultimate necessity and priority of our post-mortem Redemption. Our wise Creator displays the Cross of Divine Love, the archway between Heaven and Earth, through the lives of our tormented brothers and sisters, all the while hoping that the popping sparks that cascade from their agony like Fourth of July sparklers will ignite our passionate desire to Love in renewed Light by drawing our hearts inward where the power for the abridgement of our sinful agendas lies within the purview of our more noble sacrifices. The most stupefying enigma is truly being played-out within the heart of mankind because God must find Himself bewildered that His Divine offspring would not invoke and utilize the heavenly wisdom of Love to eradicate the incidence and need for such edifying imitations of His Son's Passion and Death. Why must there be such horrifying occurrences of human despondence and desolation, especially in the lives of the innocents, before we will marshal a sense of decency and allow the battle-cry, *No more!* to rise from our resurrected souls as we lay our fortunes along with our folly at the Holy feet of the Resurrected Savior of the world? Our Lady asks us to step forward with the valor of angelic warriors, without parceled penny or prestige, and convoke the legions of the holy blessed to rescind and revise the sorrowful consequences of our earthly compatriots and our own disheveled comportment. She pleads for us to answer the reveille of Paradise, *Come one and all to the Feast of Heaven and Earth! Cast aside all that divides you; the arrogance, the ill-will, the greed, haughtiness, and cold hatreds!* When the Holy Mother tells us things about what it is going to be like in Heaven when we get there, such as taking 10,000 years to say Amen because our hearts are pouring-out a thanksgiving prayer of such duration, it is not a figure of the confining understanding of our speech, but rather the most living and multi-dimensional articulation of the possibilities that rest in the unrestrained concelebrations of Almighty God. Her words are a revelation that there are no boundaries to the scope of Eternal hope or the parameters of the ultimate freedom of Divinity. If the Immaculate Heart of the Queen of Paradise would be warmly consoled by the experience of 10,000 years of thanksgiving to the Messianic Second Person of the Most Holy Trinity, we should be assured that our spirits will be bursting at the rapturous opportunity to offer Her 20,000 more atop these initial ten. We will feast upon Her glowing satisfaction for Eternities without end, while our miraculously-instilled genius will be engineering even loftier renditions of prized grandeur to bless, honor, and elevate Her consecration in the Redemption of humankind. This is exactly what we are commissioned to accomplish at this preciously-opportune moment in preparation for the return of our Honorable King because our salvific care of the lowly, poverty-stricken, and grieving, our re-enshrinement of the Holy Gospel in the premier alcoves of our hearts, the restoration of the preeminent values of a civilized society where children are prepared for the liberty of maturation, where abortion is a scourge that is vigilantly prohibited, and the elderly are enthroned as respected emeritus are those things which will bring tears of joy to God's beloved Queen.

All of this Truth is One, United, and Universal because every human heart understands the simplified language of Love, even though they may yet be unable to "speak" its more harmonious soliloquies with fluent inflection.

The unblemished and comprehensive body of reality is the Mystical emanation from the Most Holy Trinity who is God for every man, woman, child, and created thing ever given the fire of existence. The Christian religion is given its bodily form on the Earth as a courageous beacon of elevated Light amidst the smouldering pyres of our exile. This Divine pharos is the instrument of the heavenly Father's engagement with His beloved humanity. The Mystery seems to rest in how Eternal Oneness can remain an absolutely united Being in a Trinity of Persons; Father, Son, and Holy Spirit. If we dare to delve even a minute distance into this beatific Union, knowing in advance that our ideas will fall short of unveiling its signs, we must surpass the quantified constraints of human logic and contemplate possibilities that only the Holy Spirit can inspire. We must consider three separate, distinct Persons all simultaneously emanating from one another and living in the complete union of identity without beginning or end. Let us first consider a mirror and our image as it is reflected by it. The face that we see staring back at us is truly our likeness to the extent that the reflecting surface is able to produce it. Yet, it is still only an image since the mirror is restricted to bending light which is returned to our eyes. Thus, it can only project something that resembles us. Now, suppose there was a "super-mirror" that had the extended capabilities to reproduce not only our image in a way that our eyes could see, but also the capacity to reflect the substance of our flesh and bones, our thoughts and physicality, literally our entire being; so that if we peered into this mirror, another complete person would be seen facing us that we could reach-out and touch, and interact with as if we were engaged with ourselves in every way. As we stand before this looking-glass, both of our persons would be totally united in function and being, each emanating from and existing in unity with the other. If one decided to remove himself from the focus of the reflection, wouldn't he still be completely present and operative in the second? Would not the latter person also be present in the person of the first? It is now easy to extrapolate this situation to a trinity of beings. This is a hint as to why Jesus said that, if you have seen Him, you have seen the Father because God embodies every beatific capacity, including the ability to manifest Himself as Three Divine Persons without diversion from His unity. Therefore, it should not be repulsive to accept the Trinity of Persons; Father, Son, and Holy Spirit, as being one God just because our simple minds cannot understand Him quite yet. After all, we embrace the multiplication of our own image on a routine basis every morning while we wash our faces or shave our beards. So, with one spiritual foot placed ahead of the other, let us go forward together with these words from April of 1997 from our Heavenly Mother.

Friday, April 4, 1997 - "I greet you, My beautiful children,   *g(094)*
with a holy and reverent kiss of Love. You are My special
ones, My prayerful children whom I love with endless
compassion. My children, I know your hearts. I see your
suffering. I feel your sorrows and pray for your strength.
You are part of the faith that keeps My Son's hopes living in
the universe. Thank you for being participants in God's plan
for the destiny of humanity. Thank you for answering the call
of God without questioning why. I have come to ask you to
continue to pray for the Mother Church. Pray for all souls       *x*
who compose Her, who lead and guide Her, and who serve
Her in so many exemplary ways. You know how God loves
His Church on Earth. He asks you to know Her well, to
embellish the sanctity of Jesus' Spirit who dwells in Her.
Please pray for the Holy Father. Pray for the hierarchy, the
Bishops, priests, all those called by God to serve. Know that
in all of the longevity, Grace, and beauty of the Church, She
is still a tender and sensitive faith and order. She still knows
pain and weeps over Her lost sheep. Please pray for Her, be
kind to Her, and treat Her gently, for She is the source of the    *xx*
salvific Sacraments that are guiding you Home. She is the
blessed Body of the Salvation of humanity. Treat Her with
dignity and respect. The Mother Church is the seamstress
who made your holy baptismal garment, and through whose
grace you are kept clean. The holy and Universal Church is
God's Love for you and the vehicle through which, in faith,
you return that Love. Exult the Catholic Church over every
nation and principality! Honor Her all of your days and She
will bring you to Jesus through Me.

My children, I have never before told you of My        *xxx*
tender love for the Holy Church on Earth. I wish you to
know that the intercession of the Saints is invoked by your
petitions to God through His Faith-Church on Earth. It is
there that the Saints have left their inscription and legacy. It
is there that you are greeted by them as you enter the
doorway of the sanctuary. They relish the time they are
allowed to speak through you. They are happy to have the
opportunity to pray for you and simultaneously with you for
the peace and healing that you seek for the lost world of

humankind. When you go into the Church, especially for    *xl*
Holy Mass, you are flanked by angels who usher you to the
site from which God wishes you to observe and participate in
the Crucifixion of His only Son. The Holy Church Universal
is blessed because it belongs to Christ, the Anointed One.
Thank you for your compliance and participation in the one
Body of faith and love for Jesus. With Him, I bless you and
guide you. God knows both your heart and your faith. He
knows how you pine for peace in a world so reluctant to love.
He sees the cynicism about you and the persecution you
suffer for His sake. He also knows overwhelmingly your    *l*
impatience in waiting for the coming of His Kingdom and
justice. When your faith is perfected, you will know that He
has taken His first steps toward you. Anytime you see a
Baptism, you see the footstep of Jesus coming to save you.
When a child is fed or a sickness healed, it is Jesus laying His
foot down on His journey back to the Earth. Each time you
pray for the lost, He lengthens His stride. When you reach-
out to the lonely in His Name, your Lord increases the pace
of His steps toward the mortal world.

    My children, if all the faithful would pray in unity for    *lx*
peace and healing, Jesus would come running at full speed
back to you with the power and pace of the Champion that
He is. You already know Him and He assuredly knows you.
The pendulum came to a stop on Mount Calvary and has ever
since been swiftly swinging back to you. One day, all will see.
All will hear. Please be ready, My children, because that
pendulum is also the clapper in the bell of Creation about to
hit the other side of time, a ringing joy that will end the world
as you know it and ring-in the new age of Paradise and peace.
I promise that I will be there and help you come to complete    *lxx*
Love. I will help you put your little hands over your ears if
the joyful ringing seems too loud. I will not allow the
mightiness of the fireworks to frighten you. Stay close to Me
and hold-on to Me because that day is coming very soon.
And, it will be then that your eyes will be blessed with the
perfect vision of Mercy personified. It is then that you will
know what your life was for. The perfect purpose of your life
given by God will come peacefully to rest in your heart. Until

that day, your heart will be restless. Until then, you will ask the question, why? From now until then, you will continue to wonder "when" is "then." It is not offensive to God for you to demand His attention. That invocation is a righteous call for the elimination of every evil that befalls humankind. God has already answered your call. His solution was brought nearly 2000 years ago. You are just now realizing it. Call upon the power of the Cross! Call Jesus into the world to quench the fires that burn the human spirit, and yet, to ignite fires where souls are frozen in hatred and indifference. Call upon the Blood of the Cross to cleanse souls lying filthy in sin. That Blood is the fuel you need to carry-on your journey, the Life-Blood that can resurrect a dead world. Yes, indeed, the Life-Blood of the Church is literally the Blood of the Lamb of God who takes away the sins of the world. And, in that Life-Blood flows the Mercy of God.

This is the special Sunday that His Mercy will be especially fluent. At the designated hour of Mercy this Sunday, you will know a portion of the ringing-bell that heals the ages. Please participate in that Divine Mercy and know that God will hear you. If you have a prayer, pray it! If you have a petition, lift it up to Him! If you have a dream, dream it indeed! You awaken God's compassion and Mercy by your call to Him. God is a God of Love and His Love is for His children. His New Covenant is your only chance to board His outstretched hand about to reach your soul and recoil into the majesty of the heavens. His outstretched arms and pure sacrificial hands are that train that is traveling the Earth seeking passengers bound for Glory. And, once you have boarded, you may look to your feet and notice that you are standing on rough terrain. If you ask, God will tell you that it is where there was once a spike that pierced the holy Palm that holds you. I ask you to remember these holy things and meditate on the happiness coming now in time toward you. Thank you for listening to My words of holy encouragement. I am here because I love you. You cannot fully comprehend how I love you. Please remember that your passage into Heaven will come swiftly, and you will wonder where time went. You will wonder how your mortality could have passed

*lxxx*

*xc*

*c*

*cx*

so quickly.  Thank you for praying to heal such a wretched world.  Thank you for yearning for Heaven, for knowing the petitions and intentions of My Heart.  Though your passing days often seem strange and conflicting, know that they are a part of your passage toward Eternal Life and perpetual Light.  Hence, they are a gift from God to prepare you to embrace Him perfectly.  Thank you still for honoring Me through the Holy Rosary.  I am your Advocate, your counsel to Jesus, who is your Savior.  I sincerely love you with all My Heart."

*cxx*

Our Blessed Lady told us on this day that She greets us with a "holy and reverent kiss."  It is worth explaining the dimensions of such a signature of Love because it is very easy to have this blessing pilfered from the grasp of our faith by someone who might pooh-pooh these sentiments through their inability to function by any other criteria than their inadequate senses can provide.  In contrast, the children of God allow the maternal Grace of their Heavenly Mother to be a supportive fortress to their ever-budding faith.  Consider every corner of the globe in the passage of the generations; how many kisses have been placed upon the delicate cheeks of little children lying in the slumbering repose of their dreamy bassinets, completely unaware of the loving interaction of their mothers and fathers who guard over them like sentinels against their misfortunes and cares, who bend in humble adulation before the gift of perfect human innocence which was generated from their love.  Are these acts of sublime human affection less than real simply because the senses of these precious infants were absorbed in other things, namely the peacefulness of their sleep?  Are the enatic impulses of our Heavenly Queen somehow negated or rendered ineffective by our lack of acceptance that they are authentic and wholly representative of Her motherly care?  We cannot be sincere if we answer this to the affirmative.  Each of us is currently immersed in the darkened realms of a humanity which has been thus far lulled into believing and accepting the inconsistencies and inaccuracies of mortality where our vision is clouded by the delusions of our wanton sinfulness; an insipid condition that has cut-off our elevated hopes at the knees while still in their infancy, condemned our grandest possibilities before ever allowing them a day of justification before an impartial arbiter, and has rotted our brotherhood as ignorant purveyors of the human senses assail our innate ability to trust in the celestial motivations of the Spirit of God.  I dare say that we are a conditioned species of people who are no more equipped for conquering this darkness than David before Goliath; but we know the kiss that God bestowed upon that young lad! The heroic shepherd boy who would become a king packed a sling-shot, the confidence of a giant, and an indomitable faith in the God he trusted to the threshold of death; and we, the children of Mary, possess the Most Holy Rosary, a Faith given to us by twelve in-spirited Apostles and a Mother who reigns as the Royalty of Heaven and Earth. So, let us invoke a more dimensioned and kinetic bond of belief where the dictates of Grace can provide the functional presence of Divinity and visionary Light into the more rancid cellars of mortal existence. The Immaculate Beatitude of Heaven has always been and will continue to be fruitful, regenerative, and multiplying wherever it touches the fertile Earth. The words of God and His acts of sanctification sprout forth from His Being, ever to return in abundance; and He would have it no other way. In like measure, the warm embrace of His Queenly Matriarch animates the dignity of Her children, giving strength and peace atop the rejuvenating purity that is secured in the Sacramental waters of our Baptism. The empowering knowledge that we are personally loved and mightily protected by the Divine Mother of Human Redemption must change us for the better from the inside out; if not at this present moment, then most assuredly in the resurrected awakening from our mortal sleep when She shall raise us giggling into Her arms to begin the first blessed day of the Everlasting Ages.

The definition of human life and its celebratory purpose in the Truth of our existence is coming into much clearer focus in these waning days of our post-modern world. Our exhaustion of the intellectual and material theories of the universe has left our famished curiosity with only one frontier on which to ingratiate itself: the spiritual Domain of the Sacred Heart of the Son of God who is the Love that will ultimately and superbly fulfill every soul. The beautiful extensions of the noble human spirit have provided the palatable seasoning for this entire earthly adventure of some several thousand years; from Abraham to Isaac and Jacob, in the footsteps of Elijah and the Mosaic caravans advancing to the Promised Land, throughout the trials of kings and the reigning prosperity of God's prophetic Kingdom of Israelites who experienced deliverance from starvation and the ecstatic euphoria of victory and release from bondage, onward in the company of the Prophets to the arrival of an Archangel named Gabriel; a Fiat from the lips of a Virgin and the Mystery of God in a manger; a public revelation of human perfection heralded from the doorstep of the evangelic Baptizer; all of this has unfolded and ultimately given way to the Crucifixion and Resurrection of Incarnate Love in human flesh, Jesus Christ. The pendulum of revelation has followed the eclipsing swath of human aspirations across the history of Creation, drawing our attention to the moment when the Hand of God grasped the leading edge of the mortal veil and ripped it from before His Thrice-Crowned Divinity, unleashing Immortal Love from the Vault of Heaven with as much righteous anticipation as the starting-gates being simultaneously dropped before the thundering paths of Man O'War, Secretariat, and Seattle Slew on the same crisp afternoon upon the mystical fields of a Kentuckian paradise, leaving His Majesty to triumphantly ride the Steeds of time back into His Eternity. The Passion, Crucifixion, and Resurrection of Jesus Christ is the apodictic moment in the inflationary reams of earthly millennia when the pendulum of celestial Revelation came to its fullest extension and began its evolutionary return of deliverance to the Creator who set it in motion away from Himself at the solemn Fall of Adam and Eve. The glorious human species has been struggling with the loss of divinity since those first fateful minutes of exile where God, Himself, gave us His predestined blessing of new hope by thrusting us inexorably onto a collision-course and heart-breaking encounter with the Old Rugged Cross of His Crucified Son; all for the purpose of our Redemption and liberation from a decrepit vision that does nothing to assist or enhance our embellished imitations of the Holy Spirit of Christ living inside us.

Our Lady has continually repeated to me in our personal conversations that we cannot comprehend the degree to which She loves us; and there are certain aspects of our humanness that keep us from experiencing the caressing nature of the Holy Spirit in the totality of our senses. It is paradoxically relevant to understand that it is some of the essential elements of being mortal that are the greatest distractions from, and impediments to, our immersion in the unseen realities that we cannot apprehend. Consider the simple intrinsic capacity of the human person to think and decide based upon the perceptions that have been recorded during our maturing growth process and the pride that we have allowed to fester while cultivating such sensible attributes. Many mortal men have used their decision-making traits to reason without foundation that God is far away and never interacts with His children. They conclude, therefore, that He must either not exist or is completely separated from us in a Heaven that we may one day see after we die. The very choice to make such a fallacy in one's thinking is a dimension of the veil of our mortal exile. It is an example of how the phantoms in our minds restrict our comprehension of our Virgin Mother's Love for us. She has always encouraged me, sometimes even ardently, to stop deciding anything except for God and begin a new life of accepting every grace from Heaven through the gift of faith; effectively believing in Salvation without seeing it first. *Do not persist in your unbelief, but believe!* I have grown to never invoke any semblance of obstinance or debate with Her diamonds of Wisdom because, every time I have, I was left standing unawares in a puddle of my own embarrassment and offering an apology to Her for not trusting someone who is so overwhelmingly superior. You see, there is no elusiveness to the Hosts of Paradise. They are not hiding from us, and neither are they looking another way. I remember the games of my childhood, especially when we would play the manifold renditions of hide-and-seek. I was one of the elder children in my mother and father's brood of six, so it would always be impishly enjoyable to hide along with the neighbor children in places where the youngest were too innocent and naive to find us. They would search the house over in attempts to uncover our rather conspicuous hiding places. Even my memories today of their pure delight in taking part with the older of us is a warmth that still feeds my soul, wishing that my adult years could have these same carefree traits. Anyway, at sometime during our play each day, we would have to give the smallest ones a chance to be lost and found because it was always more fun to have someone searching-out your clandestine nook. And, on this particular occasion, my younger sister, who was no more than two or three years old, ran to my parents' bedroom, sat right smack-dab in the middle of their bed, pulled the bedspread over her head, and waited like a frozen statue until I finally finished counting. After numbering to twenty or twenty-five, I shouted, *Ready or not, here I come,!* and began my search, which eventually took me into the bedroom. As I crossed the threshold, there in the middle of the bed was a supposedly hidden little tyke who looked like a tiny ghost fidgeting in joyful anticipation of being discovered. I remember nearly beginning to laugh aloud myself because my little prey was perched in a bolt upright position beneath the coverings, concluding that since she could not see who was looking for her, neither could they see her. Yet, to this day, I recall being mesmerized by the flash of light that emanated from such an innocent composure. Of course, I completed the game by acting as if she was so well hidden that I couldn't find her, then sprung upon her hiding place and watched her ecstatically giggle with delight at finally being exposed. Our Heavenly Mother told me that this is exactly how She and our Almighty Father perceive all of us, although they can see completely through the fabric of our exilic blanket as if it were completely transparent. We are positioned under a mortal veil and naively believe that we cannot be seen, although we pine at the thought of being found. Our Holy Mother's miraculous words, *Come out, come out, wherever you are,!* are not a signal that She does not know exactly where each of us is, but rather Her call to the collective soul of God's children who are tucked beneath their errant ideologies with which they have haphazardly made their beds. She knows that our delight will be infinitely magnified on the day that our Blessed Lord sweeps the mortal covering from atop our lives. The Most Holy Virgin calls us to pray deeply from the heart because it is the domain wherein the interaction between Heaven and Earth ensues. She wishes our entire decision-making process to be focused upon the acceptance of the Cross of Jesus Christ without question, consternation, or debate. Then, the Holy Spirit will flourish in all of our rejuvenated senses; and we will be saved. As Ripley's Jack Palance used to say; *Believe it or not!*

Friday, April 11, 1997 - "My Love is with you and My Son     *g(101)* brings you peace. My dear little children, you are God's lost artwork for which He has come searching. From the ravages of sin at the influence of Satan, you were shaken and fell from display in the halls of Paradise. But, Jesus came to pick you up, to repair your souls, to restore your perfection, and to again elevate you to the holy halls of beauty for all Creation to see. I am very happy to see so many of My children lifting-up their brothers and sisters, leading them, forgiving them, and teaching them. Jesus is happy to see     *x* broken-hearted children mended through the love of others. He is proud of His artwork. Jesus' Sacred Heart is touched to see His little children wearing apparel that says, *I am special, God did not make any trash.*

My children, you are living in a world that is near its Reckoning. I tell you this constantly; and each time I repeat it, you are yet closer to that Truth. Soon you will see the destruction and obsolescence of such phenomena as complacency, indifference, egoism, and hatred. It is time for change, and the change will come by the power of     *xx* judgement. While God prefers that judgement be preceded by conversion, He will not hold the world statically in mortality for the wait. God is the only true Master of time and timing. He has already decided when to bring His Kingdom to Earth. That Redemption and Judgement is so close that He has consistently invited Me to come to Earth and serve as the *New Gabriel*. Gabriel comes with Me each time I visit the world, ushering Me and clearing My paths into your hearts so that My messages can be heard. Do not be afraid of this New World to come. Do not believe that     *xxx* you are not worthy of such Deliverance. Indeed, Redemption seeks you with as much life as you desire it. You are like a lightning rod while Redemption is the lightning. God has found you. The world was illuminated by the Cross of Jesus on Calvary like God shining a light into a dark pit. He came looking for you with the beaming Light of His Son. And, Jesus flashed your vision that allowed God to say, *Oh, there you are!* He is now reaching down to pick you up. My children, God picks you up by the heart. You speak to God with your heart in answer to His words *I love you* from the Cross. Jesus is the Truth and the Earth is His palate. The Cross is His tongue with which He pronounced the words, *It is time to come Home.* I am here today in advance of the harvest of souls. Many hundreds of thousands still labor in the vineyards for God..."

*(My brother attended the funeral of a middle age woman whom we saw nearly everyday at Holy Mass. She was very reverent toward Jesus in the Most Blessed Sacrament, while suffering a terrible physical ailment.)*

"The new Saint of the day has said, *By the Blood of the Cross, we are saved.* She is in Heaven. Please know what that means for the world. Know how happy she is to be redeemed and made new again. For all Eternity, for the perpetual Day for which you seek, she will be ecstatic. Your brother is to be thanked for coming to pray at her funeral Mass. It was very kind. He did, indeed, attend the funeral Mass of a great person. The world must come to know greatness as defined by Heaven. Please remember all the Saints. They will assuredly remember you. You are the tabernacle of Jesus' Spirit. Jesus does wish to reside in every heart. Where He lives is blessed with peace. You are the souls whose charge it is to sanctify the world you know. You are doing such work well. For many years, day after day, I have been watching you work in God's vineyard. Your labors have been sweet and your prayers very powerful. God gives your intentions and petitions power to change the world. For two decades, you have been seeking ways to interpret, understand, and overcome the world and its influences. I watched you grow and waited joyfully for many years to bring My intercession to you."

*(Our Lady then manifested visions in my heart of all those days that She patiently watched over me waiting for February 22, 1991. My heart welled-up with the peace and light-heartedness that I had as a child during my play. I began to cry as I was able to see and feel my childhood as it was miraculously brought back to my heart. Through these visions, I transcended into the joys of my past as they were presented as premonitions of my future.)*

"Those days give you cause to smile. They are behind the veil, days that are gone, but ones that you will see again from the purview of perfection. You will live the sweetest moments again. All of this hope is real. This is not magic, fantasy, or a dream. It is real and a part of the Glory of the New World Jesus brings. I am happy to bring you this Good News. There is nothing or no one that you desire in your heart that Jesus will not give you. Each day that you live, that reality comes closer. You will soon see the comets from the Light-side of Creation. They will look like tiny lights under your feet. Remember that God not only desires that you have a joyful heart, He requires it! I give you My Motherly blessing. Thank you for your prayers. I will speak to you again soon." *lxx* *lxxx*

Let's cut right to the chase and hit the Divine Truth head-on with our feet-a-spinnin', as they say. What is our ultimate goal in life? Why are we here? The more materialistic of our number are quick to retort to such questions in a carefree demeanor: *To die with the most toys!* It should go without saying that they don't have the slightest inkling as to the meaning of our existence on Earth. And, if you press them to provide a more thoughtful answer by asking, "what then?," there is either a stupefied look that comes across their face as if they had never thought about what was next, or disdain infiltrates their heart as they realize that someone is trying to mercifully thrust their soul in the direction of God and they wish to reserve the right to imitate a toddler who doesn't want to be shown the bathtub on a Saturday evening. There are others who would be overjoyed to happen upon the true reason for their trials and tribulations as they have been curious about their purpose for most of their waking moments; but they just don't know whom to trust in the ocean of dissimilar opinions. It is my hope that this last chapter has given this latter group a reason to have new faith in the witness I am extolling, and to the former a clamoring wake-up call that something holy is expected of them in the final analysis. Our necessary search to understand the most meaningful aspects of our lives begins in prayer from our deepest spirit. We will never grasp the greater dimensions that reside within us unless we abandon our worldly mindset to the meditations which flourish when our hearts are tendered to humbleness and peace. Our Lady offers this maternal advice over and again in Her tireless efforts to lead us into the depths of prayer, especially the Holy Rosary. So, what is it about the *Hail Mary* that makes God so happy? Why has the Rosary proven to be such an overwhelming power against evil in the course of history, even to this day? Foremost, it is a prayer of life-giving oneness where our souls become completely united with the sublime contemplations of the heavenly Hosts in the realms of the spiritual unseen. The Divine vision that adorns Heaven with Beauty is the Life, Death, and Resurrection of the Lamb of God which has rendered Humanity-Redeemed to be the priceless jewel of Paradise. The Holy Crucifixion of Jesus Christ on the Cross of Mt. Calvary and all the grace-filled events that led to such an unselfish immolation being conquered by the Triumph of His Paschal Resurrection is the stupendous regenerative Thought of God radiating from His Infinite Love for us, which is our protection in the time of our every need. When we enter into the chronological Mysteries of the Most Holy Rosary, our hearts are employed as willing participants within the purview of the unfolding of Eternal Salvation; and our immortal souls are donned with the same impenetrable Glory in which every Celestial Host in the Eternal Firmament is arrayed. For those blessed minutes, the meditations seen through our inner eyes of faith are synchronized with the Host Angelic Choirs who live the rapturous wonderment of the Divine magnanimity of our benevolent God; and we become the beneficiaries of the jubilation that pulsates from the infinitely hospitable mansions of Paradise that are populated with the courageous souls who have preceded us in the good fight, having already claimed their crowns to the tumultuous fanfare that only God, Himself, knows how to effect. The all-encompassing feat that we must undertake in order to realize such a miraculous prodigy as God sending His Son into the world to die for His wayward children begins in our willful acceptance that the querying syllables of the Archangel Gabriel initiated the preeminent obedience in the Immaculate Heart of our Blessed Virgin Mother. Can you imagine how this radiant Dove treasures the words of God's heavenly messenger in Her immortal soul at every moment throughout Eternity, knowing that Her faithful compliance graced the history of man with a Sacred Beatitude that will never see an end? *Hail Mary!* This, in itself, is the First Joyful Mystery of the Most Holy Rosary! Our Salvation has been miraculously wrought for the sake of humankind at the utterance of Her Fiat and a Magnificat of praise. There was not a hint of reservation in One so gentle and true; the lapse of Zechariah would never stain Her response; and Motherhood would henceforth be filled with a hallowed benediction. *Blessed are you among women, and blessed is the Fruit of your womb, Jesus,!* culminating in an ultimate stroke of petition that She would pray for us through the moment of our earthly passing into Her arms. And, there you have it! Every time a holy heart reechoes the Salutation of the Archangel Gabriel, the conjunctive essence of the Kingdom of Heaven accents the Sacred Conception of our Messianic God upon the Earth and accelerates the transformation of human existence from damnation to the final Revelation of Victory. We have all heard the blood-curdling blather which sooner or later coagulates into rejection from those who want to "decide"—there's that word again—that the Holy Rosary is just a mindless mantra of words; a supposed conglomerating distraction away from Jesus, whom we should be focusing our attention upon instead. These are nothing but nefarious excuses from infidels who do not understand the magnificent Christological power of the Rosary or what obedience to the Holy Spirit really means. If the Truth be told openly, they are simply functioning from a deep-seated hatred of anything that appears to be Catholic in nature. How's that for cutting to the chase? I rather function by this credo: Since the Queen of Heaven has been sent by God to miraculously appear and communicate His desires to us, every person who ultimately wishes to find themselves in communion with His Omnipotent Will must respond without question, discussion, or rebuttal. That is the true nature of Divine obedience. I marvel at the ignorance of those who cast aside the meditations of the Rosary because they "aren't getting anything out of it." Let me put it into a parable. Consider the plight of the Jewish people during World War II, and how they collectively suffered such horrific defilement and indignity at the hands of diabolical Nazi hate-mongers; the racism, the purging of the ghettos, families separated forever, the satanic death-trains of colossal inhumanity, incarceration in extermination factories, starvation and torture in barracks, back-breaking labor solely for the gain of their captors, and a Final Solution of murder by the millions for being nothing other than a particular race of people. Imagine being given a book written by one of the survivors of such horror; one who maintained the most beautiful parts of the great human spirit amidst such desolation; and upon giving it a cursory read, handing it back to them saying, *Sorry, I had to put it down because I wasn't getting anything out of it.*

Friday, May 30, 1997 - "Peace. The peace of the Holy Spirit    *g(150)*
is with you always. My children, the Spirit of Love protects
and guides you. He gives you Wisdom, confidence, and
good strength. My dear children, I do not come to warn you
of a terrible scorn given to mankind by God; My words do
not portend doom and hopelessness. Instead, I come
bringing you hope and happiness. Of course, the world is
filled with heresy and hatred, but such have already been
defeated by Jesus to be manifested completely in your time
upon the Triumph of My Immaculate Heart. In that, My    *x*
little children, is constant hope. Do not fear the day, for the
Light is Christ the Victor. You bask in His Holy Light. You
are cleansed by the healing waters from the side of the
Champion, pierced beautifully for your souls. I must tell you
today that unless you hope in your success, you will not
succeed. Believe in the power of your prayers and you will
be successful. Know your courage with which you convert
others and you will savor such victory. Accept the Love in
your heart as the Truth which guides your days. My
children, today I have come to remind you of the Reign of    *xx*
the King that you so adore, yet cannot see Face-to-face.
Your King is not only the King of Creation, He is also the
Prince of Anticipation. Jesus anxiously awaits the word from
the Father to return for His blessed children. At each new
day, He turns to the God of all to say, *Is this the day?* Jesus
knows His own and waits in every possible emotion to come
to take you to your mansion which He has so beautifully
prepared for you. With toil, suffering, sweat, and His holy
Blood, He built that mansion for you, and many mansions
there are. They are a New Zion for a New Man. Man-    *xxx*
Zions. Mansions. I have seen the Glory of this New
Jerusalem. I have come today to assure you of My
intercession to assist you to get there. In your heart and in
your love, you have seen this New City from the firmament
of faith. Your vision is from the perspective of your trust in
Jesus. No despair or fear can stop you from attaining this
joy. The King who reigns there has announced His desire
for your attendance at His Eternal Feast. And, the King's
wishes are always fulfilled. But, these days are the precedent

to that Glory. Now is the time that will take you there. *xl*
Yours are the prayers that will usher-in His Kingdom. You
are His evangelists. You are His baptizers. You are the last
age to say "Yes" to a salvific plan for humanity that began at
the Annunciation of Saint Gabriel. What Grace you must
now know! You recently viewed a motion picture depicting
the passage of mortal men through time. You are doing so
at this very moment because you are praying simultaneously
with all the Saints in Heaven who lived centuries before.
Prayer is timeless as your Love is timeless. I assure you that
there is no better place for you to be at this time. You are *l*
doing God's work in the vineyard where He needs you. You
are wielding tremendous power over evil and influence over
the indifferent. Please know that God is pleased with your
progress. The King is smiling from His Throne and knows
that you are a messenger of His Holy Will on Earth. This
King protects you and gives you the gifts you seek. My
children, I am grateful to God to be allowed to bring this
news to you. I am humbled by the gift He made to Me of
yourselves as My little children. Heaven does not take your
sacrifices lightly. We share in your grief and celebrate in *lx*
your joy. You are one with Heaven when you realize, reveal,
accept, and live the Life of Christ. There is no better way to
make God happy with you. As you adore Jesus, you
concurrently venerate this Mother who gives Him to the
world. So, do not desist in your hope and prayers. Do not
be despondent about the travails of a passing world. All is
said and done. It is finished. You are just now learning
about its happy ending. To the Victor-God belongs the
souls He saved. Many are among them, you have not time
to count, but all you will soon know. My children, I have *lxx*
been about the world blessing and dispensing graces. As
terrible as the world seems, it is only Satan's facade in
attempt to destroy your hope in Jesus. He will not succeed
because your faith lies in the Sacred Heart of the Son of
God, the Crown Prince who is already King. My son, your
faith is enough to bring all that you seek. Your Love can
conquer any ill. Please never dismay at the world. You
know already the Truth which Jesus has given you to know.

God has allowed the world to see an image of your Love for Him. It is especially important for you to protect that image. Before, no one had any means to determine its limitless magnitude. Now, however, if you do not emit that perfection, they will know it. I will help you to be the perfect Love that you wish to be. I am always with you and join My prayers with yours. I will speak to you again very soon. I love you."

It is an almost euphoric feeling to have all of your highest hopes for the world confirmed in these larger-than-life moments. So true are the observations that malignant heresy and viral hatred run rampant through even our more civilized cultures; the most notorious and clandestine examples being the collusive opportunists who illicitly cloak themselves in public respectability while their true agendas are completely comprised of either making indentured consumers out of the rest of the world or outright economic slaves of their fellow men in their sweltering factories of consumerism. And, equally as genuine are the prophetic utterances that have announced their impeding annihilation as the Triumph of the Immaculate Heart of Mary comes to its monolithic crescendo. Human dignity will prevail; and we will all revel in a freedom that we once only dreamed could exist. The declaration which will be engraved upon the new cornerstones of our societies will read: *Succumbed willingly to the Grace of the Most Blessed Virgin Mary.* No other station of Divinity is more prolific in these latter times; no cultivated field has brought forth a more bountiful harvest; and there has not been a more obvious display of the supernatural guidance of Almighty God by the power of the Holy Spirit. Some people become rather anxious when others speak of the Victory of the Mother of Jesus Christ for a plethora of reasons. They usually begin with the shallow refutation that it is not explicitly spoken about anywhere in Sacred Scripture that they can find, and ends somewhere in the vicinity of, *I'll believe it when I see it.* This basically means that they would not accept anyone who was sent to them with a message from their Omnipotent Maker. I have stated before that rejection has always been the defining act of the mortal human will as masses of people have spurned the loving overtures of God for repetitive centuries on end. Faith, however, is the imperishable sustenance of the spiritually bold and the lamp of ever-rising possibilities in the courageous of heart. The logical beauty of faith tells us that using the finite texts of Sacred Scripture alone as a confining barometer of the limitlessness of what God will do and the spontaneous response that He expects of us to His graceful Holy

Spirit at each moment of our lives is pure folly. Are the great victories of Saint Joan of Arc and the liberating campaign for the soul of her French motherland foretold in Scripture? Is the profound life of Saint Francis of Assisi and his imprint of divinity upon the Christian conscience of humankind prophesied explicitly in the Word of God? Where in those Holy Texts is the clear annunciations that the Great Doctors of the Church would write, how the sacrificial stigmatists would suffer, and when the littlest and most insignificant ones would be called to shame a godless world with a message beyond imagined hope from On-High? None of these manifestations of virtuous Christian Truth are prophesied directly in the Bible according to the standard which is used to pass judgement on the magnificent intercessions of the Mother of Jesus Christ. Yet, they are part of the collectively authentic works of God's Pentecostal Spirit which have flourished from the Passion, Death and Resurrection of the Messiah. So, let's snap their faithless measuring sticks in half before God, Himself, reincarnates some of our stricter nuns from generations past to place needed discipline across our knuckled pride and once and for all believe that the Holy Spirit is living and well, operating within and wholly throughout the souls of men in absolute conformity with the prophetic revelations implanted in the strains of Sacred Scripture. The Deposit of Christian Faith that is securely nestled within the Divine Heart of the Catholic Church is a function of both the articulated and recorded Teachings of Christ *and* His reverberating Actions until the end of the world in fulfillment of the requirements of our Eternal Redemption. It is the Traditional Act of the Church to advance the totality of Our Lord in Word and Deed under the imbued guidance and inspiration of the Holy Spirit through the unified soul of the children of God. Therefore, knowing that Christ, along with all the Saints and Angels, is still alive and in attendance before the purview of the unfolding end times, it is not beyond the realms of the meekest faith to accept that the Queen of all Christian Evangelization, our Mother Herself, is quite possibly, if not convincingly, initiating the conclusive transformation of man and bringing to culmination the greatest prodigies of redemptive Grace that Creation will ever see. *Indeed, all ages will call Her blessed!* Since Holy Scripture states clearly that God will raise to high places and glorify those who are faithful to Him, isn't it quite likely that we are blessedly witnessing the effects of the glorification of the Mother of the Redeemer as She wields power across the globe and the ages, too, that the greatest of saints would have died a thousand deaths to administer? The answer is a clearly definitive yes; and in that "Fiat" is the Triumph of the Immaculate Heart of the Queen of Heaven. It is a further faithful step for us to concede that She who cooperatively generated and nurtured the first Coming of Jesus Christ has appeared in Her heavenly

Motherhood to gestate the lasting holiness of the children of God in preparation for His Second Arrival in Glory. Hence, we should prepare our hearts with an even greater degree of attention so that the Final Appearance of our Savior finds us with lamps alighted with the luminosity of His Mother's Love. For anyone who may still have difficulty accepting Her prophetic revelations, please accept these next paragraphs as being from one who is an eyewitness to the miraculous intervention of the Heavenly Hosts and the ultimate Wisdom that emanates from the true Will of God.

I wish to bring to the fore a very timely message that epitomizes the supernatural intercession of the Queen of Paradise and highlights the thoughts of our Almighty Father concerning what would make us all more resemble true babes in the woods by sharing the sentiments of the Matriarch of Creation. It refers to the commutation of the sentence of capital punishment to dozens of condemned prisoners on death row in the State of Illinois by former Governor George Ryan. While I espouse no partisanship whatsoever; except my undying allegiance to the Roman Catholic Church, our Supreme Pontiff, and the Holy Communion of Saints, I sat back in my recliner before a television set on the eleventh day of January 2003 and waited for our secularly-embattled Governor to step before a microphone and offer his conscientious leadership on the topic of executing our brethren for their sins in the administration of social justice in our State. I harbored no expectations when his speech began that an elected official of any stripe might break from the long tradition of political expediency and tabulated turpitude to courageously stand as an elder statesman and child of God for fundamental moral principles. But, what every person witnessed from him that day was of such Divine Light that I am convinced that it will be recognized and hailed by the most civilized bodies of humanity until the last minutes of the world. Our culture of death took a fatal blow to its gluttonous broadside from a man who opened his childlike heart to the genius of the Living Christ and gave righteousness a fighting chance to flood the Earth with the brilliance of mercy and pardon. In union with the humanitarian giants of this century in the likes of Nelson Mandela, Desmond Tutu, Pope John Paul II, His Ecclesial College of hundreds of Roman Catholic Cardinals and Bishops, and millions of faithful Christians throughout the world, this leader among men outlaid his heartfelt reservations about whether social justice can truly exist in a system of human extermination and the vengeance it is attempting to satisfy. It was also ironic to hear Governor Ryan quote so appropriately Supreme Court Justice Harry Blackmun, the author of the infamous *Roe v. Wade* decision to allow infanticide to become the law of our land, when he said, *The death-penalty experiment has failed. I no longer shall tinker with the machinery of death.* No sooner had he finished his address when the howling outrage commenced. Over the course of the next several days, prosecutors, lawyers, victim's families, and the public at large from all over Illinois went before cameras to repudiate the Love of this visionary of peace. They placed their venomous assaults into newsprint and letters for no other reason than to attempt to justify themselves before man and God, alike, by declaring that their right to kill another person for the sake of retribution and their flawed ideas of closure was somehow their sacred duty for the preservation of America. Notwithstanding this onslaught, for one brief span of beautiful moments, the Kingdom of God gracefully thundered the Truth of the ancient Decalogue from the lips of a sinful mortal man throughout the soul of everyone within the sound of his voice, setting a monumental crest of Light into Creation that will ultimately sweep down those mighty walls of vengeance, hatred, and inhumanity that Bobby Kennedy spoke about so profoundly; and there is nothing that our former Governor's detractors can do about it. What profit is there in offering mercy, pardon, and love only to those who love you in return? Another great Man in history asked that one day. The answer is that there is no Eternal profit in seeking the destruction of created human life. This is a reflection of the inescapable Wisdom that is the definitive foundation of the Gospel of Jesus Christ and the underpinning of every civilized culture; but there are those who toss such elevated perfection away as if it were merely a wrapper on a piece of chewing gum. We live in a society that is failing because our spirit is oblivious to the sacred dignity of each human person and the Salvation of every creature who is begotten in the image and likeness of the Heavenly Father. Thereby, we react to the many difficulties and sorrows of life with a singular putrid ideology: Kill! Destroy! Abort! Eliminate! Annihilate! Segregate! Exile! Punish! This has become our undeniable national legacy to which the Lord God responds, *How you judge, so shall you be judged! By your own measure, it shall be measured unto you!* Our glorious country of liberty and shared rights is heaping the fiery condemnation of God's Almighty Judgement upon its inflated ego, which will reduce it to a smoldering pile of rubble upon which the Angels, Saints, and all repentant sinners shall stand with 40 million aborted babies hoisted atop their shoulders and executed criminals grasped in their loving embrace. There is a momentous day in the spectacular offing when the world itself will take the immortal shape of the stately hall at Northwestern University on that winter afternoon in January 2003 when a humble man spoke with humane decency, surrounded by the entire Angelic Court with all the great humanitarians of history in attendance. The ad infinitum King of all Creation, Christ Himself, will rise to the Celestial podium and proclaim with full-throated clarity that all life was, is, and ever shall be precious from the moment He first conceived its multiplicatus dimensions in His Sacred Heart. The Eternal litany of His Immortal Words will race back across the ages faster than any electronic medium could ever reproduce them and reverberate off the wall of the very first Dawn of Edenic Paradise like the song of a mountaineer echoing from a far-off canyon; and there is no way His hate-filled detractors will be able stop it. The vengeful, the haughty, the arrogant, the proud, the self-seeking, and those who believe that they have the authority to take another human life to satisfy their lingering vengeance will stand helplessly watching the God of Abraham resound His dictates of perfection for the admission of the executed into Eternal bliss as was inscribed into Creation by His Crucified Son with indelible exclamation on a horrific mountaintop 2000 years ago. Gone will be the duplicitous interviews, hackneyed editorials, and opinionated rebuttals for slandering the merciful commutation of our deserved sentences of eternal death on that blessed day because the arrogant blindness that generated the furious call for vengeance in the year of Our Lord 2003 will be reduced to ashes. Those who are guilty will be frantically licking their wounds in repentance in finding themselves to have been so offensive toward the dignity of the children of God, hoping to wash themselves clean before Final Judgement is pronounced upon them to the same degree they offered it to their enemies. I wish for no one to assume that these righteous sentiments are of my own making because they come from the Mind of God through His Virgin Mother. Like you, my spirit did not comprehend the infinite magnitude of the Divine Mercy of Jesus Christ until the Blessed Virgin Mary miraculously appeared to proffer Her pious visions to me. However, I am commissioned by the Grace of the Holy Spirit to make God's Will known to men, come what may. So, I ask you to be humbly accepting by embracing these words given by Our Lady on the Feast of the Baptism of Our Lord on the day succeeding Governor Ryan's speech in 2003. They, too, will live alongside the oratory of this native Illinois' son until the end of time.

> Sunday, January 12, 2003 - The Baptism of The Child Jesus   *m(012)*
> "My Special son, after the eloquent way you addressed the Heavens last week in our message and your absolutely profound writings for your books since then, we will speak only briefly today. I have come to pray with you today because there is never a time when I do not. I see the visions and hopes in your heart that you poured-out before Me last week; and you can see more clearly now that many questions are never easy to answer. Let Me tell you, however, of a matter that is for sure. Yesterday, January 11,     *x*

2003, the Governor of the State of Illinois, USA, pronounced both Mercy and Pardon upon the lives of every single person who had previously been condemned to die by the courts, executed outright for their crimes. There is no doubt that you listened to a speech that will live-on until the end of the world. It rivals the deliverance of the Sacred Beatitudes by Jesus Christ on the side of the Mountain. It reflects with precision the Holy Gospel of Christianity in its most essential form. This is a man who has risked scorn, rejection, ridicule, and physical danger to his life. I tell you today that Jesus Christ has gained another Saint and Doctor of the Church, a man of great means who has absolved the poor and wretched who have been given very little. I speak of a man who wept at the loss of someone very dear to him from his own hometown, and then boldly told the world that these criminals who flank him on both sides, all of them, would not die for their sins. Does this sound familiar? Governor George Ryan, whose original signature you have on a letter he sent to you, is being lauded by the greatest Angelic Courts ever to have sung the praises of a mortal man. It is both clear and obvious what the followers of evil, especially the media and the courts, will try to do to him now. I am telling you that as he leaves office tomorrow at midday, he will not only take his dignity with him, but the blessing of the Son of God that is so profound that his mortal soul will glow with Light. Imagine how the Holy Trinity has wept in thanksgiving of the change of heart of My little boy, My George, who is now the conqueror of the wretchedness of vengeance and hate. His power and conviction are nearly unparalleled in the annals of history, and certainly in the time of modern man. Forget about the Nobel Prize for Peace, this man is a walking Saint of Holy Christendom, and all should fall at his feet and wish to emulate his Grace! I thank him for his wisdom and strength, Jesus offers His Love for his every loving act, and God the Almighty Father will soon deliver him to the highest pinnacle of the Heaven He has promised. Yes, His soul will bask in a land of milk and honey with the greatest among men who ever set foot on the face of the globe....What a day!—this

*xx*

*xxx*

*xl*

January 11, 2003! What a humble man! What a moment!        *l*
What a Saint! What a bountiful heart! I wish only that you
would someday make My remarks public so all in the world
can understand... Thank you for helping Me to do so.
Please do not be too disappointed by some of the actions of
a humanity who has been taught by their predecessors to be
like they are. Every time someone like your Governor, who
leaves office tomorrow, stands-up against the howls of evil
that come from those who espouse hatred and revenge, it
drowns-out the declaration from centuries-past of, ...*What I
have written, I have written.*"

There is something to be said about our American cultural identity and
the standard Godless mindset which is sustained when men are confronted
with pious reflections such as these from the Queen of Paradise because they
are radically more sanctified than what one might encounter from the secular
multitudes of the supposedly avant garde of our gated republic. It has been
revealed by our Heavenly Mother that, despite the infrequent flashes of spiritual
brilliance which have inadvertently escaped from the mouths of the American
media through their historical tenure, their modern progressive assault against
the time-honored foundations of Christian moral decency and their penchant
for the proliferation of unchecked lust and perversion that their egoism has
wrought on our nation in the wake of their social apathy render them complicit
before the Throne of God as coopted assailants against our interpersonal
civility. And, Justice is well on its way! So, all of you who have been praying
on your knees for the Light of Love to shine again amongst men, now is your
time! The Most Holy Virgin of Mount Calvary is your Queen! And, the
following edict from Her thematic anthologies is among your most powerful
weapons!

Saturday, June 28, 1997 - "My dear, dear special little   *g(179)*
children. It is, indeed, an amazing Grace which sustains you!
The holiness and Light which you have so willingly
embraced are your guides to Paradise. They are the beacons
which Jesus has brought you to lead you Home. And yes,
you are sustained in the life of perpetual prayer. You are
perfected by all of these. The breath which sustains your life
is faith, and your love is your life itself. My children, God is

maneuvering the people He created into the positions which best please Him. You are being aligned at the right hand of Jesus to fight for Him and with Him. You have courage because you need faith, but you have valor because you invoke faith. You greet the day with the perspective of anticipation and revelation. You do not fear because God is in you. I have seen you live these realities for the decades of your lives. Today, your greeting of the world is again through a simple heart. You are sitting in the carriage waiting for it to begin its final journey Home. Imagine the eight beautiful steeds standing with dignity, strong and still at the front of your carriage. They are tall and handsome, and they occasionally turn their heads to the side just to say, *Whenever you are ready.* These mighty steeds represent the magnificent pillars upon which God has placed His hope to take you back Home. One steed represents *the pillar of Saints*, another *the Angels*, another *the Great Sacrament*, a fourth *the prayers of the faithful*, a fifth *the fruits of the Holy Spirit*, a sixth *the collective human spirit*, a seventh *the great steed called Hope*, and the eighth is *one single Hail Mary*, the power of all other pillars combined. Yes, My son, all of these pillars are the strength built by the Sacrifice of Jesus on the Cross. The horsepower that will deliver humanity to God is derived from the Blood of one Lamb. One Lamb created eight steeds. And, so stands the magnificent assembly waiting for the God of all who is sitting at the seat at the front of the carriage called Redemption to shake the reigns in His hands and nicker, *Let us go now homeward with our cherished cargo of souls. Let us go proudly to the homeland which I prepared for them.* And, then, the eight Glory horses will raise their heads proudly and walk in cadence to the beat of the mighty Sacred Heart. Their manes have been beautifully braided by the holy women of old. Their coats have been brushed by the calloused hands of those faithful to Saint Joseph. What beautiful horses are prepared to move at the initiation of God's call. When this happens, you will know. You will be both in the carriage and also watching the carriage. I have made some pretty ribbons and bows to place on this carriage of Redemption. I have given it My motherly touch. Yes, God has aligned His people, His Hosts of Heaven, His Holy Sacraments, and all the power of righteousness to bring you Home. When you hear the clapping of the hooves on the golden pavements, know deep within your heart that God's Kingdom is come. Yes, there is a distinct majesty about horses. They are strong and confident, peaceful and obedient. It is with this same majesty that God touches your lives to allow you to know the valor of a mighty steed... All of this has come from the Sacrifice of one Man, My Jesus. You will see Him Face-to-face and He will know you. And, best of all, you will know Him. Indeed, you are already one Love. I share this Truth with you in the confidence that you will continue your life for Him. You will endure many horrible battles for Jesus before He calls you Home. You will always be victorious because of your faith and your love for God and for Me. I give you My promise of Love and commitment to your Salvation that I gave to God through the Angel Gabriel. I will speak to you very soon. I love you. Goodnight."

The Kingdom of Heaven manifests great Divinity in its soul-wrenching guidance of humanity. I dare say that most of us do not understand to any appreciable degree that our entire existence is a direct function of the prefigured encouragement and masterful choreography of the Crucified Son of Mary. The inception of the word "coincidence" in our dictionaries belies the real Truth regarding our lack of vision concerning the interaction of God with His children. Guardian angels? Some mock us by saying that we must be kidding. But, let me tell you about a certain "coincidence" that flushes the not-so-obvious into the open. When I was a little boy, no more than six or seven years old, I used to climb to the highest branches of any tree in our yard in which I could find a foothold. For me, the world was somehow inspiringly different from such elevated heights, so much so that I would even take my father's binoculars with me in order to see even farther. My grandfather lived on a farm about three miles across the cultivated fields; and I would often look in his direction, hoping to catch a glimpse of him working on the lawn, or perhaps doing his chores. On one particular summer's day, I was climbing a pair of persimmon trees about a hundred yards from the house, ones that I had ascended so many times before that I could probably have done it asleep, to an altitude that was a prescription for a disaster. As I hurriedly neared its highest branches, I reached to take-hold of another one and suddenly lost my footing, sending me plummeting backward out of the tree from about thirty feet in the air. I was expecting great trauma and pain in those next few moments because I knew there was probably nobody nearby to help me. But, then, something really peculiar happened. It was as if I had leaned back onto a feathery bed as I bounced head-over-heels from one leaf-blanketed branch to the next, each one deferring to my descent. Upon impacting the last limb with my back, it gently bent to the ground to counter my weight, flipping the soles of my shoes, with me inside them, over my head one last time as I floated down like a leaf, landing upright on my feet in the grass. At that moment, with my heart racing from the adrenalin, I felt a serene peace inside me as I knew that something near-supernatural had just happened. I remember having thoughts about my guardian angel and how the branches seemed almost human, as if huge hands had extended themselves to catch me. In the most unique sense, I felt loved and protected by God in whom I had been taught to believe, but had never seen, more than ever before. I have wondered many times since why I have seemingly always been delivered from the tragic consequences of my more careless moments. Does the answer reside in seeing *Morning Star Over America*? Through my faith, I can say *Yes*.

Friday, May 1, 1998 - "My dearly beloved children, how *h(121)* thankful I am to be with you tonight, how blessed is this place to accept the Love I bring. Children, the darkest of night is just before the dawn; and you are come to that place in time. You are seeing many repulsive things, but you must rejoice because their passing is near. You are seeing a world which both denies and dishonors God: An additional signal that your Redemption is at hand. You have heard the words, *Lead, O' kindly Light.* That is the Spirit in which you live as one for God. You follow Jesus and are yet His Light for          *x* many. I have asked you to walk softly and gently upon the ground. You have consented and are soon to reap the fruits of your humility. Your hearts have stored many souls in them, the souls of the lost which you are taking to Jesus. Such is your prayer, your great task at hand. The union of your hearts resembles a titanic vessel, filled with happy souls on their journey back to Jesus. Mightily you steam away from the port with your precious load, all of them waving goodbye to all that kept them bound. But, this mighty vessel

will not sink.  This maiden ship is also My Heart, and God      xx
Himself could not sink Her.  Yes, you steam away from the
last port as the waves lap in your wake.  All of the majestic
songs play at the sight of the launching of this ship; the
angel-choirs sing in rhythm with the pulse of the waves.  I
have given this mighty vessel for you to bring to our God
the souls you know are My sweet children.  Now, upon the
high seas, you hear My Son, your Savior, tell you, *Take Her
to speed! My son. Let's spread Her wings.*  So well you are
doing what I asked so long ago, in 1991.  The fireworks
above this ship will not be a distress call, but a call to      xxx
celebration.  Let the celebration begin because the dawn of
man has come.  All of the boilers are fired and you are
steaming toward the horizon, over which you will find your
Home.  Yes, let there be dancing and merrying between the
rich and the poor!  Let the gates of division be knocked-
down as the affluent carry the feast-trays to feed those so-
long locked behind them.  Many times I have asked you to
live this hope.  It is now near the new reality as this month
of flowers has begun...Justice is served.  It is served because
you emulate the Mercy that Jesus gave the world, His Life,      xl
Death, and Resurrection, forgiveness, and Sacraments.
Indeed, vengeance is the possession of God who disposes it
to the last chamber of time, and in this bringing-forth is the
beauty of your compassion for His children.  You must
realize your very role of advocate for humankind.  Therein
lies your answer when others ask what Jesus in now doing.
Answer them by showing your living example..."

Like Jesus, Our Holy Mother speaks to us in Mystical parables because
She is inviting us to open our hearts to the vivid realms of the contemplations
of God, wherein our childlike faith becomes a sanctified plateau from which
our spirituality enjoys a more profound relationship with the Heavens that wait
in joyful hope for the collective glance of our affections.  Every Christian
knows the story of Noah and how he and his family were saved from the
Biblical flood by the direct intercession of our Omnipotent Creator who sent
such a devastating deluge upon the ancient world to cleanse it of its evil works;
notwithstanding how futilely our modern-day archeological revisionists wish to
explain away its Eternal significance.  Our Heavenly Father has been speaking

to every age through His redemptive works in which He has manifested untold Mystical allusions to the final days of the Salvation of humankind. The Ark in the time of Noah was the instrument by which He delivered His loyal followers to the culmination of their rainbowed future. Then, the Ark of the Old Covenant miraculously appeared in mortal history and the Jewish people carried it into battle in the heights of their glory days as the catalytic artifact containing the very presence and power of the God of Mt. Sinai among them. Thereupon, in due time, the Heavenly Father pierced the mortal veil again through the birth of His Only-Begotten Son; and the torch-bearing alliteration of the Vessel of Redemption fell upon the Immaculate perfection of the Most Blessed Virgin Mary who carried Jesus, our Messianic Deliverer, in Her Womb and His Spirit in Her Soul while donning the ordained title of the Ark of the New Covenant. And, finally and again, at the close of the mortal ages, the seamless ingenuity of our Eternal Father manifests the Ark of Final Deliverance in the supernatural intercession of His Heavenly Queen and Perpetual Mother as She lays-out Her Immaculate Heart before Her children as the sure refuge for all sinners before the great Day of Eternal Reckoning. Jesus Christ, Himself, prophesied that the end times which are presently upon us would be marked by the same revelrous excesses and reckless distractions that prevailed in the days when Noah entered the Ark. So, here we are. The Mystical Ark has appeared; the Woman clothed with the Sun; and the heroic souls of those who have dared to climb aboard through their Divine faith are being securely stowed in the hold of Her Love for the tempest-tossed voyage that is about to ensue at the report of the Heavenly Trumpets. And, how is this pristine Matriarch presenting Herself to the peoples of the Earth who have rejected Her supplications for generations? She is lifting Her Immaculate Heart to God in prayer and with pleading entreaties for our shared mercy and forgiveness. *Come! Come as one humanity! Raise your hearts in love! There is room for all to come aboard!*

Friday, August 7, 1998 - "My dear faithful children, I am *h(219)* pleased to return to this holy place to speak to My children that I love so heartily in return. These are the days that mark the culmination of a great amount of work that you have done over many years for Jesus. My Special child, when you were younger, you constructed rockets for launching into the skies. You are similarly making the Diary that will soar into the heavens with the force of such a rocket. You have already constructed the missile-shaped fuselage. Now, there are a great number of wires that run to the primary thrusters.    *x*

There are two hundred of them that are now being placed on their proper leads.* You are placing the fuel in the boosters by the formatting of the text. I am sent also to tell you that you will be ready for a test of main engine ignition very soon. That is when you will make one of your last passes over the work before it is staged for formal take-off. This parable is an accurate depiction of the status of your work. There are no words that can describe the appreciation that God has for your service and holiness. Many years of hard work are about to pay-off. But, you must remember to allow Me to guide you to ensure the stable flight of your Diary and the integrity of both its superstructure and infrastructure. I know the glide-path it needs and the character required to keep it on course. It needs to have the appropriate alignment to maintain its proper attitude, yaw, pitch, and roll. I am making those adjustments now. You will be pleased. You are collecting an unreproachable work. Remember the contribution made by the Angels during these latter times. Like Me, they know your heart. Also remember to pray for the intercession of Saint Dominic tomorrow in thanksgiving for the gift of the Holy Rosary. You will know all and see all in perfect understanding someday. Thank you for your prayers. I will speak to you very soon. I love you."

*xx*

* Our Lady was foretelling the Holy Rosary having 200 Angelic Salutations, after the addition of Luminous Mysteries by Pope John Paul II in 2002.

The banner successes of the children of Mary have been nurtured and guided for 2000 years and counting in both courageously apparent and securely clandestine ways. Our Lady has enhanced the power of the Christian Gospel of Love within our hearts to be administered to the multitudes of honest people who have been forced by either circumstance or destiny to engage their heart-rending challenges in the course of their ofttimes soul-shattering existence on the Earth. Inordinate tragedy and travail define the gruesome pilgrimage of the lives of everyone who makes the initial curtain call through the passing of mortal flesh. Our catastrophes are wandering like a sinister pack of lions seeking to devour our sweetest moments until we are summoned to return to the Eternal stage for a triumphant encore at the demand of the righteous Hosts of Heaven whose rosy accolades will shower upon our faces for serving well and suffering long with the graceful countenance of Christ in our designs. Many are the devout who have come to humble grips with the energetic sense of perceiving the paternal interaction of our Almighty Father, leaving them with the realization of the powerful, petitionary utility which has allowed the atrophied paraplegia of our faith to be replaced by an overwhelming certitude of convincing trust that has liberated our hopes from their wheelchair confinement. The Mother of Jesus Christ has sustained this transcending spiritual vision within us and buoyed our highest dreams to the Truths of the Holy Gospel of Her Son. There is not a New Testament century nor a geographical location on this earthen planet that is beyond the maternal benisons of this heavenly Matriarch; and central Illinois in the heartland of the United States of America, especially since February 1991, is certainly no exception. While I do not patently subscribe to the shortsighted distinctions of the comparative scrutinies that have often been assigned to different appearances of the Blessed Virgin throughout history by some presumptuous individuals; knowing as I do that each time the Mother of Christ dispenses Her intercessory Grace in whatever portion or design that God desires at any given point in time, it is a Heavenly engagement of beatific grandeur that must be solemnly respected and resolutely heeded; I humbly believe that the enormity of this magnum opus generated from the boundless Love of the Immaculate Heart of Heaven's Queen is without precedent in the contemporary annals of Holy Christendom. For anyone who would suspect that I am deluded into self-glorification by such a declaration or advancing any purpose other than what has been the commission of every follower of Christ through His Passion, Death and Resurrection, I pray that God Almighty in His Divine Charity would allow Our Lady to manifest Her Grace with such overwhelming clarity that my poor writings would be rendered meaningless in the estimation of all the Angels and Saints. But, until that moment arrives, my beautiful Heavenly Mother has told me to continue in raw confidence that all which we have prayed to come to pass on Earth may be a fashion of tomorrow's morning light. She has asked me to tell everyone to join us in this Victory because Her Love cannot be stopped. It is as invincible now as it was on the mountaintop of Calvary on the darkest day of the created world.

> Tuesday, September 7, 1999 - "Let us forever rejoice that     *i(250)*
> God has blessed His people once again, that the human
> heart has shown its courage to prevail, that dignity,

righteousness, and service are still living in the mortal world, and that a people of noble purpose have finally come to their feet for the cause of human Redemption. — My children, this is the preamble with which I ask you to carry your souls into the happy future that cannot escape your grasp, come what may. Very soon, you will have in hand a weapon which you have built with the Rosary and the Love in your hearts. Along with the Sacred Mysteries, you are about to be armed with one of the most lethal and powerful weapons against evil since God watched His Son die on the Cross. It took Him twenty centuries and your past ten years, but His Will is now being done on Earth at the brink of the twenty-first. Now, you say, ...*what can I do? What will I do?* My answer and response is that you must use your new weapon of mass-divinity to convince America that She is blessed. Allow the world to come to you, they who hunger for more! To those who say that your work is huge, tell them, *This is not the half of it!* Finally, My American children will know who I am because you have cared enough to tell them. You have given your lives to God and they will be the fortunate beneficiaries. Your labors of the past eight years and seven months have been so intense that you have reveled the hopes and imagination of the Hosts of the High Heavens. And yet, you are not even the slightest bit tired or too weary-of-mind or body to go on. A year ago, you were attaching the lead wires to the great airship that you hoped to see fly. Now, that beautiful lass is stationed upon its launchpad and will soon depart into the skies, making her way to victory. All the world will know of this righteous fate. God will, indeed, glorify the work of His own Holy Spirit if you will honor Him with the patience to watch it unfold. I promised you many years ago that I would never abandon you. I will forever keep that promise, even past the long boulevards of Eternity that will never come to an end. My dear children, words cannot suffice to explain what your holy work has meant for the world. You are filled with the Holy Spirit, the incarnate gift of peace and grace to those who are lonely and afraid. You have moved through the ranks and have come forward to lead the last age of man to their Eternal moment

*x*

*xx*

*xxx*

*xl*

of spiritual awakening. I promise as sure as I am now celebrating the solemnity of the observation of My Birth in the Church that God will afford you the opportunity to deliver every speech that rests quietly in your heart, waiting to be unleashed upon the fortunate ears who will stand by the tens of thousands to hear your every utterance, the next syllable that will soothe their aching souls and place their sorrowful hearts on the pathway to solace. I am confident that you wish to deliver them all soon! I ask you to watch with hope as this new millennium and century unfolds to reveal how your last decade of the 20th brought everyone on Earth to a renewal of faith and regeneration of hope. That is the brightest light of your holy tenure... I ask you to carry your new venue with clarity, dignity, purpose, direction, reflection, and the spirit of anticipation. I will be at your side until the end of time. There will be nothing then to stop us from uniting completely together in every way known to God... I am happy and grateful that you recognize the many ways that God has blessed you. I also ask you today to not calculate the cost. God will provide. Thank you for continuing your work. By no means are you finished, and by no means have I told you everything that God continues to allow Me to reveal. These are the days during which I am most happy because I know that the faithful service of you and your brother has yielded a most savory fruit for humankind to taste. This will make way for thousands more to join at the Feast Table in Heaven. God is already setting the places where they will sit beside the Saints who now bask in the Light of His Love. Your Diary will make it clear to the world that human contrition must precede the conversion which will result, and that holiness is the lofty perch upon which Mercy will light in your souls. Upon all of this, Jesus has placed the plume of Eternal Salvation in which every heart you are now trying to open will know and understand the reason why. I ask you to be gentle with those who will be slow to accept your work, and merciful to those who reject it outright. You know by now that God does what He does, allows what He allows, and brings everyone to the Heart of My Jesus of their own accord. That

is the savory nourishment that your work is bestowing upon
the collective conscience of all those who will embrace your
Diary with loyalty and affection. In these next weeks, I will
continue to unfold many new messages that will continue to
be a part of your next work, the foundation of which I gave
previously. Once you have that book in your hands, you will
be armed! Thank you for your prayers. I will speak to you
again very soon. I love you. Goodnight."

The wretched, the irreligious, the proud, and the atheistic worldlings
should turn their deaf ears to the prevailing sentiments that are whistling from
the distance of their nightmares because these gentle breezes bear the prophecy
of their ominous awakening to the Truth they have heretofore rejected with
balky adversity and sultry obstinance. Righteousness is prophetically upon its
feet; personified by the Crucified and Resurrected Christ; towering above their
damning fray, forming its besieging garrisons, aligning itself with perpetual
Maternity, arming the beatific warriors of the final age with the brilliant Virtues
of the Love of God, and marching in lockstep with the impenetrable Virgin
Heels that Achilles' himself would have been most blessed to call his own. The
supernatural earthquake that is providentially reverberating through the oceanic
souls of the children of Jesus and Mary is lifting a moral tidal wave that is gently
bearing down upon Creation at this most opportune moment in the unfolding
of our modern times; a monumental tsunami of irreducible Revelation that will
burst upon us like angel feathers exploding from our millennial pillow-fight
with God. Oh, there will be guffaws and giggling the likes of which our
mothers and fathers never imagined coming from their bedrooms in the days
of our impish childhood. But, let us never forget, there was always the
unsuspecting tyke who caught the final swing up-side the noggin before the
euphoric pandemonium ensued. Our Holy Mother is warning us clearly to
**D**efer **U**nwaveringly to **C**hrist the **K**ing, lest we find ourselves coming to our
senses at the unexpected sound of chirping angels making circles around our
thunder-struck heads. Why is God unfolding our Deliverance with such
Immaculate Incognita? Why has He not plainly unveiled His Dominion and
asserted His Kingship before the faithless world to miraculously abridge our
horrific encounters with evil works? For the same reason that a tiny child in
a highchair reaches for the spoon from the hand of his mother for the first
time, clumsily dips it in his bowl of strained peaches resting within arm's reach
in front of him, and begins to paint his own cheeks with fruit before eventually
finding his mouth that he was aiming for. Our Lord simply knows from the
unbounded compassion of His transcending vision that we will someday wish

to have had the opportunity to manifest His Crucified Love through the willing sentiments of our own reciprocal love for Him; without coercion, domination, or force that would taint the charitable endowment of our gratitude for our Deliverance. This is why our free will is encapsulated within the veiled boundaries of our Christian faith. Our Almighty Father has mystically preserved our sacred decision to freely return such an emulated gift of ourselves to our loving Redeemer by His kind respect for the way we ultimately choose to impart it. But, impart it to Him we must, or we will be too overwhelmed by the realization of our Eternal failure on the Day of Reckoning. Indeed, what does it profit any of us to gain the whole world and ultimately find that we never loved anyone or anything but ourselves?

Tuesday, September 14, 1999- "The blessed children whom *i(257)* I cherish, admire, adore, and embrace always remember the Triumph of the Cross. That is why you, My dear little ones, will always reside at the very foundation of My Immaculate Heart. This is, indeed, the time for which you have been praying, toiling, and struggling for many years. By all means, this is the time for which the 20th century world has unwittingly waited! The final quarter of this century will be its finest of all! Thank you, My children, for making that hope-of-God come true. You are the arms and hands of the *x* Holy Spirit in a very troubled world! This is not the time to stop, but is assuredly a time to savor. You have so nobly come to adore the Child in the Manger! Your journey has taken all of 2000 years to complete! You will be upon another Advent season very soon! The work of your hands on your first Diary is complete, and you may begin to pen your memories and sentiments for the second any time you wish. The thesis for them is My messages after February 1997, along with your recollections of these End Times, the events in your lives, the reflections you may have about the *xx* process and product of your first Diary and all similar, substantial, and additional information that you may choose to relate. I am simply telling you these things to give you a sense of continuing direction during the times when you think your days have become somewhat boring and meaningless. Indeed, evil dogs surround you. This is what you stated upon the mountains of Medjugorje, the same mountains upon which you stand in this room.

My children, it is alright to look at *Morning Star Over America* with affection and admiration. You worked long and hard to complete it. Now, the work will be from afar as it goes into the world. This telemetry will allow you to know how the world is being changed. You still have to do some fine-tuning of this fine masterpiece, but the mission is underway! All the heavens watched as you worked so hard! They saw the unfortunate delays and unavoidable stumbling blocks. But, success is at hand! My dearly beloved children, the work of your hands and the paragon of all our hearts, the *Morning Star Over America*, has been launched and is en route to celestial heights that will make all humankind look upward to God again in *faith, hope, love, trust, friendship, conversion,* and *holiness.* These are the seven who are aboard. Now, we go on, we continue, we allow it to do its work, and we re-direct our attention to the work of the valleys of the Earth, always knowing that *Morning Star* will never fall from grace. This is a new time because your greatest work in this modern century is only begun. You have been given laurels, but not to rest upon! These are the continuing countdown of the final days of mortal man on Earth, and we still have much more work to do. Please do not abandon Me, for I shall never abandon you!...”

*xxx*

*xl*

Sunday, November 7, 1999 - “My dearly beloved children, the echoes of your deliverance into the Eternal happiness for which you seek originate in your utterance of the Hail Mary. You see with enhanced vision that I respond to your plea for help with the strength of the Holy Spirit and the entire Court of heavenly angels. This is a special day of prayer because, like many to come, it is the continuation of the opening of the final ages of human mortality into the infinity of Redemption. This, My children, is why others say that My messages are repetitive. Their heart is resounding the reverberations of the single Truth of one Crucifixion. I can

*i(311)*

*x*

see the uplifting of many hearts to the Grace that I have come to bestow, those who do not yet know how to define the signal miracles and supernatural sentiments which have been flowing from Heaven into this room for nearly nine years. Whether they call it a cantation of beauty, the high-strobe of Truth, textualized music, or lessons of Love, the fact remains that something new and exciting is awakening their sleeping hearts, and they can attribute it only to someone yet to be named. They will eventually recognize and conclude that it is, indeed, their Immaculate Mother."

*(Our Lady then referred to the many boxes containing the printed and published copies of "Morning Star Over America.")*

"Do you see all of the boxes of books before you? In those holy containers is the pulsating conveyance of the relay being sent back to Earth of the Truth of My intercession from the orbiting *Morning Star Over America.* You are seeing that She is about to be known by many thousands. We must pray that this century will come to its close with a renewed fervor of hope by the many people in the western world. We must pray that they accept miracle over material, prayer over self-indulgence, and reparation over recreation. The pardon that Jesus intends for souls has been reserved for the penitent, not those whose lives have been given to the flagrant rejection of holiness without a firm purpose of amendment. The Mercy of Jesus is unconditional, but it is a fruit for the humble-of-soul. This is the acknowledgment which cannot be ignored or deflected by anyone who is bound for the beauty of Heaven... Please never shed the happiness that you were always given to enjoy. Never leave your innocent kindness behind on your journey to evangelize the world. Peace exudes from your heart because you do not fear to reprimand the spiritually indignant with the charity of Love. The Truth will always prevail, but many will try to grasp your understanding of it from your hands, reshape it into what they wish it to be, and try to hand it back to you with their skewed and erroneous visions affixed. Please do not allow their deception and distraction to cause you any grief... I am

*xx*

*xxx*

*xl*

pleased that you do not allow those who call you arrogant to take you away from continuing to profess your faith in confidence!

Between the time I began the composition of this chapter containing my aesthetic thoughts about discoverers, voyagers, and truth-faring evangelists who dare the captivating boundaries of our mortal existence in the sacred efforts of forever widening the circumference of the circle of life and these moments when the exhausted ages have regurgitated another seemingly scattered defeat onto our already excruciating hearts, a flaming lone star named *Columbia* streaked across the skies of Texas and fell thundering from the crystal blue firmament on what was meant to be a triumphant February morning. Once again, mankind has encountered the colossal morbidity of the earthly side of the Mystery of Redemption whereby Providence has thrust our childlike consciences into the solemn gallery before the Calvarian Cross to witness arm-in-arm the ageless transition of mortality into glorified immortality. Our hearts have been graced by the re-immersion in the grand vision of a flying-bassinet of septuplets being birthed into the outstretched arms of their Heavenly Virgin Mother who had waited over two millennia with eager longing for the nine o'clock hour of that dreadful morning to pluck Her seven children gracefully from their flight seats of sky-bound adventure, Mystically jettisoning them beyond the horrors of this world and wrapping them in garments befitting the most triumphant victors to have ever appeared before the Court of their King and Queen. Their names, Husband, McCool, Clark, Chawla, Anderson, Brown, and Ramon were inscribed in the Eternal Book of the Living long before they were etched in the black granite solitude of the heart-touching memorials which will remember their contributions to the expanding purposes of humankind throughout the swiftly passing ages. Henceforth, they shall never fall from Grace because they are now cloaked with their auspicious mortal passing and shall ride within the tri-clustered legacy of the Morning Star forever to come. Their new heritage is of an ecstatic lot of explorers who gaze upon the ultimate undiscovered Country, passionately striding a Paradisial trek from which they will soon return upon the wings of eagles at the side of Jesus Christ on the day when our present indistinct visions will defer to the victorious reality that all life from its inception has been perpetually snatched from the jaws of death in its most ferociously poignant moment on a summit called Mount Calvary. Our burdened hearts will drink the sparkling champagne of God's Eminent Triumph over every horrible altercation of shadow-fallen mortality that has cast grimaces of unbearable pain over our much celebrated finest hours. The Second Coming of the Savior of the World will magnify the power of His

Resurrection where success will be restored to this Creation upon all that human beings have tried to honestly hew from their inspired stewardship of this holy landscape of mortal exile. How do I know this? Because the Truth has come to me through the Miraculous Intercessor, the Most Blessed Mother, Herself; and my witness is sincere!

For twelve years and counting, the true-to-life interaction of Almighty God through Our Lady has been recorded from a willing pen; an articulation of Divinity and Wisdom that should be impugned by no good man, an epitaph of righteousness upon the stone-cold graves of mediocrity, compromise, and faint-hearted indifference; and a cornerstone for a celestial skyscraper that is rising up with majesty above the chaotic squall produced by the rebellion of those who build without holy virtue at the infernal behest of their impudent ambitions and misguided loyalties. We are truly the babes in a deep-thicket forest of faithless thinking where flying monkeys and wicked witches are the least of our worries. It is a subterfuge of outright evil to believe that the pinnacle of Messianic Truth, which is Love itself, cannot be known to its fullness, that the purveyors of any alternate earthly creed have any authority or influence before the Throne of God, and that the mortal world will not be turned upside-down in the very near offing, making the seating order at the Feast of the Blessed a more sobering reality for those who have rejected their Savior and King. This is why such a miraculous call is processing forth from this time and place, a rallying cry to the highest aspirations in the lion-hearted dreams of men. If we wish to remake the world, now is the most opportune moment, and these are the blessed of times! No one will ever regret casting their monetary fortunes into the wounds of their suffering brothers and sisters in each corner of the Earth and on every plain in between. There is nary a soul who has arrived at the Judgement Seat of God wishing that they had somehow amassed greater material wealth. So, let us pray, each and everyone, to be sentimental heroes of the highest order of loving sacrifice, one in the gallant legions of Mystical prowess, gracious victors from the outset, and confident warriors 'til the final surrender of the world into the Merciful hands of Jesus Christ.

Sunday, October 3, 1999 - My children, this is a struggle     *i(276)*
about Love versus hatred, about Life conquering death, and
about Purity defeating the lifeless stench of evil for the good
to look down-upon in joy. The battle that rages is fierce, but
it is one that has assuredly been determined. You have won
the fight because Jesus is in you, the Christ of the
Everlasting is now reigning supreme through you now. How
happy are the Saints and Angels to know that your souls are
only a mortal horizon away from joining them at the Table
of Salvation.

# Epilogue
## *Orphans and Orphanages*

I am not under the illusion that manuscripts about spirituality and organized religion will ever suffice to reconfigure the latent facts of modern history or presuppose the broader course of future events, even those that emphasize the paranormal, concelebrate the miraculous, and highlight the supernatural. However, we can learn many interesting things along the way; not the least of which is the knowledge that if we are to become the children of Light and take our youthful offspring more closely to our breast, we must arrive at the irreducible conclusion that a blessed mortal will is one that is completely soluble in the Blooded Cup of Jesus Christ. If we are to inherit that proverbial Promised Land for which our ancestors faithfully pined, God should never detect so much as a hairline fracture between His loveliness and the piety of our souls. For all the division we rend from our differences, the eloquence with which we dress our speech, and the dignity whereby we stand upright like White Oak trees in the Cunningham Forest of the Maryland Heights, we become in Jesus Christ that humane essence of Himself whom He has commissioned to inherit the Earth. The evolving criteria through which we are modernized by excruciating increments has been an opus of power and pain for our consciences and for the galvanizing of our hearts. When we pause to consider that only sixty-six years expired from the crucial moment when the Wright Brothers took to the air at Kitty Hawk in 1903 until Neil Armstrong walked on the Moon during the Flight of Apollo 11 in 1969, it gives us reason to reexamine the extraordinary sense of vogue by which the people of Earth have always met the challenges of the future despite the hindrances of the past. What our little children must learn about survival is always derived from us by virtue of the accuracy of our genius and the tenacity of our means. God has surely not been wholly filled with disdain by the many fashions we have wrought, even though we interrogated, battered, bruised, bludgeoned and killed His Only Begotten Son to prove our self-sufficiency. He has forgiven us even so, as strange as it may seem, in that He must have believed that our Eternal Salvation was worth the price of His life to get His message of Love across. Perhaps He plans to mete-out a punishment that is commensurate with our defiance of His Truth when our time in exile is through. It seems as though we are fully aware of the degree by which Love keeps us betrothed in familial and patriotic ways; but, before the Son of Man became Incarnate, humankind never quite understood what Divine affection really was. Who would have guessed 2000 years ago that the common link between men would include more useful pursuits such as the sacrificial holiness by which we now turn our attention to ameliorating afflictions like worldwide hunger, inordinate nakedness, paupers dying on the curb, prisoners emaciating to nothing in dungeons below the ground; or that we would ever be privy to knowing that there have been billions of certifiable Saints that have passed beyond their graves who feel blessed to have finally died? There are Merciful Works of the Holy Spirit that we might have never known, such as the admonishment of our fellow sinners, instruction of the ignorant, counseling the doubtful, comforting the sorely aggrieved, offering patience to the ones who are lost, forgiving their offenses, and praying for humanity everywhere, both on the Earth and for the departed souls who have slipped beyond the surly bonds into the presence of their God.

At 11:21 a.m. on April 20, 1999, two deranged teenagers walked into Columbine High School in Littleton, Colorado and began shooting their classmates and teachers, then turned their weapons on themselves. While it might be appropriate for Americans of all stripes to look down on them as though they were the epitome of random evil, perhaps we should make a more critical evaluation of the conditions that led them to commit such an atrocious act. They were marred by the inner-violence that they learned from their environment because when they were born, they had no firearms in their hands, they harbored no hatred toward any of their peers, and they exuded no symptoms that would have led their doctors or parents to believe that they would be nothing less than benign little boys. What happened? Is it not true that they were tantalized by the American nightmare in which capitalistic greed kidnapped them from their birthright of Grace and caught them sleeping inside a trap of materialism, interpersonal competition, and freelance hatred? They were abandoned and betrayed by a nation that has declined to wrap its very purpose inside the rapture of human Love. When we speak of orphans and orphanages, we draw to mind those little children whose parents have either died or have forsaken them; and there are far too many of them in every corner of the globe who are in need of adoption by loving foster parents everywhere. But, the kind of orphans to which I am referring for the purpose of this book are the multiple millions who still live in stable homes and decent neighborhoods, along wide-track drives and suburban boulevards, who see their parents not in the way of "mother and father" of the vintage 1950s vein, but as their enemies who are only holding them back from outgrowing their childish inhibitions before they have the opportunity to defeat them for themselves. Some of our offspring see their guardians as robotic devices who have left them to discern the meaning of human life on their own eclectic terms. As I have stated throughout this manuscript, such irresponsible rearing is the basis for the desecration of the nuclear family, the devaluing of the human person, the loss of our sense of purpose, and a source of untold violence. However, by espousing the Holy Gospel of Jesus Christ, our progeny will become leaders of a heralded age of new mysticism and promise. This is the raw potential in which God first gave them life, the very same innocence that was written across their little brows when their families carried them home in cotton bundles from their respective obstetric wards. Indeed, untold millions of them have become victims of the brinkmanship which is the mantra of our U.S. secularism that is headed for the dust. As I have stated before, the endless prattle of the television set is their main distraction from the inviolate hallowedness for which every heart must yearn before our mortal age is through.

If we agree that God is sovereign, but then continue to refuse Him room to shine the luminescence of His Kingdom wherever He may choose, we are nothing less than boldface liars and are blinded by our own pride and vices from seeing His Truth march on. Time will be the bespectacled teller as to whether we finally held-out against Him in favor of some type of equilibrium between our own platitudes and the solemnity of His Peace, as though we own the legitimacy to subject His Love to the throes of such debate, conjecture, or our infamous art of whitewash compromise. Perhaps it would behoove us to recall that Christ is vastly more refined in matters of mystery and logic than any analytical thought we could ever bring to mind. The High Priest is our Creator; and we are but His creatures. Quite simply put, if human life can be compared to a friendly game of Canasta in which we are to meld sets of seven cards together, He is always the dealer; we can never force His hand; the world is down to its last penny ante, and He's got the elusive Ace of Spades tucked neatly up His sleeve. We may assume that we hold dominion over the universe just because we are the stewards of the Earth, but the Heavens are on the offensive right now, and too many of us are struggling to regain control. No matter what the media spotlight might expose or lofty speeches we may hear from the rostrums on Capitol Hill, we Americans are nothing more than a puny pot of pugnacious caricatures who are too quick to start a brawl, nearly impossible to appease, slanderous with our tongues like loose battle shards into unsuspecting flesh, stoic to a fault, consumers to the max, and so isolated from the rest of the globe that it would be our next thought to seek another planet upon which to transplant the United States of America and blast this one into pieces with our hidden stash of nuclear bombs, watching it smoldering in the panoramic vision of the rear-view mirrors of the USS Starship Arrogance. Absent of inheriting some miraculous righteousness that seems too elusive to us now, our backs are pitted against the wall of the evil in the world; and we appear to not be too concerned that the guns of Satan's firing-squad are trained at point-blank range against our foreheads. So, when we think of poor orphans and orphanages, let us recall everything that went wrong in the past because we declined to foresee the effects of our sins on our progeny in the future. Let us extend our supplications to include not only those children who are lonely in their beds in barracks-like halls around the globe, but those who have their own little "kingdom" in the rich neighborhoods of the West. Let us pray for the haughty people who believe that their sons deserve the best of everything they were never quite able to conceive, even though their opportunism always comes at the expense of the suffering of indigenous peoples in lands which lay many thousands of miles away. Jesus is trying to tell us that there is a transparent nexus between our spiritual economy and His Divine Justice which is composed of the invisible discernment by which all righteousness prevails. And, it is by this essence that every Christian must moor his soul to Our Lord's Harbor of Grace and Eminent perfection in the likes of the Most Blessed Virgin Mary. At a time when the world is being terrorized by rogue religious extremists, the Holy Gospel of Christianity seems to have been pigeonholed into anonymity and reduced to a breathy whisper over low-watt radio airwaves and in the rearmost pages of our newspapers at the bottom of the latest obituary columns. We have learned through the benefit of 20/20 hindsight that our existence has been forced by rich moguls and oil magnates to be more anesthetized by error than focused upon the Truth; more corporately corruptible than spiritually Divine, and not even slightly conducive to the cultivation of the heart by which the Holy Spirit is already bracing us for God's incorporeal infusion of exculpatory Love.

Perhaps not so many other people would feel this same way about our country if they did not recognize that there is such inequality among our peoples, that we are segregated not only by our national origin and the color of our skin, but also by our status on the socioeconomic scale. How could it have happened in the most prosperous nation in the world that over 60 million people have no medical insurance or means to pay for treatment during bouts of severe illness or terminal disease? We drive along our gated communities and see doctors hand-washing their shiny new Viper sports cars and quarter-million-dollar touring buses, and then turn on the news and hear them complain that their malpractice insurance premiums are too high for some of them to maintain their office hours. And, yet, according to Marlo Thomas of that same St. Jude Children's Hospital about which I spoke in Chapter XII, the cost to treat one child with acute lymphoblastic leukemia (ALL), the most common of childhood cancers, with a standard 30-month protocol is a whopping $280,000. This is for one patient; and they have 4,300 of them on active status during any given day! It is no wonder why good will in America is so difficult to come by these days. If there is cynicism in the United States today, it is because we have closed our eyes not only to the horrible suffering of our little children, but to those who are otherwise physically healthy while their souls remain famished for our Love. There is no excuse for this because there are no ruthless dictators in America forcing them into sweatshop labor like they do in other foreign nations. No representatives from our government travel the neighborhoods to tack decrees or edicts on our door posts, mandating our participation in public elections. Even in light of these facts, we are still oppressed by our lack of knowledge as to how to make the best of our democratic freedoms. I continue to have confidence that the Good Lord is on our side; but we should fear Him like captive POWs trembling in their shoes because of the just reprisals from Heaven that He is about to visit upon our land. If He should act sooner rather than later, we must do more than simply take it in stride. We all belong to the overbearing responsiveness by which we are to keep our hopes for fairness alive—that witty and tangy tartness which tells us that the Divine Truth is about to burst into our dark reality, and that it is only a spoonful of deifying medicine and one more gruesome nightfall away. If Jesus Christ is truly searching for the "little kid" in each of us, should we not return to that simplicity by eradicating everything about us that is ugly, untoward, and unseemly in His sight? Are we not His leaven activists on the Earth whose authentic quest for piety revolves around the undefiled propensity of the Holy Spirit to accomplish anything God wishes to do through us by the Book? After all, did we not learn to read and write in first and second grades so that, by the third, we could stumble through His parables about being Jesus' little lambs and the propagating wildflower around His feet? As for America itself, it is not a pleasurable prospect to be so critical of our beloved homeland. But, if God is displeased by the way we are raising our children, would we not be committing blasphemy against His Holy Paraclete if we did not become His enunciated Fruits of Love for them? Are we not doing them a horribly grievous disservice by wrapping their future in our national colors of red, white, and blue in the race for material goods when the Son of Man is waving black "layover" flags in our faces at nearly every turn? Even though we may ignore them, we eventually find ourselves draping them across the metal badges of our martyred police officers and firemen when another one of them lays-down his life battling the constant ferocity of unchecked human sin.

We do not sense the darkness that has overshadowed the twinkling in our newborn children's eyes because they open them to the very world in which they will eventually close them again in death. The great miracle-worker Anne Mansfield Sullivan Macy (1866-1936) was the woman who taught Miss Helen Keller, who was born deaf and blind, to communicate with the rest of the world. She spent thousands of hours in faithful devotion toward the goal of helping Helen break-out of her shell of extraordinary physical incapacitation to become, herself, one of the greatest U.S. authors, teachers, and lecturers ever known. They shared a supernatural union as Helen succeeded in comprehending the facets of human reasoning, the implications of life beyond the parameters of a sensuous handicap, and into the realms of learning why other people sing, laugh, and dance. Through patience, diplomacy, external rewards, gentle prompting, kind discipline, and the determination of a saint, Annie Sullivan taught Helen Keller to become one of the most visionary educators of modern times. Not only that, Helen's personality was as viable as any Hollywood entertainer, which was in stark contrast to the drab and phlegmatic oratories of her seeing and speaking counterparts. She lived from 1880-1968, and did more to enhance the deep cultivation of the heart of our republic than all the U.S. presidents accomplished from their bully pulpits combined. One of the reasons this is so striking is because it places the obstinance of modern-day Americans in a rather unique perspective. What can we expect our little children to learn about fairness, forgiveness, and civility when in July 1997, Joseph Roger O'Dell III was put to death in the Commonwealth of Virginia a few hours after he was married in prison for a 1985 murder he said he did not commit? To add demagoguery to this tragedy, then-Governor George Allen said his decision to reject executive clemency would not be influenced by a petition for mercy from Pope John Paul II and Mother Teresa of Calcutta! And, even though his lawyers argued unsuccessfully that a new DNA test would have exonerated their client, a Federal Appeals Court refused to grant a stay. It is widely known that the last thing a condemned man would ever do is tell a lie while on his deathbed. So, Mr. O'Dell turned to one of the relatives of the victim and said, ...*Eddie, I did not kill your mother.* Well, it is far too late now for anyone to reverse course, even if they should locate someone else who is found to be responsible for committing the crime, because they executed J.R. O'Dell at 9:16 p.m. on Wednesday, July 23, 1997 by injecting lethal chemicals into his veins, whereupon he met his God and Maker. But, what does this same Creator think about the acts of people like the merciless former Governor of Virginia, jurists in their chambers, and the executioners who stuck the needle in his arm? I will refer you to the Virgin Mary's sentiments in Chapter XVI of this book for the answer to that. And, what do our children learn when they see public administrators flagrantly turning a callous ear to the pleading of such religious giants as the Vicar of Christ in Rome, Italy and a humble nun who became a Nobel Peace Prize laureate in 1979 for upholding the dignity and sanctity of human life in the alleys, gutters, and ghettos in the capital city of West Bengal along the Hooghly River in the Republic of India?

It does not take very long for our compassionate elected officials to be flushed out of public office by a majority of the American electorate because the egocentrism that sends many voters to the polls is a rather high-maintenance item. Indeed, I have had my name on the ballot before, and I have already calculated the risk of damaging my own reputation when I write books like this one, knowing with full anticipation that moderate people everywhere might view me as a religious zealot who has nothing better to do than magnify the faults of the rest of humanity. I have only one question in response to them. Would I have in any way strengthened our potential to do better in the sight of God if I would have cowered in my den at home and kept my opinions to myself? I think, perhaps, I would rather be perceived as a Christian fanatic than to have the Son of God grab me by the throat someday in the Hereafter and tell me that He gave me the gift of voice and the true Wisdom of the Holy Spirit, but I repugnantly refused to empower either one of them. Besides, there are already a sufficient number of American citizens who see outright evil forces running rampant in our streets and invading private homes who look another way like spineless invertebrates, pretending that such things never happen so they do not have to get involved. There is nothing radical about begetting from ourselves the best of everything having to do with the righteousness that Christ has afforded plentiful venues to extol. We are remiss, repulsive, and negligent when we decline to heed Him. Jesus seeks in humanity precisely what the Holy Scriptures and the Catholic Catechism espouse; the desire for Love, curiosity for spiritual revelations, obedience to God's Truth, compassion for humanity, Wisdom in Christian faith, servitude in our good works, trust in the Omnipotence of the Holy Trinity, recourse in the power of prayer, and belief that we will all ultimately be saved. By the Sacred Mysteries that God has revealed, we who are Christians compose His Mystical Body not only in an Eternal fashion, but also in the present. He relies on our participation in the same way our living obedience is bequeathed to our own children. If we Love them to the degree of hope by which our souls will ultimately be judged, we shall not fear that they will wander astray or become dismayed by our example of Christian faithfulness. There is probably not a parent alive who would not give their offspring the best of what this world has to offer in knowledge, virtue, the common good, equality, respect, solidarity, morality, and comfort. And, whether we believe it or not, God has blessed us with a land of surplus in which to succeed; ample resources, unqualified instinctiveness, broad avenues of Light, familial bonds, meritorious Grace, respect for life, and purity of heart. It is now up to us to wield these things not only to the betterment of ourselves and those significant others we hold so dear, but also toward the development of Creation at large; so that all our reactions, motivations, and intentions are connected within a global unity of gracious peoples in the Sacred Heart of Christ and the Kingdom where we serve. We are free to complain all we might about the unfairness of His denying our ownership of Cadillacs, ocean-front properties, and the like; but the swelling of the tide of Love forces our change of heart against such extravagance. On the brighter side, however, odds are well in our favor that we will never be gulped-up by a giant whale or see night-visions of Hellfire and brimstone in our sleep. We have far greater concerns to worry about than to be harried by the stature of our standard of living; things like duty, honor, sacrifice, prophecy, Providence, modesty, justice, understanding, fortitude, and Truth. Let us never forsake these seeds of human perfection while we protect and nurture them in the minds, hearts, souls, and conduct of our impressionable children. They are the rightful property of God; as are we; and it is into our custody that He has placed them for now. We must make the most of our age in leading them to the professorial brilliance of Eternal Love, lest they eclipse our seniority by becoming our spiritual teachers, and we their chosen vanquished.

# My Mother's Eyes

*I've got my Mother's eyes and my Father's hair.*
*Does anybody really care? It's getting cold out here.*
*Well, I keep walking with my head held high,*
*with my head to the sky, with my Mother's eyes.*
*And, my Mother's eyes are with me*
*in the darkness that's been paid for.*
*I'm just a nameless stranger, don't know why.*
*Have I seen all that I could?*
*Have I seen more than I should*
*with my Mother's eyes?*
*And, my Mother's eyes are with me*
*in the chilly winds of Autumn.*
*If I ain't here by Winter, she'll know why.*
*I say all that I dare.*
*I've seen more than my share.*
*Forgive me if I stare with my Mother's eyes.*

–Tom Jans and Bette Midler     1980

## Message Transcription Citations

| 1991 | *a* | 1998 | *h* |
|------|-----|------|-----|
| 1992 | *b* | 1999 | *i* |
| 1993 | *c* | 2000 | *j* |
| 1994 | *d* | 2001 | *k* |
| 1995 | *e* | 2002 | *l* |
| 1996 | *f* | 2003 | *m* |
| 1997 | *g* | 2004 | *n* |

001-366 day                    *x - cx* line

# Reader Notations

www.ingramcontent.com/pod-product-compliance
Lightning Source LLC
Chambersburg PA
CBHW060252100426
42742CB00011B/1730